DEATH IN A PRAIRIE HOUSE

Terrace Books, a trade imprint of the University of Wisconsin Press,
takes its name from the Memorial Union Terrace, located at
the University of Wisconsin–Madison. Since its inception in 1907,
the Wisconsin Union has provided a venue for students, faculty, staff,
and alumni to debate art, music, politics, and the issues of the day.
It is a place where theater, music, drama, literature, dance, outdoor activities,
and major speakers are made available to the campus and the community.
To learn more about the Union, visit www.union.wisc.edu.

Death in a Prairie House

Frank Lloyd Wright and the Taliesin Murders

WILLIAM R. DRENNAN

TERRACE BOOKS
A trade imprint of the University of Wisconsin Press

Terrace Books
A trade imprint of the University of Wisconsin Press
1930 Monroe Street, 3rd Floor
Madison, Wisconsin 53711-2059

www.wisc.edu/wisconsinpress/

3 Henrietta Street
London WC2E 8LU, England

Library of Congress Cataloging-in-Publication Data
Drennan, William R.
Death in a prairie house : Frank Lloyd Wright and
the Taliesin murders / William R. Drennan.
       p.   cm.
Includes bibliographical references and index.
ISBN 0-299-22210-1 (cloth: alk. paper)
   1. Wright, Frank Lloyd, 1867–1959.
2. Wright, Frank Lloyd, 1867–1959—Friends and associates.
   3. Borthwick, Mamah Bouton, d. 1914.
   4. Architects—United States—Biography.
   5. Spring Green (Wis.)—Biography.   I. Title.
       NA737.W7D74   2007
   364.152´30977576—dc22   2006031765

ISBN 0-299-22214-4 (pbk.: alk. paper)

For
BETH
SARAH
JOHN PAUL
EMMA JANE

It would be easy to regard [his] personal inconsistencies as mere peccadilloes that fade into irrelevancy when set against Wright's undeniably brilliant artistic achievements. Certainly there is much to be learned by moving beyond the distractions of his formidable personality to confront his buildings directly. The trouble, unfortunately, is that Wright himself clearly believed his architecture to be an organic expression of the very personality that, in many ways, seems so problematic.

William Cronon

Those who are alive receive a mandate from those who are silent forever. They can fulfill their duties only by trying to reconstruct precisely things as they were and by wresting the past from fictions and legends.

Czeslaw Milosz

Contents

Acknowledgments

Felix Raab somewhere notes that studies of this sort, "like good deeds in a naughty world, require no apology." Perhaps not, but they do require the grateful (if inevitably incomplete) acknowledgment of help where it was found.

Such help normally begins in libraries, research foundations, historical societies large and small, other archives, and from the knowledgeable and helpful people who run and staff those places. For example, Margo Stipe and Indira Berndtson of the Frank Lloyd Wright Memorial Foundation, Scottsdale, Arizona, were remarkably helpful to me, both at and after the time I spent there during my sabbatical semester. Closer to home, Craig Jacobsen, Public Access Manager at Taliesin Preservation, Inc., in Spring Green made his expertise available (and set me straight on some important matters). Early in my inquiries, I depended heavily on community libraries throughout southwest Wisconsin, all of which served me well as repositories of both print materials and local lore. Among them are the libraries in Dodgeville, Spring Green, Baraboo, Mineral Point, Reedsburg, Richland Center, and Sauk Prairie. Later in my research, the more specialized services of academic collections were generously offered up by the Wisconsin Historical Society, Madison; Sauk County Historical Society, Baraboo; Memorial Library, University of Wisconsin–Madison; the Karrmann Library, University of Wisconsin–Platteville (Eugene Nemetz was particularly helpful there); and the University of Wisconsin–Baraboo/Sauk County Savides Library, whose director at the time, Jim Bredeson, and his staff exhibited limitless patience and collegial support.

Indeed, my colleagues throughout the University of Wisconsin Colleges have been seamlessly supportive throughout the project. Former Chancellor Bill Messner; Associate Vice Chancellors Greg Lampe and then-Interim Provost and Vice Chancellor Margaret Cleek; Colleges Professional Development Committee Chair Professor Asif Habib and

Professor Janet LaBrie, his counterpart in the Colleges English Department; UW–Baraboo deans Aural Umhoefer and Michael Brophy; and Colleges English Department chairs Linda Ware and Ken Grant—none of these could have been kinder, especially in shepherding my sabbatical application through administrative mazes.

Help came from less traditional sources, as well, including the Barbados Department of Archives (thank you, Cherri-Ann Beckles) and the Department of Anatomy at the University of Wisconsin–Madison (thanks to Phil Schadler, Jim Petterson, Robert Schlotthauer, Kristen Zehner, and Wayne Roohr). And thanks to Beryl and John, whose visit and inquiring minds fortuitously prompted this whole undertaking.

Local experts on Wright and Taliesin—both recognized, much-published scholars and those who confine themselves to the role of zealous observers—provided encouragement and direction throughout my investigation; among these are the wonderful Carla Lind of Dodgeville; Therese Evans, also of that town; the amazingly hospitable John Korb; the town of Plain's Joe Wankerl; and Mildred Forseth of Barneveld. I am especially grateful to architect and Taliesin Fellowship member Charles Montooth, who graciously paved my entry into the Memorial Foundation's irreplaceable archives in Scottsdale.

Special thanks are due to Raphael Kadushin and Adam Mehring, among my clear-eyed and painstaking editors at University of Wisconsin Press. *Il miglior fabbro*, both. I am equally grateful for the intelligent, sensitive, and spot-on edit supplied by Jane M. Curran and for the instructive corrections suggested by Taliesin Preservation, Inc., historic researcher (Mary) Keiran Murphy.

Finally, this journey, like all others, proved happy only because I could share it with my wife, Beth, through whose love all labors are lightened and through whose mind all things make sense.

DEATH IN A PRAIRIE HOUSE

Prologue
The House across the River

Who can set bounds to the possibilities of man?
Ralph Waldo Emerson

In this story, I am God.
Frank Lloyd Wright

Throughout the otherwise tedious spring and summer of 1911, the dusty Wisconsin town of Spring Green, in southern Sauk County, was gifted with a welcome and unexpected diversion, one that had sparked a flurry of interest, rumors, and gossip among the villagers—all 730 of them. Just down the road, across the Wisconsin River in neighboring Iowa County, a house was being built, such as none of them had ever seen. Month after month, from behind the trees that wreathed the river's farther edge, hammers sounded and saws rasped. Ponderous horses hauled vast cartloads of local limestone, mined from an outcropping only a mile distant, up the steep hill to the building site. While its designer at first dismissed the project as a mere "cottage," the structure was emerging as an outright mansion in the eyes of the townsfolk and area farmers. Many of them, in fact, had been put to work on the house, which was set into—not on top of—a graceful knoll overlooking the fertile river bottom land known locally as "the valley of the God-Almighty Joneses"—a reference (at once grudging and admiring) to the doughty family of Welsh pioneer farmers who had settled there and who had

3

ultimately produced, on his mother's side, the nation's most influential architect, Frank Lloyd Wright, then forty-four years old. It was said that the house was intended for Anna Lloyd Jones Wright, Frank's aging mother, who had bought the land on which it would sit.

The locals were being quite consciously deceived.

The deception was abruptly unmasked on September 8, when the *Chicago Examiner* first broke the story that the house going up across the river was actually intended as a "love nest" or "love cottage" (the *Examiner*'s reporter coined the suggestive phrases, both of which gained wide currency) for Frank Lloyd Wright and his paramour Mamah Borthwick Cheney, the architect's erstwhile neighbor in the posh Chicago suburb of Oak Park.

Even isolated Spring Green knew about Mamah: Frank had already run off with her once before—to Europe, that time—deserting his wife Catherine and their six children. And now he meant to live in quite blatant sin with his illicit "soul mate" just outside this staid, conventional farming village.

Predictably, the town was outraged. Pastors sharpened their pencils and set to work on denunciatory sermons. The newspaper editor cast about for a vocabulary sufficiently purple to express his fury. In time, there was even serious talk that the citizens of Spring Green should mobilize, take arms, and forcibly evict the errant couple from their hillside retreat. And three years later, the house—Taliesin, as it came to be called—would provide the setting for the most horrific single act of mass murder in Wisconsin history.

What *could* Frank Lloyd Wright have been thinking?

1

Prelude to Murder
The Architect and the Feminist

I know how obstinate and egotistic you think me, but I'm
going on as I started. I'm spoiled, first by birth, then by train-
ing, and . . . [finally] by conviction.

Frank Lloyd Wright

Sooner murder an infant in its cradle than nurse unacted
desires.

William Blake, "Proverbs of Hell"

For such a bucolic place, Wisconsin has been the unlikely home to a
disproportionate number of murderers whose depravities have etched
themselves into the collective American consciousness.

Ed Gein, for one. He was arrested in 1957 at his Plainfield "death
farm," which was decorated by bowls made from women's skulls and by
lampshades and chairs fashioned from human skin. A bled and gutted
woman hung in the barn. Gein, who possessed a belt made from nip-
ples, became the prototype for the chilling character Norman Bates,
first in Robert Bloch's eerie story "Psycho" and then in Alfred Hitchcock's defining film. He inspired as well the figure of Buffalo Bill in
Thomas Harris's best-selling *Silence of the Lambs.* And the arch-fiend
Hannibal Lecter in that novel owes much to another Wisconsin killer,
the Milwaukee cannibal Jeff Dahmer.

But in terms of their compressed ferocity and their subsequent impact on cultural (as opposed to popular) history, the high crimes and
misdemeanors of Gein and Dahmer pale in comparison to the murders
committed by the nearly unknown Julian Carlton on August 15, 1914, at
Frank Lloyd Wright's Taliesin near Spring Green, on the forested
banks of the Wisconsin River. Carlton's rampage resulted in the most
murders that had ever been committed by one civilian at one place and
time in Wisconsin history: the murders at Taliesin, therefore, have been
rightly called the state's crime of the twentieth century. Moreover,
unlike the crimes of Gein and Dahmer, Carlton's killings are still
shrouded, some ninety years later, in mystery, debate, and evasion.

And Carlton's murders are noteworthy not merely because of their
inevitably sensationalistic aspects; his crimes transcend the mere unhappy calculus of body count. Consider: the murders involved the century's single most important residential design and the country's most
celebrated and distinctive architect. One of the victims was among the
nation's most conspicuous feminists. The crime was broadcast in print
by a journalist who was so celebrated that his persona became the pro-
tagonist of a staple of the American theater. Further, the accompanying
fire destroyed nearly all of the domestic copies of the folio containing a
retrospective of Wright's work to that date, thereby retarding full American recognition of his achievement for untold years. And finally, scholars and critics have argued persuasively that, in the wake of the Taliesin
murders, Frank Lloyd Wright's designs become markedly (and understandably) more insular, more labyrinthine, even more fortress-like.
Accordingly—given Wright's legions of admirers and imitators—the
slaughter at Taliesin may well have exerted a significant influence on
American residential design throughout the remainder of the twentieth
century.

Yet despite all this, the murders have received surprisingly short
shrift from Wright's vast number of chroniclers. Even as the production
of Wright biographies has emerged as a booming cottage industry
(Wright is the most written-about artistic figure since Michelangelo),
the murders at Taliesin are most often treated as a poignant transitional
event in the great man's convoluted journey toward eventual achievement, confirmation, and glory—a kind of fiery, tragic prelude to the
Imperial Hotel, Fallingwater, and the Guggenheim. One of Wright's

chief biographers dismisses the murders in a single paragraph. In the wake of those seven savage deaths and the destruction of Taliesin, another source notes merely that "This incident marked a rupture in Wright's career."

Well, yes. But perhaps it is time to treat the murders—not to mention their victims and their perpetrator—as something more than footnotes to Wright's ultimate artistic triumph.

Of course, the Taliesin murders, like all murders, do not exist discretely like flies in amber. Rather, they have their own peculiar genesis, their particular genealogy. . . .

—⊡—

It begins with one mystery and ends with another.

The first mystery is this: Why did Frank Lloyd Wright, a committed champion of domestic virtues and a driven artist on the very cusp of achieving his life-long professional ambition, desert his wife Catherine and their six children in 1909 (and again in 1911) to run off with Mamah Cheney, thereby crippling both marriage and career at a single blow? And the second mystery, inextricably bound up with the first: Why, on a blazing summer afternoon five years later, in a frenzy of blood and fire, did Julian Carlton take away everything Wright had left?

The two mysteries exist as twin dancers in a common dance, spinning in a mirrored hall. Still, it is convenient (if factitious) to separate them and regard them one by one.

As for Wright's desertion of his family, glib answers suggest themselves in battalions. Sins of the father, for example: Wright's father had run off (or, arguably, had *been* run off) from his own brood back in 1884, and Wright never spoke to or saw him again. Or perhaps, in the parlance of a later day, Wright simply experienced a midlife crisis, a nervous breakdown, intimations of mortality. Or money problems, a perpetual Wrightian difficulty. Or maybe, some say, he was afraid of success, or of ennui, or of any sort of personal or professional equilibrium. But the puzzle does not surrender itself to pat reduction of this sort.

Nonetheless, one must start with the father, if only because he is a neglected figure. After he leaves Anna Wright, their two young daughters, and their teenage son Frank, history pretty much forgets him. But William Carey Wright is himself an absorbing, compelling figure, one who exerted a greater influence on his famous son than has often been acknowledged. Certainly that famous son was reluctant to make such acknowledgment; he and his rapaciously doting mother, notes a recent biographer, conspired "to diminish the father, to the point where he could be seen to have performed a service not much loftier than that performed by St. Joseph."

William was a New Englander by birth (if not, in some ways, by temperament) at a time when a cultivated man from the green and leafy East could prompt as much enchantment as suspicion among rural midwestern folk. And cultivated he certainly was, although not in any area that promised quick or even long-term riches: he was accomplished on the violin, pianoforte, and organ and was a wonderful orator of the new school—down to earth, not flowery. He was handsome, irresponsible with money, congenitally free-spending. (Even his loving daughter Lizzie conceded that "he had no financial sense whatever.") But he composed waltzes and rondos. He adored Emerson. He dressed with a distinct flair. He crafted violins by hand. When in 1859 he wandered into the village of Lone Rock in remote southwestern Wisconsin, he must have struck the locals as impossibly sophisticated, a bon vivant. Or as much a bon vivant as a nineteenth-century Baptist could be: his father, back in Connecticut, was a celebrated Baptist preacher, and William intended to be one, too, having already taken up and discarded what were to him the less lofty callings of medicine and law.

Within a year of turning up in Lone Rock, the instantly popular Wright, despite his lack of formal credentials, was named Richland County circuit court commissioner. In fact, he was the first lawyer ever to hang out a shingle in Lone Rock. Then it came into his head to run for superintendent of the county school district, and on just his second try and mostly on the power of his undeniable charm, he won. One Wright biographer sees William as among "life's darlings: he never met a single person who did not like him." Not, at least, until he married Anna Lloyd Jones.

Anna, from little Bear Creek, was one of the teachers now under his supervision, and quite by chance she had some very distant relatives in common with Permelia Holcomb Wright, William's wife. Deep into her twenties at this time (like her son after her, she lied about her age throughout her long life), Anna was already considered a spinster. Her features were pinched and severe, a facial characteristic that she passed on to her son, at least in his later years. She was a fine horsewoman and carried herself in a no-nonsense, masculine way. Her two younger sisters, Nell and Jane, had been to college. But like many rural schoolteachers of the day, Anna herself had little formal education.

She was, nonetheless, of good stock: born back in Wales in 1839, she could trace her ancestry, through her mother's clan, back to the Lloyds of Castell-hywel—an area referred to by more orthodox natives as a "black hole of Unitarianism." Her father's forebears included the first Rev. Jenkin Jones, a prominent figure in the development of the rebellious Arminian church, which had split from Calvinism over the doctrines of irresistible grace and predestination. For Anna, all this family history trumped her superintendent's claims to have sprung directly from the line of William the Conqueror, and she was immensely proud of her heritage, even haughty about it.

The Lloyd Joneses had made their way to America from Wales in the mid-1840s, more in pursuit of religious liberty than in hopes of improving their material lot in life. (By then they were all radical Unitarians, a breakaway faith that had evolved from Arminianism's left wing.) This is not to say that they were not desperately poor at the time of their exodus: the journey by sail from Britain to New York and then by wagon and canalboat to the Helena Valley cost them nearly everything they had, including Anna's three-year-old sister Nany, who died miserably of a fever between Utica and Rome, New York. Once in Wisconsin, however, the clan—dominated by farmers, builders, preachers, and educators—began to prosper, so that by the time that Anna met William Wright in the early 1860s, the Lloyd Joneses were among the Valley's most distinguished, prosperous, and distinctive extended family. These theological outcasts even flaunted a suitably defiant, if presumptuous, family motto: "Truth against the World"—meaning, of course, *their* truth.

Anna's father and the clan's patriarch, born at the tail end of the eighteenth century (the same year that Washington died at Mount Vernon), was the Bible-packing, circuit-riding Richard Lloyd Jones (called "Ein Tad"), a tall and thickly bearded figure so intimidating as later to be understandably confused in young Frank Lloyd Wright's mind with the prophet Isaiah. He was "lion maned and mercury tongued," a Wisconsin poet recalled. Over the course of twenty-three years, his wife

Mary Thomas ("Ein Mam" or "Mallie") turned out children, and by 1853 Richard found himself surrounded by ten surviving progeny who, in short order, collectively established the Lloyd Jones dynasty in the Helena Valley. Son Thomas (Frank's early mentor) became the family builder, while his brothers John, James, and Enos farmed. The latter-day Jenkin, like his namesake, was a Civil War hero and famous Unitarian preacher who, down in Chicago, socialized with Susan B. Anthony and Booker T. Washington. Anna taught school, as did her sisters Nell and Jane (after Frank's birth, everyone referred to these two maiden ladies as simply "the Aunts"). Margaret and Mary, a bit older than Anna, married prominent area men. So William Wright's eastern breeding aside, Anna had ample reason to be proud of her own lineage.

Then, in 1863, William's wife Permelia died following the delivery of a stillborn infant, leaving William with their three small children. His subsequent courtship of Anna Lloyd Jones—and her avid reception of it—seemed to make sense on both sides.

True, he was fourteen (Anna maintained *seventeen*) years her senior, short (Anna, like her bewhiskered brothers, was notably tall) and, alas, a Baptist. But at least he was a man with a religious calling; the numerous Lloyd Jones brethren could iron out his theology later. Like Anna's family, he was a decided "dry" on the temperance issue. Further, his education, easy charm, impulsive generosity, good looks, and bubbling musicality were all calculated to stir the heart of the workbound and housebound Anna, whose own artistic sensibilities, such as they were, had been effectively stifled in provincial Bear Creek. Accordingly, there is every reason to suppose, from Anna's side, that this was initially a love match, not a mere flight from the calumny of spinsterhood.

For his part, William needed a wife, and his children needed a mother figure. In Anna, both would be largely disappointed. Brendan Gill quite nakedly asserts that the "single irremediable error" of William's checkered life was his union with "the ambitious, half-mad, sexually cold, and drearily self-righteous Anna Lloyd Jones."

Such an assessment carries with it the conviction inherent to hyperbole, but it may not be entirely fair: many women of a warmer, less volatile, less tiresome nature than Anna's might well have found William hard to live with. True, he was in many ways a lovely, admirable man— gifted (even brilliant), gentle, and long-suffering. But his heart would remain always with his first family, he never acquired the knack of making money, and he was constantly on the move, pursued by creditors. Down deep, in fact, he probably did not care all that much about money. He was an idealist who had migrated westward to disseminate music, oratory, culture, refinement, and high thought, especially New England Transcendentalism's sunnily optimistic gospel of reason and self-reliance. It may have pained him to see his family in want (as they constantly were), but his vision of the American Dream had infinitely more to do with self-fulfillment and the enlightenment of others than with the accumulation of personal wealth. And on those terms, there is a sense in which he succeeded: at the time of his death in 1904, almost every midwesterner whose life he had touched felt enriched and somehow ennobled by that contact. Still, there is a core of truth in his son Frank's assessment when he refers to his father's life as a long and losing battle, a "vain struggle of superior talents [against] untoward circumstance."

Despite some grumblings among the Lloyd Joneses, William and Anna were duly married, probably in August 1866, and some eight months later the new family departed for the nearby market town of Richland Center, where William, now an ordained Baptist minister, had been commissioned to preach and to supervise the construction of a new church building. Here their son was born on June 8, 1867 (not 1869, as that son and Anna would maintain throughout their lives). Emerson, Longfellow, Melville, and Whitman were still alive. The Civil War had ended just two years before. A scant thirty-eight million people lived in the United States.

The boy was dubbed Frank Lincoln Wright; William venerated the recently murdered president and had eloquently eulogized him back in Lone Rock. (Almost seventy years later, critic Alexander Woollcott would complain that friend Frank's prose style was entirely too "Lincolnesque.") Frank, immediately and obsessively adored by his mother, joined an ample household that included William's three children by his first wife Permelia—Charles (then eleven), George (nine), and little Elizabeth Amelia ("Lizzie," about seven). But there would never be a question as to who was Anna's favorite.

In Richland Center, William scored an immediate social success. The town's newspapers vied with each other in their celebration of this welcome newcomer's contributions to the cultural and spiritual life of the community. But also in Richland Center begins (or perhaps continues) an intractably recurring, predictable pattern in William's life: he charms, he impresses, he enchants, he preaches, and then he leaves. And, more important to Anna, he leaves without making money. A recent biographer truly observes that the proud and talented William "excelled at everything but turning a profit."

He and Anna did continue to make babies, however: by the spring of 1869, another was on the way, and the Wrights moved to the Mississippi River town of McGregor, Iowa, where Mary Jane ("Jennie") was born. Anna found herself as housebound and as pinched for cash as she had been as a single woman back in the Valley amid her outsized brothers. But at least she had Frank, on whom she doted almost pathologically. He was destined for great things, she assured him (and herself) repeatedly.

Barely two years later, dogged by money troubles, William and his family were on the road again, first to the Lloyd Jones redoubt, near Spring Green, and then back east to the outskirts of Pawtucket, Rhode Island, where William sought to rebuild a church. In her five years of married life, Anna had already undergone three wrenching relocations.

Unable to resurrect the local church, William was ultimately reduced to accepting donations from his adoring congregation in order to keep food on the table. Under pressures of this sort, Anna, as a wife, was emerging into a caricature of a shrew; as a stepmother, she was evolving into something out of the Brothers Grimm.

Anna seems to have singled out Lizzie, William's youngest child by Permelia, as the primary target of her venom. In her unpublished memoir, Lizzie recalls some of her childhood in Iowa and Pawtucket under Anna's roof:

> As I grew older, [Anna] used to tell me that she hated me and all my Mother's people. . . . She not only beat me till I was black and blue all over but threatened me with some terrible things, and especially if I should tell my father about her treatment. . . .
>
> One . . . time when he was at home and up in his study, she was frying meat at the stove with a long two-tined fork. . . . She got at me for something or nothing and grabbed me by the hair and held my head back and jabbed that fork at my face and said she would put my eyes

out. . . . I remember one time she was pounding beefsteak with a heavy hardwood roller with sharp ridges all over it, made for the purpose, and she pounded me all over my back with it until I was black and blue and sore but not bleeding. . . . I could never please her, no matter how hard I tried. She admitted sometimes that she hated me and all my mother's relatives; she said she would like to have all our heads laid over a log and take an ax and chop them off. I do not know whether her mind was just right or not. She seemed to have periodical spells when she got "mad hysterics" and raved like a maniac. Then she would be sick in bed for a day or two and I would have peace.

On another occasion, in the dead of winter, Anna threw well water on Lizzie, so that her clothes froze to her body. In an act that must have called for the most excruciatingly delicate diplomacy, William gently inquired of the intimidating Lloyd Jones brethren whether there was a history of insanity in the family. The offended brothers would allow only that Anna possessed what they called "a most tremendous temper."

In 1874, for her own protection, William packed Lizzie off to Permelia's relations. In due course, his two sons by his first wife also left to fashion their own lives. Anna was gratified: by her reckoning, the much-despised Wright children were departing ("For Anna," asserts one observer, "[they] ceased to exist"), leaving only genuine Lloyd Jones young ones at home. Especially Frank. Anna seems not to have cared much for her two daughters by William, while, according to one account, she "appears to have regarded her son as the consequence of a sort of virgin birth, for which she deserved and took all the credit." In all his copious autobiographical writings, Frank Wright hardly mentions his sisters and never refers to his three stepsiblings; his father is largely dismissed as an ineffectual martinet. "His parents," a biographer notes, "seemed to exist only for him." In sum, Frank's birth, less than a year into Anna's marriage, had already signaled an early but permanent alteration in the family's dynamics, a seismic shift from the father to the son. Even one chronicler of the family who is habitually kinder and more tolerant toward Anna than are others acknowledges that she "turned on Frank the full force of her starved emotional needs," often in disturbing ways. Maginel, Frank's younger sister, observed that Anna "gathered all the strands of her yearning, wove them together, and fastened them once and for all to her son. He was more than her child. He was her protégé, her legacy. He would accomplish what she and her husband could not. From the start, her devotion to Frank was overwhelming, and as it grew, the gulf between her and father widened." Frank himself conceded the point: "She [Anna] lived much in [me]."

This peculiar and much-discussed matter of Anna's attachment to and influence upon her son finally escapes our full understanding. In her old age, she once confided to Frank that her own childhood in the Valley had been hard and truncated; "she had felt hemmed in all her life by circumstance," she said. Her younger daughter perceived in Anna an incessant yearning "for some elusive thing, something that refused to take shape . . . and make itself known." Clearly, such comments bespeak the frustration of an ambitious will. In a brilliant review piece on Edna St. Vincent Millay, *New Yorker* writer Judith Thurman remarks on how frequently writers and other artists spring from mothers such as Anna, "exceptional women disappointed in marriage and thwarted in ambition and desire who give all and ask for nothing except that the special child live gloriously enough for two." Thurman speculates that, in taking up that burden, the child assumes a task "inherently impossible to finish," yet somehow "fundamental to art."

In any event, following five years in Rhode Island, the nomadic Wrights were inexorably on the move—first to William's father's house in Essex, Connecticut, and then, in 1875, to Weymouth, Massachusetts, where William had accepted another call to preach. Once again, William's parishioners fell in love with him, as he espoused the Baptist worldview with his characteristic vigor and eloquence.

Then, three years later, an odd thing happened: William abruptly announced that he had become a Unitarian, abandoned his astonished Baptist flock, and moved his poverty-plagued family back west, to Madison, Wisconsin, where there was hope at least for some financial support from Anna's family.

Not enough has been made of this religious conversion; most often, like the move to Madison (and therefore to the environs of the Helena Valley), William's theological about-face is seen as a further concession—a "sop," it has been called—to his wife and the Lloyd Jones clan, a quid pro quo for their help. And it is certain that the intervention of the eminent Jenkin Lloyd Jones, a kind of Unitarian bishop in

Chicago, oiled William's easy transition into the Unitarian mission field. But surely there must have been more to it than that. After all, by this time William was approaching his midfifties. Like his father and numberless ancestors before him (and indeed like his son Charles after him), William had spent much of his professional lifetime as a preacher, proclaiming the triune nature of the godhead, urging the salvific efficacy of Christ's sacrifice on Calvary, and defending the New Testament accounts of Jesus' miracles. For him to renounce all of this presumably heartfelt doctrine and then to embrace his wife's intensely liberal Unitarian creed with its specific denial of Christ's divinity is a shocking or at least remarkably dramatic step. Perhaps finally it was William's lifelong veneration of Emerson—the one enthusiasm he shared with Anna, the young Frank, and all the Lloyd Joneses—that accounts for the lurching reversal: the Transcendentalist movement, of course, was rooted in the New England Unitarianism of such influential religious thinkers as William Ellery Channing and the luminous Orestes Brownson. But whatever his motive, one effect of William's conversion was that he thereafter preached much less and began to see himself primarily as a teacher of music, not of salvation.

In fact, after a summer sabbatical at Hillside, William set up shop on Pinckney Street in Madison, then a city of only 25,000, heralding his enterprise as a "conservatory of music" and offering instruction in voice and in nearly any instrument. And he actually bought—not rented—a house on Gorham Street, near the shoreline of picturesque Lake Mendota. The family could certainly have used the enhanced living space: although William's children by Permelia were now gone (Lizzie, still charging Anna with spoiling Frank rotten, returned for a time to attend high school in Madison), the Wrights had a new daughter, the initially fragile Maginel, born in 1877 back in Weymouth. And for the first time young Frank now had his own room, on the door of which he posted such stern adolescent warnings as "Sanctum Sanctorum" and "Keep Out!" The music conservatory could not meet the family's financial needs, however, and one day hardy Uncle James drove a produce-laden wagon, with a cow in reluctant tow, forty one-way miles from Hillside to the Madison house so that "Anna's children," as he pointedly called them, could have some fresh milk and decent home-grown food. Soon William, properly humbled, was compelled to supplement the family income by preaching in the Valley and by taking his well-tuned tonsils out onto the lecture circuit yet again.

Meanwhile, Frank, always a lackluster student, matriculated at the Second Ward School and then at Madison High, from which he ultimately dropped out. But an education of a different and more meaningful sort had been opened to him: for something like eight straight summers, Uncle James came to Madison and took Frank off to the Helena Valley to "make a farmer" out of him. Anna's feelings about all this must have been mixed. On the one hand, Frank was being ushered into more intimate identification with the Lloyd Jones clan and was thereby being further dissociated from his increasingly superfluous, redundant father; on the other, Anna's tearful separations from the son on whom she had pinned her all her hopes for personal vindication must have been genuinely painful. She even had to cut off his golden curls.

Those summers were painful for Frank, as well. True, a half-century later in his *Autobiography,* he would wax rhapsodic about the glories of the Wisconsin countryside, the transcendent joys of agrarian life, and "milkweed blossoming to scatter its snowy fleece on every breeze." But most of this was mere Emersonian pap: in reality, James rousted the boy from bed at four every morning and worked him to exhaustion, so that Frank ran away on at least three occasions. Years later, in a private conversation with an apprentice, he would bluntly sum up his real take on farming: "It's all pulling tits and shoveling shit." The mature Wright certainly appreciated and even deified "Nature" (he commonly and reverentially capitalized the word), but it was a nature at one remove, more to be admiringly observed and philosophized about from a respectful distance than to be earthily and intimately experienced on a working Wisconsin farm.

And back home on Gorham Street, William and Anna's marriage was spiraling out of control toward its inevitable crash. At age ninety-three, William's father had died, leaving his son enough money—if just enough—to pay off the accrued family bills. But somewhere around February 1883, in the wake of a violent fight over the paltry remains of his inheritance, Anna announced that she loathed the ground on which her hapless husband trod, and she evicted him from the marital bed, relegating him to what he complained was "the coldest room in the house." After at least a year of such treatment, and following some eighteen years of a marital union that he characterized in his court deposition as "unhappy from the start"—he alleged even physical abuse at Anna's hands—William filed for divorce on grounds of desertion. Anna, counseled by the Reverend Jenkin Lloyd Jones and the Valley brethren, did not contest the action; in fact, biographer Meryle Secrest speculates that William's desertion reflects the ultimate success of a long-term and quite calculated campaign on Anna's part.

In any event, William packed the few scant possessions he could carry with him (his violins, mostly) and left the Madison house and Anna and their three children. Frank records that he never spoke to or saw him again. Maginel asked her mother what she should tell inquisitive neighbors about her father's abrupt disappearance. Anna's reply was typically curt: "Say he's dead."

William drifted back to where his heart led him—to the children of his first family—and he spent the remainder of his days in his characteristically itinerant manner, teaching music in various midwestern states. He died at his son Charles's house near Pittsburgh in 1904 after making sure that his body would be transported back to Lone Rock to lie beside Permelia, the wife he had loved. Frank *Lloyd* Wright—by now he had discarded the middle name chosen for him by William and adopted one more to his mother's liking—was nearby at the time of his father's funeral and burial, but he did not attend. If Anna gloated, finding justification in this pointed and hostile act of filial neglect, she ought not have: when she herself finally died in 1923, Frank did not bother dropping by her funeral, either.

—🔲—

In his *Autobiography,* Frank Wright broods over his own culpability in the divorce of his parents. In truth, his role in the breakup makes for an intriguing psychological study, especially given the awful events that would unfold in Oak Park and Spring Green a quarter century later. A biographer perceptively discerns "a kind of tragic pattern [that] emerges from even the little that is known of William Wright's story." And it is fascinating—even eerie—to observe how that same pattern plays itself out once more in the life of William's famous son.

Actually, in many ways the two were remarkably alike. For all the subsequent palaver (much of it generated by Frank himself) about

Anna's influence on Frank—her prenatal visions of his becoming "an Architect," her purchase of the fabled Froebel blocks with which his boyish hands first fashioned geometric patterns—a good case can be made that the young man actually turned out to be very much his father's son.

On a superficial level, Frank inherited William's diminutive stature. But perhaps this physical legacy is not so superficial, after all: Frank drafted his residential designs with reference to what he called "the human scale," by which he meant his own modest stature. Visitors to Taliesin and other Wright-designed houses are forever bumping their heads on beams, lintels, and the edges of cantilevered roofs. Gill charges Wright with committing "psychological blackmail upon anyone taller than he."

More fundamentally, they shared a maddeningly cavalier attitude toward money and the practical aspects of life that was coupled (often helpfully) with an easy, winning charm. William was in debt most of his days and much preferred buying violins to supplying clothes or beefsteaks for his family; still, his parishioners could not help but cherish him. Similarly, Frank spent a lifetime either avoiding creditors or charming them into capitulation. For example, he once owed his Sauk County neighbor Ed Kraemer a sizeable sum for delivered limestone, and Kraemer confronted him over the matter on the street. Looping up his arm to cast it around big Ed's shoulders, Frank purred, "Ah, Ed, what's a little money between friends?" Much later, in 1936, Frank infuriated Herbert Johnson when the final costs for the Johnson Wax Building in Racine, Wisconsin—a Wright masterpiece—ran many times over budget; but then Wright turned on the charm, and Johnson ended up giving him two further commissions. ("Do you hypnotize your clients?" baffled colleagues asked Wright.) A sheriff once took up residence in the children's playroom in Frank's Oak Park home for a night while the architect scraped up enough money to pay off an old debt. Anna Wright would have had parallel and doleful memories touching upon her difficult days with free-spending William.

But despite their frequent setbacks, Frank and William shared as well an indomitable sense of self-assurance and correspondingly gregarious, even evangelical, natures. Frank indeed would come to see his profession as a kind of prophetic, semi-priestly calling, akin in its way to his father's old call to a variety of fiery Baptist pulpits.

Both had problems as parents, too. In his *Autobiography*—that odd and oracular outpouring of habitual unreliability and occasional real beauty—Frank claims that William never loved him at all, alleges some harsh treatment (if not outright abuse) at his hands, and records a possibly apocryphal episode in which he, Frank, beat up his father in a fist-fight. However accurate these accounts, it is certain that Frank's young sisters, Jennie and Maginel, were deeply troubled by William's departure from home and hearth. Years later, in the wake of deserting his own six children, Frank confessed, "I never had the father-feeling"; elsewhere, he asserts that his real children were his buildings and that he detested the word "Papa." As an adult, his son John remarked, "I often wonder now why he didn't leave sooner."

Both William and Frank were ardent advocates of Emerson and, through him, of a glorification of radical individualism, an idiocentrism that social historian Quentin Anderson calls a celebration of "the imperial self." In fact, more than one scholar correctly locates the primary source of Frank Wright's intellectual debt in the person of Emerson, "whose respect for nature and whose comments on architecture provided the young architect with a groundwork upon which he would build a complex, philosophical justification for a personal architectural expression." In 1959, at Frank Lloyd Wright's funeral, someone inevitably read Emerson's famous lines "Whoso would be a man must be a nonconformist. . . . Nothing is at last sacred but the integrity of your own mind." Father William could have hardly demurred.

Finally, William bequeathed to Frank his passion for music. Young Frank played piano and viola in the family orchestra. When he left home for Chicago in 1887, he had seven dollars in his pocket; upon arrival, he immediately spent one of them to attend a concert. More importantly, even Frank conceded that his father had taught him "to see a symphony as an Edifice—of sound!" This spiritual linkage between musical composition and architecture may well have been William's most important and lasting legacy to his son. One observer aptly summarizes Wright's debt to his father: "Temperamentally and physically, the two were very alike, and Anna Wright's awareness of this resemblance must have caused her many a rueful shake of the head: no matter how vehemently she pressed her claim to a total possession of Frank, genetically he was a Wright and not a Lloyd Jones."

One last similarity: It may be that there was one favored woman in each of their lives. For William, it was Permelia, beside whom he had himself buried in the chilly little village of Lone Rock. For Frank, it was Mamah Bouton Borthwick. He had himself buried near her, as well, on the grounds of the chapel at Hillside, in the very shadow of fabled Taliesin where she had so hideously died.

All of that, however, came much later.

—🔲—

Given this natural consanguinity between father and son, the question then arises: Why did Frank side so determinedly with his mother (with whom he had his own problems) throughout the divorce action, a stance from which he never budged? True, William had probably been a somewhat distant father figure for his three children by Anna, and no doubt the adolescent Frank clashed with him from time to time. Anna, conversely, was routinely supportive of her son. Still, it seems hard to account for Frank's passionate championing of his mother's cause. He must have been aware of her mistreatment of Permelia's children, for example, or of the various calculated cruelties she had visited upon William himself over the years. Nor could it have been lost on him that his mother flatly lied about her marriage's failure. For one thing, she falsely represented herself, not William, as having been the plaintiff in the divorce action. She also depicted herself as the blameless victim of a whimsical, unprovoked desertion, a discarded woman who had been shamed as a divorcee in the eyes of the community and punished for crimes of which she was ignorant. "In actuality, of course," a biographer reminds us, "Anna had been the defendant against a lonely and frustrated husband who had apparently clung to a deteriorating marriage long after it was salvageable." The perceptive Frank surely knew all this. A quarter-century later, moreover, he would replicate William's flight from domesticity. Why, then, did he cling to his mother's charade with such fierce tenacity?

At the time of the divorce, young Frank clearly wanted to identify himself with Anna's branch of the family: he seems to have admired their stability, their interdependence, and their sense of established place. And much later in his life, his defense of his mother—formalized into words decades after the divorce—provides an analogical defense, some say, of his abandonment of his own first wife and family in 1909 and 1911. According to this credible view, Frank embraced Anna's grotesquely distorted version of events so that he could portray her, however inaccurately, as a heroic martyr, sacrificed on the altar of society's narrow moral sensibilities for the crime of pursuing her own worldview and of exercising the integrity of her particular ethical vision. At the time he wrote the *Autobiography,* such a portrayal served Frank's personal ends well, as one Wright scholar demonstrates: "Just as Anna had suffered during her 'persecution,' so had he [Frank] been publicly condemned for doing what he felt was right [in deserting his wife and children in 1909]. Just as she had been 'punished' for her courage, so had he been ostracized for acting openly and honestly. As Wright saw it, he and his mother had suffered similar unjust fates, and the parallel between their lives gave him a certain solace. Identifying with Anna's interpretation of her marital difficulties gave him a crutch to lean on during his own predicaments."

Those "predicaments" began in 1887, when Frank, who had run off to Chicago against Anna's wishes, fell in love with a high school girl named Catherine Lee Tobin.

—◫—

Much has been made about how little formal education Frank Lloyd Wright received. He always claimed to have left the University of Wisconsin in his senior year, but that was a lie. He probably attended one year only, in 1886, and he studied engineering there (at least in a desultory way), not architecture. He did some construction work on the campus's Science Hall, and he claimed to have witnessed the collapse of a wing of the nearby State Capitol building, which had been erected on a foundation of shoddy materials. If so, Wright learned the implied lesson well. When the Kanto earthquakes of 1922 and 1923 leveled much of Tokyo, the Wright-designed Imperial Hotel held firm. And when his Midway Gardens in Chicago was torn down, the contractors hired for the purpose went broke, because the building so stubbornly resisted the wrecking ball.

Some further good came out of his college year in Madison. A university dean and professor of civil engineering, Allan D. Conover, was starting up a local architectural practice, and he hired Frank as a laborer at the Science Hall site. More importantly, he also taught him the rudiments of drafting and some elementary principles of engineering. And between semesters, back at Hillside, Unity Chapel was being built, the Reverend Jenkin having decided that the Helena Valley Joneses needed a proper place to pray. Jenkin hired Chicago architect J. Lyman Silsbee for the job; Silsbee had done the design for Jenkin's All Souls Unitarian Church back in the metropolis. But it is likely that young Frank played a significant role as draftsman for the chapel and that he contributed to the sanctuary's interior design and decoration. This experience served to augment what Frank must have already learned about the essentials of the building trade from Uncle Thomas during those long summers months spent on James's farm.

In any case, and on the solitary basis of this spare background in the profession, young Frank Lloyd Wright now fancied himself prepared to commence his architectural career. In the early days of 1887, after pawning some of departed William's books, he immediately set off for Chicago, which had become a mecca for ambitious architects from around the country ever since the Great Fire of 1871 had gutted vast expanses of the city. Very much his father's son, he left behind him a flock of Madison creditors.

Anna may have been prepared for and even have helped choreograph William's defection, but she was not prepared for this one: she wanted Frank close to home and continuing his studies. She fired off a fusillade of letters, entreating him to return to Madison, and even recruited brother Jenkin to her campaign. The preacher backed her with the full weight of his considerable authority, predicting somberly that in Chicago Frank would merely "waste himself on fine clothes and girls." Frank, who (at first, anyway) had no intention of wasting himself at anything other than purposeful work, steadfastly refused to come home. Anna must have felt in some way betrayed—she had made enormous personal sacrifices to help him through his one year of school—but it was always her way to forgive him anything. Soon enough, she swept up her daughters and took the train to Chicago to find Frank and keep a steady eye on him. By late 1887, she was again living with Frank, this time in the home of her friend Augusta Chapin in suburban Oak Park.

The portly Miss Chapin was an ordained Universalist minister, an extraordinary novelty for a woman at the time.

Ironically, Frank's connection with Jenkin had won him his first job in the city, as a tracer of drawings for his uncle's own architect, Silsbee. Through Silsbee—also the son of a Unitarian minister—Wright met and shrewdly cultivated the friendship of yet another preacher's son, the young draftsman Cecil Corwin, who soon was lending the newcomer money and sharing his lodgings with him. More importantly, Corwin provided him entrée into the cosmopolitan ways of the big city and became his social mentor, teaching him how to dress, where to eat, what cultural events to attend, and with whom to be seen. Wright himself confessed his need for such instruction, finding Corwin "so much more developed than I. So I began to go to school to Cecil."

Again, Frank—a comparative provincial for whom such things as telephones, cable cars, and electric lights were new—learned his lessons dutifully and well. Before long, he was cutting a bold figure in Chicago, frequenting expensive restaurants, revamping his wardrobe, and, as in Madison, living light years beyond his means. He repeatedly demanded raises in salary from Silsbee in a futile effort at keeping up with his inflated expectations of what the world owed a young man of his talents, spiritual sensibilities, and newly refined appetites.

And as always, he kept an opportunistic eye out for the best chance. It was not long in coming. The design for the projected Auditorium Building, the decade's plum commission, had fallen to the thriving firm of Adler and Sullivan. In eager response, Wright ditched Silsbee after less than a year and, following a brief stopover with another firm, signed on as a draftsman with the great Louis Henri Sullivan, "Father of the Skyscraper," ultimately securing a five-year exclusive contract. As part of the arrangement, Wright was asked to agree that he would not leverage his new position in order to "moonlight" or "bootleg" his own residential designs during off hours, as so many unscrupulous young architects were doing. Frank promised that he would not. At the time, he may even have meant it.

—▣—

For the moment, Wright was content to learn at Sullivan's knee, to evolve into "a good pencil" in the hand of the burly, brilliant man he called his *lieber Meister,* his "beloved master," one of the few people in his life to whom he would ever defer. Toward that end, Wright worked with ferocious focus and indefatigable energy, until the day his own drawings finally became indistinguishable from Sullivan's. He quickly assumed the mantle of his master's favorite—a fact so self-evident and so rankling to the firm's other draftsmen that it prompted fisticuffs and even a knife fight in the studio. Frank took pride in occupying an office that adjoined Sullivan's. He asked for raises and got them, becoming (at sixty dollars a week) the highest-paid draftsman in Chicago and, by 1889, the practice's chief designer. Sullivan's enthusiasm for his new acolyte, his "other self," may have partaken of the erotic: Wright was an attractive, charming young man, and Sullivan harbored distinctly homosexual leanings. But Wright was a painfully shy virgin—Anna had taught him, from her experience with William, that sexual contact of any kind was a "contamination"—and he was in the studio of Adler and Sullivan only to learn architectural design. He did learn, voraciously and rapidly, soaking up knowledge and influences like a sponge. It was an education that lasted him a lifetime and that changed the American residential landscape forever.

"Form follows function," Sullivan famously (if none too originally) argued. What he was really asserting was the need for a distinctly American architecture, in contrast to the neoclassical European designs that were in vogue at the time, all Beaux Arts colonnades and Romanesque arches. "Walk for a few blocks through the streets of our city where 'good copies' abound," Sullivan bemoaned, "and you will find a different civilization on every corner and subcivilizations aplenty in between— and yet nobody laughs!" What was needed, Sullivan maintained in his own vague way, was an architecture worthy of the brave *terra nova*, reflective of democratic, Emersonian ideals and emerging honestly and naturally out of such considerations as setting, materials, and purpose. It would fall to Wright, ultimately, to realize Sullivan's inchoate vision.

If the path of Sullivan's career in Chicago reflects the grimly inevitable rise-and-fall parabola of Sophoclean tragedy (one that Wright, in his own way, would reprise), its apex was certainly the grand opening of the Auditorium Building on December 9, 1889. That magnificent opera house, four years in the making, was Chicago's most impressive pile, encompassing offices, shops, a four-hundred room hotel, a theater, and the world's largest concert hall. From its stage, the celebrated Spanish soprano Adelina Patti sang on opening night for a packed house; even the president, Benjamin Harrison, was there. Wright had played a small but helpful part in the auditorium's design, and he giddily recalled that Sullivan's tuxedoed men "all floated upon [the city's enthusiasm] like small ships in a grand pageant."

But an abrupt reversal in Sullivan's fortunes, his peripeteia, was already in the works. The World's Columbian Exposition—people called it more economically "The World's Fair"—was held in Chicago in 1893, and it instantly and effectively smothered everything fresh in American building design. Under the classicist Charles Atwood and his partner Daniel Burnham, the fair's construction chief, practitioners of the emerging Chicago school were routinely snubbed in favor of New York architects who favored drearily atavistic Romanesque and Beaux Arts designs. Sullivan was most conspicuously shunted aside, permitted to exhibit one sole building, which, while quite wonderful, became lost "in a great wave of Greek temples, Roman baths, and classic arches." The millions who attended the fair went home to demand dignified and restrained buildings like the ones they had seen there. For Sullivan, the writing was on the decidedly traditionalist wall: he was doomed. "The damage wrought by the World's Fair," he foretold, "will last from half a century from its date, if not longer."

Wright could read the signs, as well. The nation, he said, had come to a pivotal juncture, and 1893 was the "fateful year in the culture of these United States. They [were] about to go Psuedo-Classic in Architecture." That very year, he and Sullivan acrimoniously broke off their relationship, ostensibly over Wright's "bootlegging" of a number of residential designs on his own time, including the Blossom (1892), Parker (1892), and Gale (1893) houses, for which Wright had duplicitously cited Cecil Corwin as "architect of record." Sullivan felt personally as well as professionally betrayed; his confrontation with Wright, says Gill, resembled "a lovers' quarrel." But the sagacious Wright knew a sinking ship when he saw it, and he had no intention of lashing himself to its hull. Once the star among Chicago architects, Sullivan was down and out by 1909. "With the future blank," he wrote in a lachrymose letter to Wright, "I am surely living in hell." He died in 1924, an utterly broken alcoholic. Toward the end, the *lieber Meister* was reduced to begging handouts from his former disciple.

But while the World's Fair had been an unalloyed disaster for Sullivan, it was not so for Wright. The official Japanese contribution to the exposition was a half-scale model of the Ho-o-Den temple pavilion, a compellingly delicate seventeenth-century design—sweeping horizontal lines, natural wood and stone materials, translucent screens, and interlocking modular construction—that seemed to emerge organically out of the ground. Wright looked at the buildings long and hard. He was enchanted; his aesthetic sensibility would never be the same. The "Prairie house" was about to rise from the ashes of Sullivan's ruin.

—◨—

According to a recent biographer, that same 1893 Columbian Exposition celebrated an "emerging American type" of young womanhood—"tall, with well-formed limbs, radiating good health, vigorous and suitably virginal, yet at some level aware of her budding sexuality." Red-haired Catherine Lee Tobin, "Kitty" to her intimates, might well have served as a model for this new ideal of feminine beauty, a veritable Gibson Girl in the flesh. Moreover, she was vivacious, bright, charmingly opinionated, refined, and rich: her doting parents—Kitty was the family favorite—were well-heeled Unitarians living in Chicago's fashionable Kenwood district on the South Side. And despite her precocity, Catherine seemed perfectly willing to subjugate herself utterly to the will and needs of whatever man she happened to marry, however demandingly narcissistic he might prove. She aimed, in sum, to be the perfect Victorian wife.

Wright had first spotted her at Uncle Jenk's All Souls church in 1887, the same year he joined Adler and Sullivan. He met her formally at a dinner and dance where he was dressed up in a military costume out of Victor Hugo's *Les Miserables* and seemed enamored of the clanking sword that came with the outfit. He literally collided with Catherine as he ran toward a group of friends, knocking foreheads with her and falling with her to the floor. The next anyone knew, she was saving him a seat beside her at All Souls, and the two were scarcely seen apart. She was only sixteen, a student at Hyde Park High School. Frank indicated that he planned to marry her. His mother was equally determined that no such thing should happen, ever.

In order to make some sense out of Anna's intractable opposition to the match, one must finally question whether she was willing to share her son with any other woman. After all, the proposed union was exceptionally and self-evidently promising. In fact, a good case could have been made at the time that it was Frank who had been dealt the better hand. Catherine was a prize catch. She was beautiful, intelligent, moneyed, and resided several social steps above the struggling young architect who, only a few years before, had been little more than a Wisconsin farmhand with a knack for design. Moreover, Kitty was no dim-witted debutante. She was sensible enough to discern Frank's flippant disregard for practical matters, for example, and she took swift and effective steps toward getting his finances in order, at least for a while. Finally, her love for the promising young man was authentic and passionate. Frank had long dreamed of an ideal mate, some "intimate fairy princess," as he put it, a "muse [and] selfless helpmate" who would unconditionally adore him (as Anna did) and spur him on to professional glory. In Catherine, he seemed to have located just such perfection in a potential life partner.

But Anna, whatever her motives, objected. Over the next two years, she repeatedly attempted to sabotage the relationship. Her initial tactic was to confront Frank directly and appeal to his ego, always a soft spot. "Have you thought of the consequences," she asked him, "to this young girl of your singling her out to the exclusion of all others?" When that approach failed, she wheedled Cecil Corwin into advising his friend against a hasty marriage. But Frank instantly saw through that clumsy bit of subterfuge. Desperate now, Anna alerted Catherine's parents; alarmed, they shipped their daughter off to northern Michigan for several months.

All of Anna's efforts, however, finally came to nothing. Frank and Catherine were married in Uncle Jenk's Silsbee-designed All Souls on June 1, 1889. Wright was a week shy of twenty-two, Catherine barely eighteen. It rained all day. Catherine's father wept during the ceremony, and Anna fainted dead away. Perhaps she found at least some consolation in Frank's selection of the honeymoon spot: the Helena Valley, the domain of her Lloyd Jones kin.

Upon his return to Chicago, Wright told Louis Sullivan about a choice residential lot that he had spotted in suburban Oak Park and on which he wanted to build a house. Sullivan loaned him five thousand dollars for the purchase but warned him sternly against cost overruns in the home's construction. Frank said he would be careful.

Meanwhile, he and his new bride were living with Anna and Frank's sisters in the close quarters of furnished rooms, and his mother had already begun casting at Catherine the same vitriol that she had tossed young Lizzie's way years before. "Poor Kitty," Maginel later lamented. "She didn't deserve so forcible an adversary as my mother." Frank seems to have done little or nothing to block even Anna's most excessively nasty assaults on his young wife. When he was away at work, the thoroughly intimidated Catherine took to hiding in closets. And she can hardly have been cheered by the fact that Anna had sold her Madison house for cash, vowing to move in next door to Frank and Kitty's new home.

—▣—

Oak Park—like bucolic Spring Green later on—at first seems an odd choice of residence for Frank Lloyd Wright, whose premeditated flamboyance eventually became the stuff of legend: the town prided itself on its propriety, manicured lawns, good schools, and its spiritual remove from Chicago, just to the east. Oak Park, its residents boasted, was "where the saloon stops and the Church steeples begin." Actually, Frank's bohemian flamboyance came upon him only later, after he was established and successful. For now, he wanted someplace conventional and respectable—a good place to build a career and raise a family. Staid, leafy Oak Park filled the bill nicely. "Saint's Rest," people called it. "So many churches for so many good people to go to, I suppose," said puckish Wright.

The house he built there at 428 Forest Avenue for him and Kitty was itself fairly conventional—on the outside, at least—recalling Silsbee's and H. H. Richardson's East Coast "shingle style." It was finished by the early spring of 1890, just in time for the birth of the couple's first child, Lloyd. For Wright, however, no house was ever truly "finished": he kept tinkering with the design, never quite able to leave it alone. He had the sublimely nonsensical (but vaguely Whitmanesque-sounding) motto "Truth Is Life!" carved into the mantelpiece. He obsessed over the placement of the furniture, constantly moving it around for just the right effect. Later, as more children arrived, he added a vaulted playroom and then, in 1898, a separate drafting studio. In the words of one observer, the residence grew like Topsy, becoming an outright "laboratory for many of [Wright's] experiments in domestic architecture." Frank's vow to Sullivan notwithstanding, construction costs came in wildly over the initial budget. This tendency on Wright's part to exceed—indeed, to pretty much ignore—projected costs would recur stubbornly over the next nineteen years, during which time Frank built some twenty-nine homes for his frequently irritated Oak Park neighbors. But despite his well-earned reputation for budget busting, Oak Parkians could not get around the fact that the residences he built for them were beautiful, wonderful. "It is like living within a work of art," gushed one satisfied customer. In fact, the tidy streets of the suburb eventually evolved into a virtual museum of Wright's architecture.

True to her promise, Anna moved into an existing Gothic Revival cottage just around the corner; she had purchased the place promptly after Frank bought his Forest Avenue lot. And predictably, her quite unmerited torment of Catherine picked up seamlessly from where it had left off. "As a child bride," records a Wright biographer, "Kitty [was] no match for her calculating mother-in-law. One of the most difficult aspects of marriage for Kitty must have been living next door to the one person who (as everyone knew) would always try to drive a wedge between her son and any woman perceived as a rival."

In an exercise of almost superhuman patience, Catherine nonetheless played the role of "the dutiful daughter-in-law to the dragonish Anna Lloyd Wright with remarkable competence." She set up a kindergarten in their new house. She joined clubs, involved herself in various civic causes, and earned herself a reputation as a model wife, mother, and hostess. There were problems, of course: Anna's incessant meddlings, the pangs of repeated childbirths, rumors of infidelities, and Frank's penchant for spending considerably more than he brought in. Still, Catherine was permitted perhaps a decade and a half—say, from 1890 to 1905 or so—of relative marital happiness. But no more than that; and when the end finally came, it was dreadful.

Having broken with Sullivan in 1893, husband Frank immediately set up shop in the Schiller Building on Randolph Street in Chicago with long-time friends Cecil Corwin and Robert C. Spencer Jr. The degree of collaboration among them is uncertain, however: Wright brought his work home, doing his actual drafting at Oak Park in the warm (if increasingly disruptive) familial glow of pretty Catherine and their ever-increasing number of offspring. Six children made their appearance in brisk order: Lloyd (in 1890), John Lloyd (1892), Catherine (1894), David (1895), Frances (1898), and, finally, son Llewellyn (1903). Wright, in his few off hours, played the role of indulgent *pater familias* to the hilt, thundering out Beethoven sonatas on the player piano, hosting countless clambakes, romping cheerfully with the children in the wondrous playroom, and playing boisterously with them on his green Oak Park lawns. His children were denied nothing, and it is easy to see all this paternal indulgence as a reaction against Wright's own childhood background of penury, emotional chilliness, and want. And as if his own progeny proved insufficient to satisfy Wright's parental instincts, he gradually became a father figure to the dozen or so apprentices and draftsmen who came to work over at the attached studio. Even clients and other admirers were welcomed into the extended family circle. "The [Oak Park] house was filled with noise and laughter," Maginel recalled, and son John remembered his father as "an epic of wit and merriment that gave our home the feeling of a jolly carnival. . . . There were parties somewhere all of the time and everywhere some of the time. . . . It was fun just to have him about." On a distinctly sourer note, one neighbor grumbled, "If that fellow Wright doesn't stop having children, he'll overcrowd this town."

So despite his later dismissive comments about fatherhood, Frank seemed to have entered into domestic suburban life with enormous zest and exuberance. While Catherine ran her kindergarten and household and busied herself with worthy civic endeavors, Frank competed in genteel horse shows, affiliated himself with exclusive organizations for local bibliophiles and literati, designed area golf and tennis clubhouses, and blithely accumulated speeding tickets by roaring through town in his specially modified Stoddard-Dayton sport car, nicknamed "The Yellow Devil." The family quickly won the respect and affection of the community. "Mr. Wright is held in high esteem by his neighbors," purred the *Oak Park Reporter.* They joined Unity Church, the local Universalist congregation, and vacationed together fashionably at Hillside, spending time there at Uncle Jenk's Tower Hill School of Religion and Ethics. Home life, in sum, appeared to suit Frank Lloyd Wright.

At the time, all this rampant domesticity accorded wonderfully well with what had become Frank's guiding philosophical light, one fueled by the popular Arts and Crafts Movement, an impulse that harbored important implications, he thought, not just for design, but for the moral shaping of life itself. Remaining influential until World War I, the movement had its origins in the philosophy of the English poet and artist William Morris, who—dismayed by the shoddy, duplicative furniture being cranked out by industrial machines—established a workshop that produced only hand-made furniture, textiles, wallpapers, and stained glass of severely simple design. The result was an outright revolution in public taste.

Furniture maker Gustav Stickley brought the idea to America and founded the *Craftsman,* a periodical that became the movement's principal voice. At his own shop in Eastwood, New York, Stickley built simple "mission style" furniture out of natural materials, an act of open rebellion against both Victorian ornateness and machine technology itself, the rise of which he correlated directly to a decline in quality craftsmanship. Englishman C. R. Ashbee, who first visited Wright in Oak Park in 1896 and who remained his friend for forty years, became an Arts and Crafts proselytizer, founding the Guild of Handicrafts in the late 1880s. Yet another advocate was Elbert Hubbard, the celebrated peddler of humanistic rationalism. Like Ashbee, Hubbard was a frequent visitor at the Oak Park house. Wright was so impressed by him and his Roycrofers—an Arts and Crafts commune and publishing house in East Aurora, New York—that he took to emulating Hubbard's shaggy hairstyle and theatrical manner of dress. The business executive Darwin D. Martin, justly called a "colossus in the life of Frank Lloyd Wright," was Hubbard's protégé and worked for Hubbard's brother-in-law John D. Larkin, founder of a mail-order soap empire, a company that commissioned Wright to design its massive administration building in suburban Buffalo. And Wright would have instantly recognized in the movement a reaction against the vapid classicism championed by the 1893 World's Fair, the exposition that had so brutally wrecked Sullivan, his cherished *lieber Meister.*

More to the point, Wright had assessed the movement correctly: Arts and Crafts, one social historian observes, was in fact "advocating a set of principles, not [just] a style":

> Today, the idea that an architect has an obligation to encompass the values of an ideal society in his work has been unfashionable for decades. But when Wright first began independent practice in Chicago, he was just one of a number of architects . . . who saw the possibilities offered by the new [Arts and Crafts] movement, which was as much Romantic as it was reformist and revivalist. . . . In championing a return to humbler styles notable for their beauty and fitness of purpose, young American architects could talk about a need for an architecture that was untainted by foreign influences, that was home-grown, a quintessentially American architecture that they all, in one way or another, were competing to invent.

Just as modern industrialism produced ugly furniture, it also produced homes and families that were fractured, alienated. It was the job of the new breed of American architect to remedy this social contagion. As Ashbee's biographer puts it, "Ask any Arts and Crafts man to give an account of his work and he would talk not only about techniques and materials, but also about the status of the decorative arts . . . work, nature, [*and*] *the home.*" On both personal and professional grounds, therefore, Wright's attraction to Arts and Crafts seems natural, even inevitable.

In 1901, however, Wright broke with the movement on one salient point. At Jane Addams's Hull House, he gave the most important speech of his life, "The Art and Craft of the Machine," the first defiant, unabashed embracing of mechanization by an American architect. Both the audience and the venue of that speech were apt: the Chicago Arts and Crafts Society, of which Wright himself was a founding member, had been established at Hull House in 1897. In the speech, Wright drew upon all his evangelical heritage and Welsh charm to urge the rather obvious point that "the machine is here to stay." Sullivan himself had been an advocate of the machine—the skyscraper, for example, would have been unthinkable without it—and Uncle Jenk frequently used his bully pulpit to praise McCormick's mechanical reaper. Rhetorically calling forth a diverse cloud of witnesses—from Tolstoy to John Ruskin and from Morris to Victor Hugo—Wright argued that machinery, in the proper hands, could actually enhance natural materials, revealing inner glories that might otherwise remain obscured. After all, "The beauty of wood lies first in its qualities as wood," and if machinery could aid and abet in the production of beautiful materials, its prudent use could be only to the good. "Genius," he said, "must dominate the work of the contrivance it has created." Further, steel framing and reinforced concrete, like wood, should be considered natural resources; he spoke paradoxically of "native forests of steel, concrete, and glass." These machine-produced materials would liberate the modern architect from his obsequious bondage to the confines of the antique past, to "the meager unit of brick arch and stone lintel." One day, some visionary artist, some poet in stone and steel, might infuse the machine itself with "the thrill of ideality—A SOUL!"

Wright then changed gears, shifting into his prophetic mode and taking Hugo's *Notre Dame de Paris* (1831-1832) as his text. In that novel, Hugo proposes that it is always and everywhere the impulse of the artistic spirit "to perpetuate itself," to "leave some trace" of its having existed. Until the sixteenth century, therefore, the poetic soul naturally gravitated toward architecture, the most permanent of the arts. With the invention of the printing press, however, all this changed: suddenly, a sonnet might outlast a cathedral. As a result, Hugo maintains, artists fled the field, and architecture lost its native originality, withering inexorably into a series of pallid imitations of the dog-dead Greco-Roman past. During the Renaissance—that "setting sun which we all take to be the dawn"—the "book [was to] kill the building," and architecture itself crumbled into ruin. (Hugo here precisely foreshadows the views of Wright's hero Sullivan and, even more pertinently, of his idol Emerson: "The American who has been confined, in his own country, to the sight of buildings designed after foreign models, is surprised on entering York Minster or St. Peter's at Rome, by the feeling that these structures are imitations also—faint copies of an invisible archetype.")

What, then, could be done to restore architecture to its former monumental glory? Nothing much, Hugo confesses, unless by chance the "great accident of an architect of genius might occur in the twentieth century," some audacious and rebellious soul who would turn his back on the received tradition, start new with a freshly scrubbed tabula rasa, and recapture all the art's potential creativity. Could Wright be so hubristic as to imagine that he himself was the single redemptive rebel whose nativity Hugo had prophesized? Wright implicitly answered this question in his own speech when he substituted "in the latter days of the nineteenth century" for Hugo's somewhat later timeline, intimating that architecture's savior was already standing before those dubious elders of the Arts and Crafts Movement gathered at Hull House on that frosty March evening in 1901.

The important fact, however—his vatic self-image aside—is that Wright, save for his championing of the machine, was in all other ways a committed disciple of Arts and Crafts principles and ideals, especially as those pertained to marriage and home life. Indeed, it was his lockstep allegiance to what has come to be called conventional "family values" that makes the events of 1909-1911 so maddening a puzzle, an enigma so resistant to reduction or excuse.

Wright most clearly demonstrates his adherence to the home in the composition of his own body of work. For example, although the practice at Adler and Sullivan had specialized in large commercial building projects, Wright devoted himself while in their employ almost exclusively to residential designs. And after his break with Sullivan, he maintained that trend. As late as 1909, Wright had constructed only three significant structures that were *not* residences: the Larkin Administration Building, Unity Temple, and—for Aunts Nell and Jane—the Hillside School, back in the Helena Valley. The rest of his amazingly prolific output over those years (nearly 250 designs) consists mainly of houses.

On a personal level, the centrality of the idea of the home for Wright probably grows out of hard-won life experience—again, out of the contrast he must have drawn between the solidity of the Lloyd Jones clan as opposed to the nomadic uncertainty of his own boyhood years. But philosophically, his allegiance to home and family clearly owes much to the Arts and Crafts Movement as well: it has been convincingly argued that the entirety of Wright's architectural philosophy was grounded in the Arts and Crafts idea that a house was no more—and distinctly no less—than a palpable expression of marital fidelity and an idealized domesticity.

That indebtedness finds direct expression in Wright's co-authorship, with William C. Gannett, of an elaborately printed Arts and Crafts–style book entitled *The House Beautiful* (1896-1898). In 1895,

Gannett had given a well-received sermon that provides the book's text; the volume's spectacular decorations in red and black are Wright's work, and his name appears on the title page with Gannett's. Ninety copies were cranked out in the River Forest stable that Wright had designed for neighbor William Winslow's Auvergne Press. The homiletic text hymns the sanctity of the marital union and of the ideal home, "a building of God, not made with hands." Within such a dwelling, the married couple could establish a bulwark against everything tawdry, threatening, or immoral. Their union and the house itself were sacred things, sacraments that fostered such virtues as discipline, sacrifice, and self-control. Wright could not have agreed more; according to his most trustworthy biographer, "Perfection was [for Wright] an entirely domestic scene, the felicity of two people in love, surrounded by beauty, in a hidden paradise." A stanza of the text's closing poem, Courbet's "Lovers in the Country," strikes that same chord:

> I dreamed of Paradise—and still,
> Though sun lay soft on vale and hill,
> And trees were green and rivers bright,
> The one dear thing that made delight
> By sun or stars or eden weather,
> Was just that we two were together.

A fine dollop of treacle, to be sure—but it does capture Wright's most heartfelt convictions at that time and for some time to come. Home life for him was a kind of substitute for religion. Or, more accurately, it *was* a religion. Desperately seeking solace in a post-Darwinian world that seemed to preclude the faith of his fathers, one British Arts and Crafts architect found residual comfort in the same place that Wright found it—in the home: "Belief in the sacredness of home-life is still left to us, and is itself a religion, pure and easy to believe. It requires no elaborate creeds, its worship is the simplest, its discipline the gentlest and its rewards are peace and contentment." Frank Lloyd Wright believed that new doctrine and seemed determined to erect both his personal and professional life on what he took to be its sure foundations.

And then, in 1909, he abandoned his wife and six children to run off to Europe with the neighbor lady.

But if Wright's sudden decamping from domestic life prompts astonishment on moral and philosophical grounds, then a second consideration only compounds the enigma: for in abandoning his Oak Park family, Wright simultaneously threw over his architectural practice, so energetically and painstakingly put together over the course of twenty-two years. And despite Wright's later testimony to the contrary, that practice was robust, routinely receiving accolades from both his peers and the general public. As one observer points out, Wright "was conquering the profession . . . and there seemed to be nothing on the horizon [circa 1909], not even a tiny cloud, to indicate that his fortunes might change."

Wright's conquest had its origins back in his apprentice days with Adler and Sullivan, when, in 1891, he designed the Charnley House in Chicago, modestly dubbing it "the first modern house in America." Characteristically, Wright positioned the Charnley's fireplace centrally, in the very heart of the home and on a direct axis with the front door. In keeping with Arts and Crafts conviction, Wright felt that the hearth was emblematic of family togetherness, "affirming the sacramental nature of the institution of marriage." In the reserved and formal Winslow House (1893), Wright's first independent commission, the vast reception hall serves a similar function, asserting "the sacredness of home and hearth." In sum, the Winslow has been seen as an overt evocation and manifestation of that "house not made with hands" called for so hopefully, if so vaguely, in *The House Beautiful*.

Wright entered into private practice in 1893 with an impressive total of twenty-five designs already under his belt. He was not long in making his impact felt on the profession, garnering unprecedented attention for a practitioner in only his twenties and early thirties. He was already a prominent Chicago figure by 1900, to the point that his friend and colleague Robert Spencer Jr. felt justified in presenting a compendium of Wright's designs for the respected journal *Architectural Review;* in the accompanying article, Spencer calls Wright "a perpetual inspiration" to all his colleagues and intimates. But perhaps the first great breakthrough came in 1901 with the publication of Wright's own *Ladies' Home Journal* article, "A Home in a Prairie Town," in which he announces the birth of the Prairie house, "a functional and aesthetic breakthrough," one that aimed at no less a goal than to "preserve and strengthen proper family living." It is said that this pivotal article provided Wright with the mental clarity he needed to prompt a full decade of prodigious creativity. Fully half of the displays at the Chicago Architectural Club exhibition of 1902 were of Wright's designs, indelibly stamping him as the acknowledged leader of the younger Chicago architects and of the emerging Prairie School. The man was only thirty-five.

Early evidence of Wright's preeminence was the groundbreaking Highland Park house he designed for Ward Willits that same year. This residence was quickly judged "the first masterpiece among the Prairie Houses" and "an image of modern times"; before long, its creator was acknowledged as nothing less than the "great original interpreter" of modernity. Comparable triumphs followed for Wright throughout his Oak Park years, including an unprecedented one-man exhibition at the Chicago Art Institute in 1907 and a 1908 full-issue review of his work in New York's infinitely prestigious *Architectural Record*. In fact, new honors and commissions kept coming in, right up to the fateful day when he fled both home and practice at once.

Wright's success was grounded in his grand conceptions of the Prairie house specifically and of what he called "organic" architecture generally. Not that the ideas were entirely original with Wright. As early as the 1840s, while Richard Lloyd Jones was still leading his family on their arduous trek halfway across the continent, the American sculptor Horatio Greenough was writing a letter to Emerson: "Here is my theory of structure: A scientific arrangement of spaces and forms to function and to site . . . color and ornament to be decided and arranged and varied by strictly organic laws, having a distinct reason for each decision; the entire and immediate banishment of all make-shift and make-believe." Emerson found in turn that Greenough had anticipated "the leading thoughts of Mr. [John] Ruskin on the *morality* [his emphasis] in architecture." Elsewhere, Emerson complained, "I know not why in real architecture the hunger of the eye for length of line is so rarely gratified." Wright intended to satisfy that hunger.

By "organic" architecture, Wright—like Greenough and Ruskin and Emerson before him—meant buildings (homes, mostly) that adhered to the laws of nature and that, through their design and their use of indigenous materials, were tied to the native landscape. In Wright's hands, such houses were typically low lying, like the midwestern prairie itself, and featured wide, cantilevered roofs—Emerson's horizontal "length of line"—that hovered over open, free-flowing interior spaces. The idea, Wright said, was to abolish "the box," those square and cramped cubicles that too often characterized American interior design. The floor plan of the Prairie home was intended to promote convenience, freedom of movement, and togetherness; and the house itself should be so much a part of the ground on which it stood that it would seem to dissolve, almost, into the landscape itself.

Emerson had written, "We feel, in seeking a noble building, [one] which rhymes well . . . that it is spiritually organic." Wright's residential designs were attempts—most often successful attempts—to transform that Transcendentalist model into wood and stone, space and light. It is not surprising, therefore, that his houses found quick and widespread acceptance among his clients—most of whom, like him, were themselves suburban Unitarians of a decided, even evangelical, Emersonian bent. In Wright's work, such clients discovered "a philosophical expression not foreign to their own . . . steeped in the tradition of the organic from the New England transcendentalists to the American wilderness painters and romantic poets."

If Emerson had found his poet in Whitman, he found his architect in Frank Lloyd Wright.

—◙—

Mrs. Queene Coonley discovered in Wright's houses "the countenance of principle," she told him, and in 1907 she gave him a carte blanche commission to build her a terraced mansion in suburban Riverside. She must have fascinated Wright endlessly. Both she and her husband Avery were heirs of enormous fortunes, but she had spent her earlier years, like Anna, as a kindergarten teacher. Now she was an idealistic advocate for women's rights. Her theological views, like his, were dissenting and liberal. And, of course, she was rich, a condition in life that Wright was increasingly seeing as a prerequisite to personal freedom: on this occasion, at least, he could build the kind of house that *he* wanted to build, unrestrained by considerations of budget.

The result is "the palazzo among prairie houses," certainly one of the greatest of Wright's Prairie designs. Wright himself thought that the Coonley House was "the most successful of my houses from my standpoint." Indeed, the architect's utter satisfaction with his creation prompts one critic, Norris Kelly Smith, to speculate that "perhaps it was not built for [the Coonleys] at all," but rather represents the kind of roomy, "populous" house that Wright would have liked to build for himself. "By contrast," Smith reflects ominously, "[Wright's] crowded little house in Oak Park must have seemed insufferably cramped and confining."

And, indeed, it is certain by this time that Wright's home life was striking him as irritatingly narrow. His children were numerous and noisy; not even the separate Studio that he had built on the Oak Park property could insulate him from their disruptive forays into his workplace. "Things began to smash," he wrote later. "Cries to resound. Shrieks. Quarrels and laughter. . . . Destruction of something or other happened every minute." Local creditors hounded him endlessly. Suburban life itself, once a goal to be achieved and celebrated, now seemed oppressively provincial and inimical to the full expression and fulfillment of the imperial self.

And, yes, Catherine bored him: no longer the golden girl of the 1890s, she had made the fatal error of becoming a matron. While her love for and devotion to Frank remained steadfast, the demands of childrearing and Oak Park social life had left her, Frank reckoned, intellectually moribund. She seemed not to think much about matters that did not involve home and family life. Someone like Queene Coonley might agitate for women's rights and for emancipation from domestic drudgery, but Catherine remained supremely content with her own lot in life. A successful husband, six healthy children, and a pretty shingled house: this homely trinity sufficed for her.

It did not suffice for Frank. Increasingly restless, he borrowed some money in 1905 and sailed to Japan with Catherine and the Ward Willitses. Frank looked at Japanese buildings with an admiring eye, as he had back in 1893 at the World's Fair. He bought several expensive prints. Mrs. Willits resented his overt neglect of Catherine and was infuriated when she discovered Ward and Frank cavorting in a Tokyo bathhouse;

she did not speak to Wright again for thirty-eight years. By the time they came home, fissures in Frank's marriage, deniable before, were beginning to appear clearly to everyone, probably even to Catherine herself.

Already a bit suspect in the eyes of his conventional neighbors, Frank was becoming less and less the model Oak Park citizen. He let his hair grow long, Hubbard-style, and he affected flamboyant dress, like his father before him. He self-consciously played, in short, the role of *artiste*. By suburban standards, guests at his house became ever more exotic, even bizarre. Visitors included the likes of Rabindranath Tagore, a hirsute West Bengali poet-prophet—hardly someone to introduce to an Oak Park businessmen's club.

Wright stopped going to church—even to the immensely liberal Universalist church at Unity Temple, which he had imaginatively (and economically) built out of poured concrete for the local congregation. Unity Temple, one critic avers, "remains [at once] the most modern and the most traditional church built in twentieth-century America," which is a foolish thing to say. What pleased Wright most about his design, it seems, was that the resulting building does not look like a church at all. "In fact," notes a more sober observer, "it would take a theologian who was also an architectural scholar to find any evidence from the building that Christian worship was to be carried on there." The theatrical designer Norman Bel Geddes took a glance at the place and said, "It looks fine, Frank. What is it—a library?" Someone suggested that Wright should have paid more heed to the building's intended use. "I don't give a damn what the *use* of it is," the architect tartly replied. "I wanted to build a building like that."

But he did care, of course: the design coincides quite nicely with Wright's personal theology at the time and is supposed to symbolize the unity—one might say the leveling—of God and man. "Why not build a temple to man," Wright asked, "in which to study man himself for his God's sake?" He liked the way the place turned out. "I was feeling," he wrote, "somewhat as I imagine a great prophet might. . . . *I* had made it come true. Naturally, I well remember, I became less tolerant, and I suppose, intolerable. Arrogant, I imagine, was the proper word. I have heard it enough." An ideal church, he added, should also be "a good-time place." Like a Tokyo bath hothouse, perhaps.

Wright, who had worked so hard for so long, began to have a good time. He took the Japan trip, for example. And later he was repeatedly seen barreling around Oak Park in his conspicuous yellow sport car in the company of clients' wives. Rumors flew.

Frank was only conducting business, loyal Catherine maintained. He "is as clean as my baby," she said. But over in England, Kitty's correspondent Janet Ashbee knew better—and knew that Kitty knew better. "I feel in [Catherine's] background somewhere," she sensitively wrote, "difficult places gone through—knocks against many stone walls—and brave pickings up from sloughs of despond . . . and I am certain I hear too beginnings of a different kind of sadness—a battling with what will be an increasing gloom and nervousness . . . in her husband. . . . As yet she is almost a girl still—slender and lovely . . . and when she laughs you forget the tragic lines round her mouth."

Most often Frank's companion in the sporty Stoddard-Dayton was Mamah Borthwick Cheney, so handsome, intellectual, lively, and cosmopolitan. And, like him, a restless suburban "outsider."

—┐◻┌—

H. Allen Brooks has discerned a persistent profile that emerges when one surveys Wright's residential clients during the Oak Park years. Typically, says Brooks, those clients "were mostly upper-middle-class families in which the husband was a businessman (often an executive) with certain technical or engineering skills. . . . One or both spouses might have a strong interest in music or theatre, and apparently they were more independent-minded than the average person." Such an outline fits Edwin and Mamah Cheney seamlessly.

Mamah (pronounced "may-muh"), like Wright, was a child of the Plains, having been born in Boone, Iowa, in 1869, the year of birth that Wright duplicitously claimed for himself (he was actually Mamah's senior by two years). Her father, a machinist with the Chicago and North Western Railway, had risen through the ranks to the position of superintendent of the line's repair department. He moved his family to Oak Park, where Mamah and her two sisters attended the local schools. She apparently met her future husband at the University of Michigan. Mild-mannered Edwin Cheney (pronounced "chee-nee") was majoring in electrical engineering, while gregarious Mamah interested herself in languages and literature. In his own unassertive but persistent way, Edwin pursued Mamah for the better part of a decade, proposing frequently. Her response was decidedly tepid; she picked up a master's degree in teaching and wandered off to lonely Port Huron, Michigan (the boyhood home of Thomas Edison), working there as a librarian for five long years. Only after the death of her mother and the approach of her own thirtieth birthday did she at last condescend to give her reluctant hand to loyal, dogged Edwin. She moved back to Oak Park and married him in 1899. They honeymooned on the Continent. A son, John, was born in 1902, followed by a daughter, Martha, some four years later. Mamah took classes at the University of Chicago, studying under the popular novelist Robert Herrick, whose socially conscious works must have appealed to her. She began to entertain literary aspirations of her own.

With the birth of their son, she and Edwin decided to build a house. Like so many of their neighbors before and after them, they consulted the local man, Wright.

2

Scandal in Oak Park

The reality of the house is order
The blessing of the house is community
The glory of the house is hospitality
The crown of the house is godliness

Frank Lloyd Wright, 1905

(inscribed on the fireplace

at the Heath House)

No prostitute on the street as such is a social menace. She is a symptom—it is the wife with the soul of a harlot "protected" by marriage in practices that evade all responsibility who is the "menace."

Frank Lloyd Wright, 1915

It is a commonplace to point out that Mamah Cheney, in terms of her artistic temperament and capricious personality, much more resembled Frank's two future wives, Miriam Noel and Olgivanna Hinzenberg— and indeed his mother Anna—than she did Catherine. But there is good reason to believe that Mamah met Frank through Kitty: they were both members of Oak Park's Nineteenth Century Women's Club (so was Grace Hemingway, toddler Ernest's mother) and were frequently mentioned together on the social pages of the town newspaper.

In 1903 (the year that Llewellyn, his last child by Kitty, was born), Wright began plans for the Cheney residence on nearby North East Avenue. The red brick house, which was ready for occupancy by June

1904, is among the best of Wright's small designs. The door to the home is accessible only after negotiating a maze-like garden path, and the overall impression of the place is one of coy withdrawal from the gaze of outsiders. Inside, however, Wright's characteristically free-flowing floor plan—rooms were delineated only by columns and the placement of furniture—made privacy difficult, and friends of the Cheney children reported spying on Frank and Mamah as they "spooned" on the library couch. Prairie houses were designed, after all, for promoting family unity, not for concealing suburban adulteries: the Cheney House, like so many of Wright's designs, features a "cross-axial" arrangement, centered in the domestic hearth. An alarming irony is therefore at work here: Wright had designed a "family values," Arts and Crafts–type house for a family unit that he was about to destroy.

How early the affair actually began is hard to determine with certainty. One enduring and probable account has it that Wright was infatuated with Mamah at first glance and that the 1905 Tokyo trip represented a last-ditch attempt by the Willitses and other Oak Park neighbors to dissuade Wright from persisting in his potentially ruinous liaison. On the other hand, Frank scarcely needed to be coerced into a voyage to Japan, a nation whose art and architecture had fascinated him since the Expo back in 1893. (By the end of his life, he had traveled to Japan no fewer than seven times.) Further, he borrowed heavily—including from Ward Willits—to finance the jaunt, at a time (when was there *not* a time?) when his personal debts were already crushing; this was not just a casual pleasure cruise intended solely for the testing of marital waters. And, of course, Mamah had a child by Edwin as late as 1906.

But whenever the sexual relationship commenced, by 1909 free-thinking Frank and Mamah were openly sharing the good news of their love with their respective spouses, and Frank began to ask Catherine for a divorce. "Eddie" Cheney—despite his long pursuit of and obvious devotion for his wife—took it all in stride; according to Wright biographer Brendan Gill, Edwin "gains a certain distinction in history by dint of his seeming never to have raised his voice." Perhaps he was intimidated by the spirited Mamah or by Wright himself. A neighbor of Edwin described him as "middle-aged, dark-eyed and bald. You could hardly call him a Don Juan, but he was so charming and gracious that he didn't have an enemy. Whereas Frank Lloyd Wright was very swash-buckling, a buccaneering type." (Five years later, Frank would visit upon poor Edwin an infinitely greater cause for provocation, but again the placid engineer remained bafflingly mute.)

For her part, Catherine was properly stunned. She asked Frank for one year of grace; if he still wanted a divorce after that time had elapsed, she said, she would grant him one. Privately, in letters to friends, she fervently hoped for and confidently anticipated an eventual return and reconciliation. He did come back, briefly, late in 1910, but then he took off again. For good, this time.

—🔲—

At the height of his success, Wright's abandonment of his practice (and, not incidentally, of his wife and six children) has justly been called "a conundrum that [defies] analysis." Of course, the bare fact of the puzzle's intractability has prompted countless attempts at just such an inquiry.

Some observers, for example, see Wright and the Studio, in 1909, as having absorbed a series of professional setbacks, most notably the fail-ure of the palatial design for the Harold McCormick estate, a disaster that Wright forecast as prefiguring the demise of the Prairie School itself. Further, this argument has it that Wright had soured on his marriage and was determined not to be lumbered by an unwanted wife. But others are deeply skeptical of this "official" version of the desertion, one promoted only years after the fact by Wright himself and simply parroted by his sympathizers. A host of competing critics argues that Wright's career, far from teetering on the edge of ruin, was actually flourishing at the time. From this perspective, and given his nearly un-broken string of stunning triumphs, the idea that he ran away as a result of artistic neglect or rejection seems absurd.

Why, then?

One early biographer speculates that Wright was undergoing a "ner-vous breakdown."

More plausibly, Wright scholar Robert C. Twombly suggests that the man was a victim of his own success: namely, that his work, while widely admired, was inexorably being reduced to a "type" or "style," rather than being correctly appreciated as a distinct and complex

American response to "fundamental social and cultural questions." In this view, Wright's ego had been tweaked by the reflexive tendency of architectural critics, through "specious categorization," to equate his own work with the formulaic efforts of his imitators and his inferiors (by which, of course, he meant everyone—including Sullivan). Accordingly, the years 1907-1909 comprised for Wright a frustrating professional "denouement" from which he devoutly wished to extricate himself. "Increasingly," says Twombly, "he saw himself as a free spirit, as a creative artist who had earned the right to take liberties with rules and customs," including the narrow rules of suburban propriety and the custom of marriage itself.

Others make note of Wright's lifelong tendency "to invent emergencies when they failed to develop of their own accord." Perhaps the man simply could not tolerate any sort of equilibrium in his life or in his life's work.

Some have seen the magnificently horizontal Robie House (1910), with its gravity-defying cantilevered roof so suggestive of an airfoil, as a metaphor for Wright's determination to fly away from his Oak Park sorrows.

Norris Kelly Smith agrees with Twombly that by 1909 Wright "found himself imprisoned within the confines of a fashionable convention" of his own making. But Smith maintains that Wright felt trapped not by success but by failure—specifically, the failure to reconcile his Transcendentalist ideals regarding personal freedom with the public demands of architecture. His design for the Coonleys, with their unlimited budget, had been a great treat; but how could Wright honestly "compare himself with Whitman and Thoreau while putting his art in the service of such multi-millionaires?" In a word, architecture for Wright had become "inherently inimical to his Emersonian ideals," to the point that he "could not go on."

The best potential witness, of course, is Wright himself; but he is either evasive or pontifical on the subject. His Nietzschean defense of his actions, as presented to his Spring Green neighbors in 1911, will be dealt with later. In his memoirs, however, Wright first adopts a tone of helpless puzzlement, a rhetorical throwing up of his hands: "Because I did not know what I wanted I wanted to go away," he writes. "What I wanted I did not know. I loved my children. I loved my home. A true home is the finest ideal of man, and yet—well, to gain freedom I asked for a divorce." The decision threatened to tear him apart, he says, but he found relief by riding out into the countryside north of Oak Park on his horse Kano, reining in the steed only long enough to leaf through some Whitman.

Then he switches into a pedantic mode, leaning heavily on the philosophy of Ellen Key (pronounced "kay"), the Swedish feminist whose works Mamah had been busily translating. In Key's books, he discovers that his desertion of wife and children, far from constituting an act of betrayal, actually reflects steadfast loyalty to a number of lofty ethical principles, among them the notion that "marriage not mutual . . . is worse than any other form of slavery" and is in fact indecent and "barbarous." Further, marriage is in no way a sacrament—here he makes an irrevocable break with the Arts and Crafts convictions he had so recently championed—but rather a mere "civil contract between a man and woman" and therefore subject to cancellation on either side, once the knot of true love unravels into a less than "mutual" relationship.

On this latter point, at least, Wright is not so much indebted to Key as he is to the established traditions of his own dissenting forebears back in Britain. For example, the ancient legal codes of Wales, finding precedent in Celtic law, regarded marriage "as an agreement rather than a sacrament, [one that] could be ended by mutual consent." And in Wright's defense, the idea of escape in the name of freedom has a long and even defining tradition in American life and letters: Huck Finn flees the madness of the Widow Douglas and "lights out for the territories"; Melville's Ishmael, "tormented with an everlasting itch for things remote," sets sail aboard the fated *Pequod;* Rip van Winkle runs from the madness of his wife to the beckoning, somnolent mountains. Thoreau leaves settled Concord for wild Walden; Emerson leaves settled Unitarianism for wild Romanticism.

It is no accident, perhaps, that all these tales and figures date from the nineteenth century. "To the core of his being," historian William Cronon reminds us, "Wright was a nineteenth-century romantic, steeped in idealist traditions that reached back through Louis Sullivan and Walt Whitman to the New England Transcendentalists and beyond." Cronon supplies the subtlest available inquiry into the mystery of Wright's desertion, anchoring it firmly in that one seminal figure whom both the Wrights and the Lloyd Joneses venerated: "To understand . . . Frank Lloyd Wright today, one cannot avoid a serious encounter with Ralph Waldo Emerson." Having cut himself off so terminally from the precepts of the Arts and Crafts movement on whose foundations both his professional and personal lives had been erected, Wright sorely needed an alternative worldview that would serve to vindicate and even celebrate his decision to leave Kitty and the children. Emerson afforded him just such a perspective, a less-traveled-by road out. "Trust thyself," the sage of Concord had preached; and Wright *did*, to the point, Cronon concludes, that "he felt wholly justified in ignoring the niceties of conventional behavior . . . if they got in the way of his higher truths." After 1909, such "truths" could always be paraded out "to rationalize actions whose motives were sometimes less [than] pure." Eventually, they became "quite literally his religion."

To which might be added this: the Lloyd Jones tradition in religion— always radical and dissenting—had measurably devolved over the years, ultimately bearing only a misty ancestral kinship to the relative orthodoxy of, say, Grandfather Richard, who at least had carried the Good Book in his saddlebag; Frank now carried Whitman in his. By this time, Uncle Jenk, in a further lurching step toward rampant secularization and ecumenism run amok, was now presiding over a house of worship dubbed the Abraham Lincoln Centre, a "good time place" where any belief—or none at all—could be freely exhorted from the pulpit. By 1909, indeed, the faith of Wright's fathers (and mother) could hardly be said any longer to bear the weight of the word *theology*. Cronon writes, "Unitarianism's impatience with traditional Christianity, its refusal to impose any formal doctrinal test on its adherents (not even the divinity of Christ or the existence of God), its eagerness to ransack all the world's great religions in its search for sacred meaning, its tolerance of iconoclasm and individual eccentricity, its embrace of science as a necessary part of any modern search for enlightened knowledge, its humanism, and above all its faith in the unity of spiritual truth—all of these values were made to order for the likes of Frank Lloyd Wright." And it will be recalled that Wright declined to attend even *that* church.

In his memoirs, Wright refers to himself in childhood as "the young rebel"; he always saw himself that way. The Transcendentalists' earlier revolt against the lifeless, arid Unitarianism of their time is mirrored in the warp and woof of Wright's own life. Hence his veneration for Emerson. But Emerson's rebellion, in embracing much that was novel, inevitably discarded much that was of value in the older tradition, not least the authority of the Church. The result was that Wright, despite his much-vaunted "spirituality," had no real spiritual authority to call upon in weighing his decision to leave Kitty and their children. He had drifted quite happily into the cult of selfhood, as extolled by Emerson and by such latter-day free thinkers as Hubbard. He could make his own rules, he thought. Indeed, it was only by being true to his own impulses—"being honest," he called it—that he could define himself and assert his artistic eminence. No guiding star, other than his own will and his own sense of genius, need be consulted. "Hold on to your little light of reason," counseled Hubbard's agnostic friend Robert Ingersoll. "He who would tell you to put it out is a preacher." And Wright, unlike his father (for once), had no intention of being a preacher or of following what seemed to him to be threadbare and ultimately unreasonable moral codes, fit only for the common herd.

Ultimately, therefore, one answer as to why he deserted Kitty is, simply, that he *wanted* to and that there existed no external check or sensibility to prevent him from doing so. Quite to the contrary: only in leaving his wife, Wright became convinced, could he fulfill his highest moral obligation—that of being true to himself. The bald fact that he wanted unfettered converse and sex with Mamah Cheney became, for Wright, merely a tangential and occasional consideration. According to his moral arithmetic, if he desired to live openly with Mamah, and if society forbade such a union, then society, by definition, was in error. He honestly wondered why others—Kitty and the children, for example—failed to grasp the logic of it all.

Brendan Gill confidently asserts that Wright's embrace of Emerson and Key is factitious and intended only "to mitigate the guilt he feels at his selfishness. In Wright's place, only a monster could have failed to feel a large measure of guilt, and Wright was far from being a monster." But it is entirely possible to concede Gill's second point while disputing his first, just as it is entirely possible for any person to locate an existing credo—or even invent a comfortable new one—that is congenial to his character and then to embrace that belief system with a whole heart. It is very probable that Wright felt no guilt at all.

And anyway, it would be all right: his mother Anna had suffered similar difficulties following her divorce back in 1885; she, too, had been pilloried for her resolute determination (again, this was Frank's take on it) to live her life in accordance with her own vision and had stood up to the resulting slings and arrows with equanimity. Anna, if no one else, would understand. "I go to the cross," Frank sighed after deciding to leave his family. But he knew he would not have to go alone.

—◫—

The logistics of Wright's escape present their own puzzles: where some observers see well-calculated planning, others discern only spontaneous chaos, an overnight decision resulting in a "hurly-burly flight from Oak Park." But everyone agrees that it all began quietly enough, with a letter from Berlin.

Early in 1909, Kuno Francke, a German-born Harvard professor, dropped by the Oak Park studio to say that he was impressed by Wright's work. "But where will you be when America gets around to all this?" he demanded of Frank, or so Frank tells us. "Do you expect to live a hundred years longer?" No doubt Wright preened at this bit of recognition, if even at second hand, from Europe: after all, the good professor had received his doctorate in aesthetics from the University of Munich.

Some months later, no doubt at Francke's recommendation, Wright received a written invitation from Ernst Wasmuth, who presided over a prestigious art publishing house in Berlin: if Wright would prepare the drawings, Wasmuth wanted to publish a massive portfolio of his collected work, everything from houses and public buildings to a mortuary and a tennis club. Here was an opportunity for Wright to test his ideas in the crucible of the Old World, to extend his influence throughout the Continent, and to produce a "primer for a new American architecture." The offer could not be refused: he immediately set his draftsmen to work and began to plan the trip. He told Mamah all about it.

That June, Mamah announced to Edwin that she and the children were going to Boulder, Colorado, to visit a pregnant friend of hers. Always obliging, Edwin seems not to have objected. Although he testified later that he had harbored suspicions about the junket, he also had grounds to consider it a good idea: Oak Park was rife with rumors about

Mamah's affair with Frank, so her brief exile to the Rockies may have seemed prudent.

In October, however, Edwin received an enigmatic and troubling communication from his wife. Her friend had died in childbirth, she said, and Edwin was to come to Colorado at once to pick up the children, then aged seven and three. But by the time Edwin got there, Mamah was long gone.

Two possibilities now obtain. Either Mamah traveled directly to New York, or she first dropped by Oak Park, in Gill's words, "to utter an ultimatum to Wright. Certainly [Wright's subsequent] conduct was that of a lover who, after long delays, had been forced to make an irrevocable choice."

It certainly was: in one day—late in October 1909—Wright sought furiously to divest himself of the architectural practice that he had been laboriously cobbling together for over two decades. To finance his escape, he borrowed money on all sides, collecting advances on commissions from Chicago clients and pawning fistfuls of his precious Japanese prints. As for the Studio itself, he simply gave it away. After several rebuffs, he was finally able to turn it over to the first person who would take it—a no doubt befuddled young German-born architect named Hermann von Holst, whose own architectural vision had nothing in common with Wright's and who indeed was chiefly known as a designer of conventional church buildings. One biographer's gloss is entirely plausible: "Perhaps that was not a day for rational decisions."

That job done, Wright slipped home to announce his abrupt departure to a tearful Catherine. He turned to his son David, then thirteen, and told him that he was now the man of the house. He left the boy with a grocery bill for nine hundred dollars. When interviewed seventy years later, David was still indignant.

Clearly, it is at this point that parallels break down between William's desertion in 1885 and Frank's in 1909: as Twombly points out, "William C. Wright had left home having failed to cement strong group ties; his son fled to escape them." Or as son John puts it, "Maybe the technique was hereditary, but in my father's case he was not asked to leave."

Asked or not, Frank took a fast train to New York, met up there with Mamah, and sailed for Europe.

It took the local press only a week or two to track him down, and when they found him, the story set off shock waves back home. On Sunday, November 7, the *Chicago Tribune* drew back the curtain on the most sensational scandal to titillate the country since Harry Thaw, three years before, had shot and killed architect Stanford White for seducing Thaw's wife. The *Tribune's* Berlin correspondent, in poring over the register of the Hotel Adlon, had found that a "Mr. Frank Lloyd Wright and wife" were registered there. Indeed, Kitty had already sent Frank a postcard there in care of his Berlin publisher, containing a message that managed to be both pitiful and subtly assertive at once: "My Dear: We think of you often and hope you are well and enjoying life, as you have so longed to. From the children and your wife, Catherine L. Wright." On the other side of the card, pointedly, was a photo of a church, Frank's own Unity Temple.

Wright, the *Tribune* blared, was responsible for "an affinity tangle . . . unparalleled even in the checkered history of soul-mating." An armada of reporters descended on Catherine's Oak Park doorstep. A minister by her side, stalwart Kitty was ready for them.

She handled herself with masterful dignity, issuing a shrewdly con-ciliatory oral statement, her voice breaking only on occasion:

> My heart is with him now. He will come back as soon as he can. I have a faith in Frank Lloyd Wright that passeth understanding, perhaps, but I know him as no one else knows him. In this instance, he is as innocent of wrongdoing as I am. . . . He is honest in everything he does. A moment's insincerity tortures him more than anything in the world. Frank Wright has never deceived me in all his life. . . . Whatever I am as a woman, aside from my good birth, I owe to the example of my hus-band. . . . I shall make no appeal whatever to the courts. I stand by my husband right at this moment. I am his wife. He loves his children ten-derly and has the greatest anxiety for their welfare. . . . I feel certain that he will come back when he has reached a certain decision with himself. When he comes back, all will be as it has been.

Regarding Mamah, Catherine was notably less appeasing. Mrs. Cheney, she said, was "simply a force against which we have had to con-tend," a disembodied agency of evil, a latter day *belle dame sans merci* who, for the moment, had bewitched blameless, unsuspecting Frank with her "queer ideas." Disregarding the fact of her own former friendship with Mamah, Kitty averred, "I never felt that I breathed the same air with her. It was simply a case of a vampire—you have heard of such things." (*Vampire*—an interesting word choice. Before long, Frank would be using even less tempered diction against Kitty, because she would not grant him a divorce.)

The press strove to extract an interview from poor Edwin, but he was typically mute. "I don't care to talk about this matter at all," he informed frustrated reporters.

Affronted local clergy *were* talking, however. In a sermon entitled "Affinity Fools," for example, the Rev. Dr. Frederick E. Hopkins of Pilgrim Congregational Church mixed any number of barnyard images, finally likening Frank and Mamah, in their passion, to "an old setting hen"; inevitably, "one day there is a splash, and both have tumbled into the same old hog pen where thousands have tumbled before them." Nor had Hopkins exhausted his porcine metaphor: "If you have gone down into the refrigerating rooms of a big packing house and looked at a row of pigs' faces hanging on their hooks," he pronounced, "you have seen a perfect picture of affinity fools unmasked."

Meanwhile, carefree Frank and Mamah, dreamily oblivious to the commotion they were prompting back home, lazed away their golden days in Europe, happy as, well, pigs.

—◻—

Oddly, perhaps, the honeymooning couple did not spend all their time together, at least initially. Instead, Mamah found a flat in Berlin and took a teaching job at a seminary for young women, while Frank hustled off to the villa "Fortuna" in Florence to work on the portfolio in sunnier climes. He was joined there briefly by his eldest son Lloyd, nineteen years old by then and himself a budding architect, and by the Studio's draftsman Taylor Woolley. Under Frank's supervision, the two worked together on the drawings during 1909 and 1910. Many other renderings had already been completed back at Oak Park, often by the magical Marion Mahony, Wright's most talented delineator and designer. Mahony, an MIT graduate, had been with Wright on and off since 1895; in 1898 she had become the world's first female licensed architect. It was Mahony who had introduced Wright to von Holst, the man who took over the Studio upon Wright's departure. Mahony was so close to Catherine that Wright had posed the two together for a formal portrait photo. More to the point, her drawings for the Wasmuth folio were amazing, wonderful.

That folio—finally completed in June 1910—emerged from the presses as a two-volume boxed set entitled *Ausgeführte Bauten und Entwürfe von Frank Lloyd Wright* (Finished Buildings and Designs of Frank Lloyd Wright); it comprised some one hundred plates, illustrating seventy buildings and projects undertaken by Wright between 1893 and 1909. Its impact on European architecture was immense, immediate, and lasting—"an event," claims one critic, "that modified the course of architecture in central Europe."

Among the first to see it were the great Mies van der Rohe and Walter Gropius, both then working at Peter Behrens's Berlin studio. Mies was effusive in his praise, depicting Wright as nothing less than a messianic figure:

> We [young architects] were ready to pledge ourselves to an idea. But the potential vitality of the architectural idea of this period had, by this time, been lost.
>
> This, then, was the situation in 1910.
>
> At this moment, so critical for us, there came to Berlin the exhibition of the work of Frank Lloyd Wright. . . .
>
> The work of this great master revealed an architectural world of unexpected force and clarity of language, and also a disconcerting richness of form. Here finally was a master-builder drawing upon the veritable fountainhead of architecture, who with true originality lifted his architectural creations into the light. Here, again, at last, genuine organic architecture flowered.
>
> . . . The dynamic impulse emanating from his work invigorated a whole generation. His influence was strongly felt even when it was not actually visible.

Mies began adopting Wright's cross-axis as a basis for design, as in his Barcelona Pavilion of 1929; Gropius played variations on Wright's drawings for the Mason City (Iowa) Bank and Madison's Yahara Boat Club; Theo van Doesburg and the Dutch De Stijl movement were similarly affected. If it had been Wright's goal to make his mark on the Continent, he had succeeded beyond his dreams.

Frank had been in the habit of staying with Mamah in her Berlin apartment whenever he came to the city to consult with Wasmuth. Now he brought her back with him to Italy, to Fiesole and his cream-colored villa above Florence. Years later, he rhapsodized over their life together there:

> How many souls seeking release from real or fancied domestic woes have sheltered on the slopes below Fiesole!
>
> I, too, now sought shelter there in companionship with her who, by force of rebellion as by way of love was then implicated with me.
>
> Walking hand in hand together up the hill road from Firenze to the older town, all along the way in the sight and scent of roses, by day. Walking arm in arm up the same old road at night, listening to the nightingale in the deep shadows on the moonlit wood—trying hard to hear the song in the deeps of life.

And so on: Wright, freed from his editorial duties, seemed intoxicatingly happy. He and Mamah were inseparable now. He read his Ruskin, and she translated Goethe and Ellen Key, the Swedish proto-feminist and free love advocate who had proved so useful to Frank in justifying his break with Oak Park. Hand in hand, they tramped through the city and countryside. Frank especially admired the Villa Medici, set so harmoniously into a gentle hill and haughtily surveying the Tuscan countryside below. He went so far as to make a preliminary sketch for a "Studio for the Architect, Florence, Italy," suggesting day-dreams of settling down with Mamah in that congenial place. But more likely he was already imagining a Villa Medici of their own, set into an American hill—not an Italian one—with a view of green and golden fields.

Still, in a letter to his English friend C. R. Ashbee a few months earlier, he appeared to strike an ambivalent note about the Oak Park desertion and his relations with Mamah:

> I think you will believe that I would do nothing I did not believe to be right—but I have believed a terrible thing to be right and have sacrificed to it those who loved me and my work in what must seem a selfish, cruel waste of life and purpose. I have never loved Catherine—my wife—as she deserved. I have for some years loved another. . . . I took her with me when I sailed for Germany. . . .
>
> I cannot ask others to countenance the thing I believe to be right when I know it may, yes, it *must* seem wrong to them.

... What a traitor I must seem to the trust that has been placed in me by home, friends, and not least the cause of Architecture. ...

I wanted to square my *life* with *myself.* ... I want to *live* true as I would *build* true, and in the light I have I have tried to do this thing.

Much of this is vintage Wright, of course—all those conditional *seems*, for example, and his old argument that open adultery is somehow more honest and "true" than a clandestine affair. But what is one to make of that unsettling clause "I have believed a terrible thing to be right"? Despite his later rationale in the letter, does Frank hint here that his spiritual and sexual odyssey with Mamah has proved "a terrible thing," an unforeseen mistake of dreadful dimensions? Or is he merely confessing, finally, that the consequences of his acts have been "terrible" to others— to family, friends, and clients—but not necessarily to himself? In either case, he does seem to imply that the bloom may have been off the Florentine roses and that a terrible gamble had been taken, and lost.

Or maybe not. Perhaps the Ashbee letter represented no more than an initial shot over the bow in a long, calculated campaign, the inchoate outlines of which were already taking shape in Wright's head—a plan that, if successful, would lead him back to the Midwest and ultimately to a rural villa built just for Mamah, sheltering her securely beneath its broad, cantilevered roof.

Indeed, within a few months he was again writing Ashbee, this time to announce that "The fight has been fought—I am going back to Oak Park to pick up the thread of my work and in some degree of my life where I snapped it. I am going to work among the ruins, not as any woman's husband, but as the father of the children, to do what I can for them. . . . But I have been cruel. I have hardness in my soul. I have destroyed many beautiful things—in the hope of putting better things in their place."

"Better" for *whom*, one wonders. In any case, he sat down and wrote to Catherine, spelling out the conditions for his return. Those stipulations mirrored the ones suggested in his letter to Ashbee: namely, that he and Catherine would no longer share normal marital relations (a marriage not "mutual" still being tantamount to "slavery"), but that they would at least be together and put up a good front for the sake of his children and, more centrally, of his work. Further, he would give up

Mamah, though not his love for her, and he would remain her protector. Still, he told Catherine, "he feared by staying with [Mamah] that he would grow to loathe her." Then he wrote a long defensive letter to Anna, excusing his actions on the grounds that his family had failed "to give him emotional support in his time of need."

The prospect of going back to Oak Park galled him. "I dread the aspect my return must wear," he wrote to his mother.

> I am the prodigal—whose return is a triumph for THE INSTITU-TIONS I have outraged—a weak son who, infatuated sexually, has had his passion drained and therewith his courage, and so abandoning the source of his infatuation to whatever fate may hold for her—probably a hard, lonely struggle in the face of a world that writes her down as an outcast to be shunned—or a craven return to another man [i.e., Edwin], his prostitute for a roof and a bed and a chance to lose her life in her children . . . while I return to my dear wife and children who all along "knew I would" and welcomed by my friends with open rejoicing and secret contempt.
>
> Why must this be so?
>
> I enclose the letter written a week or more ago to Catherine telling her the basis upon which I wish to come to my work and the children—I think it is well you should know of it.

(How oddly typical of Wright to assume that he should share with his mother the most intimate details of his married life.)

He took his lover to Paris, left her there, and sailed for home.

—◻—

"Mr. Wright reached here Saturday evening," Catherine wrote Janet Ashbee from Oak Park, "and he has brought many beautiful things. Everything but his heart, I guess, and that he has left in Germany." Understandably, Kitty was feeling sorry for herself. "Womankind," she wrote, "seems to be so moveable a feast, easily sold and easily bought and passed around and tossed away and no mercy except from outsiders."

He had suddenly appeared in Oak Park on the night of October 8, 1910, and the unprepared town was stunned. "W[right] was dressed," wrote his startled former client W. E. Martin, "to closely resemble the man on the Quaker Oats package" and apparently was quite authentically dismayed by the unexpected coolness of the town's reception.

Women turned aside as he passed them on the street, and former friends crossed the road to avoid him. The local Presbyterian minister was preparing a sermon in which adulterous man was portrayed as one who has "lost all sense of morality and religion and is damnably to be blamed." "I may as well admit that I am a social outcast," Frank told Martin, who felt constrained to drive Wright home from the station along deserted side streets to keep from being seen with him. Nonetheless, Martin perceived that Wright "evidences but little signs that he himself is ready to eat any humble pie."

In fact, Meryle Secrest interprets all these curious machinations of late 1910—right down to Frank's specific choice of Martin to help him with his luggage—as discrete and necessary parts of a grand scheme, hatched back on the sun-drenched slopes of Fiesole the previous summer. First, sufficient time had to pass so that Mamah could get a divorce from Edwin on the grounds of her own desertion. Second, Wright's plan would require money, and Martin's brother Darwin had pots of it. He had proved to be a soft touch in the past, credulous of Wright's bluster and helpless in the face of his charm. But Darwin was a man of conventional morals, and it was therefore crucial that he first be informed that the prodigal had returned, was at least conditionally repentant, and was living in his own house with his own wife. Who better to reveal this reassuring news to Darwin than his own brother?

Darwin D. Martin, it will be recalled, was chief executive with the Buffalo-based Larkin Company, the prosperous mail-order soap firm with which the flamboyant, free-thinking Elbert Hubbard had also been connected. It had been Darwin who had won Wright the commission for the company's administration building (1904), a mammoth pile that gracefully managed to transfer Prairie house concepts to a large commercial structure, one that featured any number of Wrightian innovations, including metal furniture, wall-hung toilets, central heating, and a primitive air conditioning system. Frank had also designed Darwin Martin's magnificent house in Buffalo, and Darwin seemed to hold him in almost brotherly affection. In Darwin, Wright had identified an indulgent banker for his ambitious and still secret scheme.

Within four days of his return, Frank was writing to Darwin and playing the role of the reformed sinner to the hilt. Of course, he asked for a loan. He needed money to renovate the Oak Park house, he said, and he had to pay an installment on the Wasmuth edition and pay off the debt that would free up his valuable collection of Japanese prints. Martin dutifully scolded him, and then, over the course of the next two months, coughed up some twenty-five thousand dollars—a staggering sum in those days. Frank reassured him: "I suppose you have a lurking suspicion that Wright having been swept off his feet once may be again—if he gets large sums in his hands—but this is wide of the mark. . . . Go cautiously as you like you will find no trickery." In order to remodel his own Oak Park house into apartments for rental income for Catherine and the children, he talked Darwin into giving him a "trust-deed" loan; however, Darwin soon discovered that Frank, employing a favorite tactic of his, had already sold off partial equity in the house to a variety of people, thereby creating an intractable tangle of legal knots. Still, Frank even got Darwin to pick up the mortgage on Anna's house so that she could invest, as Frank put it, in "a small farm up country." Frank praised Darwin lavishly for his largesse; generous but clear-eyed Darwin countered, "What you term 'a fine nature and a good heart' is commonly termed 'sucker.'"

Using Darwin's money, Frank bought back his Japanese prints, which he then promptly sold for over twenty thousand dollars. That done, and his stern vow to Catherine notwithstanding, he hurried to the coast and jumped on the first ship he could find that would take him back to Mamah.

—┑▣┌—

When he returned once again to Oak Park, early in 1911, the intricate campaign was entering its final stages.

Four years before, Uncle James—that seemingly indestructible bearded goliath who once, so long ago, had driven his produce-laden cart to Madison and who had futilely sought to make a farmer out of Frank—had died suddenly and horribly in a farming accident, having entangled his leg in the wheel of a steam-driven tender; two of his co-workers were scalded to death in the same mishap. James left behind a wife and seven children.

And, as it turned out, a mountain of debt. His death gradually brought to light a shameful secret: James had overextended himself in a series of ill-timed land speculations, undermining the economic foundations of the entire Lloyd Jones fiefdom at Hillside. Anna alone was unaffected and was therefore in a position, on behalf of her favored son, to buy a thirty-one-acre parcel of Helena Valley land—that "small farm up country" to which Wright had alluded so offhandedly to Darwin Martin.

Over the years, Frank became justly famous among his apprentices for his uncanny capacity to absorb mentally every feature of a given plot of land. Every swell, undulation, contour, and tree: Wright memorized land like an earnest actor memorizes his Shakespeare. And from his long summers on Uncle James's farm, Frank knew this property that Anna had bought for him particularly well. He recalled, for example, that it was dominated by a verdant, majestic knoll, so reminiscent of that Tuscan hill into which, centuries before, Renaissance architect Michelozzo had set the sprawling Villa Medici.

Frank's pencil moved furiously across paper, his talent concentrated to pinpoint focus, like sunlight seduced through a prism. He forwarded the resulting blueprints to contractors in Spring Green, and construction was underway by April 1911. In a letter to Darwin Martin that same month, Wright mentioned in passing that he ought to "see about building a small house" over in Spring Green for his mother Anna.

Meanwhile, Mamah returned to Oak Park, but not to Edwin, whom she sued for divorce that August, the requisite two years' absence having elapsed to establish legal desertion on her part. Edwin, characteristically, did not contend the action. He was awarded the children, a disposition that seemed to suit Mamah just fine. Indeed, one of the things that had most attracted Frank to Mamah was her relative indifference toward her son and daughter, who, even while nominally in her care, had been routinely foisted off on a series of nurses and boarding schools. Unlike Kitty, she had largely freed herself from her offspring to pursue the world of ideas—including Wright's ideas—and Frank found that choice admirable and compelling.

—▯—

Once work on the emerging structure at Hillside was far enough along to receive her properly, Frank took Mamah to the Valley and ensconced her in Taliesin, as he called the place on which he had been laboring so hard. "Shining brow," the word means in the lilting tongue of his forefathers; it is also the name of a mythological Welsh bard, "fostered in the land of the Deity" and "able to instruct the whole universe." Knowing what we do of Wright's robust self-esteem, therefore, it seems likely that the house was named as much for its architect as for the "shining brow" of the Wisconsin hill that it embraces. Taliesin has truly been called Wright's "architectural self-portrait," his "alter ego."

"I began to build Taliesin," Wright said, "to get my back against the wall and fight for what I saw I had to fight." The defensive language is appropriate: one of several ways to look at Taliesin is as a fortress within which two errant lovers could barricade themselves against a hostile and deeply suspicious outer world. It is no accident, for example, that the house is positioned on a hill (as opposed to in the Valley) or that its interior design provides a panoramic view of the countryside all around. It would be hard for anyone to approach Taliesin without being observed.

A second and more conventional way to look at Taliesin is to see it as the apotheosis, the culmination of all that is best and most appealing in the tradition of the Prairie or "organic" house. Setting to work on the place, Wright proclaimed, "There must be a natural house . . . having itself all that architecture had meant whenever it was alive in times past. Nothing at all I had ever seen would do." (Which was not quite true, of course: he had seen the Ho-o-Den pavilion and the Villa Medici, for instance.) The vaguely J-shaped building—or, more accurately, series of connected buildings—was constructed of only local materials: the stucco walls were mixed with raw sienna and the yellow sands of the Wisconsin River; the masonry was rectilinear fieldstone mined from a quarry just down the road and integrated so subtly into the plan—like natural outcroppings—that "it was not so easy to tell where pavements and walls left off and ground began"; timbers were finished to resemble "gray tree-trunks in violet light." The complex, abstract pattern of roofs became itself a kind of landscape; the shingles were allowed to weather into the hues of overarching branches. "My house," the architect concluded, "is made out of the rocks and trees of the region," becoming "part of the hill on which it stands." Indeed, Taliesin could rightly be called the ultimate exercise in "architecture as the direct imitation of nature."

Third, Taliesin—like Monticello or Walden or Brook Farm before it—can be linked to the venerable American utopian tradition of agrarian self-sufficiency, of morality derived from the soil. Wright's ambition, both philosophical and practical, was eventually to make the place, in addition to a residence and drafting studio, a self-sustaining farm: the original design called for a granary, an icehouse, stables, a power plant, and an independent water supply. Farming, after all, was integrally bound up in Wright's background, even if it was not exactly in his blood. From Taliesin's horizontal ribbon windows, Frank could survey the ripe, undulating fields that his grandparents and uncles had worked so long and so hard and that, at least in retrospect, he had learned to love and call his own. "I saw it all," he claimed, "and planted it all and laid the foundation of the herd, flocks, stable and fowl [even] as I laid the foundation of the house." Much of this noble idealism is leavened with nonsense, of course. Brendan Gill insists that Wright's Taliesin "wasn't a farm at all, it was an estate. It was a rich man's estate. And he didn't have any money." Still, the fields of Taliesin in later years—in between bankruptcies and unpaid mortgages and foreclosures—would supply a fair amount of produce, meat, and dairy goods for its owner, workmen, and apprentices and would allow Wright to play the part of lord of the Jeffersonian manor—a role he found infinitely more conducive to his spirit than he had the dirty, odiferous experience of working the ground himself as a boy on Uncle James's acres.

And finally, it is possible to see Taliesin as a symbol—one that silently but powerfully comments upon the lives and love of its residents. Wright himself invites such an interpretation: "Hill and house should live together each the happier for the other. . . . Yes, there was a house that hill might marry and live happily with ever after." This perfect, organic union between hill and home was quite consciously intended to reflect Frank's union with Mamah, the woman for whom, he said, "Taliesin had first taken form." And, of course, Wright had himself in mind in the house's symbolism, as well. Significantly—and contrary to his pre-1911 designs—the domestic hearth is not on Taliesin's central axis; rather, the living room is at the center, surrounded by windows and suggesting a free-floating suspension in open air. The aesthetic argument seems to be that here the individual was now central, deified, and supreme, shouldering aside the erstwhile primacy of the family unit. Frank's grandson, Eric Lloyd Wright, would later affirm that Taliesin, for his grandfather, "was a sanctuary" and that "to him it was a sacred thing that was happening [there]."

That was decidedly *not* how the local people saw it, however. Nor did they see Taliesin as fortress, Prairie house, agrarian ideal, or symbol. Rather, when Frank moved in permanently in December 1911, the residents of Spring Green tended to regard Taliesin as merely a house in which Frank Wright and Mamah Borthwick were, well, "shacking up," however elegant the shack. And these close neighbors were furious. A Chicago reporter fanned the flames of local hostility, claiming that he had spotted Frank carrying Mamah in his arms as they forded a stream on the property, Mamah displaying "a good deal of lingerie of a quality not often on display in that part of Wisconsin." Confronted with the news back in Oak Park, a tearful Catherine tremblingly denied that any of this could possibly be accurate. Through her daughter Catherine, who had become the family spokesperson, she issued a simple statement to the press: "Just say for Mr. Wright and Mrs. Wright and all the little Wrights that we don't know anything about this awful story and [that] it must be untrue."

But it was true, of course, and Frank finally decided that it was time to talk to the local folks. He would explain himself to their satisfaction, he thought; he would explain everything. He picked, of all days, Christmas to summon a reporter from the *Chicago Tribune* to Taliesin.

Standing that afternoon before a great roaring fireplace, he greeted the *Tribune*. Mamah sat nearby, wrapped in an Oriental gown. Wright himself wore a robe of bright crimson — an unfortunate sartorial choice, perhaps, given the occasion.

Following initial pleasantries, Frank prepared to read his well-polished statement. Going into the presentation, he must have calculated that he had every reason for confidence. After all, during his years abroad with Mamah — a sojourn that the mean-spirited press liked archly to call his "spiritual hegira" — he had been reading his paramour's translations of Ellen Key and her insights into marital slavery and the joys of free love. And of course he had Emerson and Whitman by heart. Therefore he felt — hubristically, no doubt — that he was perfectly prepared, through the *Tribune*, to deliver an eminently rational and persuasive justification of his behavior to Chicago and to his less-enlightened Spring Green neighbors.

It did not go well.

Mamah Borthwick, the woman for whom Taliesin was built (Wisconsin Historical Society, WHi-3970)

Taliesin, southeast elevation, ca. 1911 (Wisconsin Historical Society, WHi-29061)

Taliesin courtyard, looking east toward the residential wing (Wisconsin Historical Society, WHi-35055)

Taliesin courtyard, working wing, and a sculpture by Richard Bock, used in the Susan Lawrence Dana house in Srpingfield, IL (Wisconsin Historical Society, WHi-29065)

Draftsmen at work in Taliesin studio, ca. 1911 (Wisconsin Historical Society, WHi-29068)

A triptych of the Taliesin living room, dominated by its Wrightian hearth (Wisconsin Historical Society, WHi-29071)

3

"A Peculiar Establishment"
Life at Taliesin, 1911–1914

Every actual state is corrupt. Good men must not obey the
laws too well.

Ralph Waldo Emerson

Every house is a missionary. I don't build a house without predicting the end of the present social order.

Frank Lloyd Wright

Love is moral even without legal marriage, but marriage is immoral without love.

Ellen Key, *The Morality of Woman*

If anything, Wright told the *Tribune* reporter, his marital break-up was
the fault of Anna and of Catherine's parents: he and Kitty had been
much too young to marry back in '89 and should have been prevented
from doing so. (It was convenient for him to overlook the fact of established parental disapproval on both sides before the marriage.) His wife
and he were two entirely different personalities, he said, and over the
years their differences had become tragically evident. Catherine lived
essentially for the children, while he lived for his buildings.

Moreover, he continued, his abandonment of his children would
prove to be good for them in the long run. If he had stayed at home in
Oak Park, he would no doubt have yielded to the temptation of molding

the children in his own likeness; as things stood now, they were free from his dominant personality, with "room in which to grow up to be themselves." "When they get a little older," he added, "I hope they will see me in another light." Further, Wright said that by leaving he had spared the children the miasma of "coldness and falsehood in the atmosphere they breathed."

Indeed, considered from a particular slant, there had really been no desertion at all. "I haven't abandoned my children or deserted any woman," Wright asserted, "nor have I eloped with any man's wife." All this, of course, would have come as news to Edwin and Catherine. But Wright explained himself: "Mrs. E. H. Cheney never existed for me. She was always Mamah Borthwick to me, an individual separate and distinct, who was not any man's possession. The children, my children, are as well provided for as they ever were. I love them as much as any father could." Besides, he pointed out, "In a way my buildings are my children," and certainly he had been faithful to his "ideals in architecture," by which he meant "something organic: something sound and wholesome, American in spirit and beautiful, if might be."

At this point, Wright, who was now pacing up and down the room, seems to have finished his prepared statement. But the reporter coaxed him into responding to some questions. For example, could he not have found some way to pursue his profession while remaining within the family circle?

Not a chance, Wright replied. "Mrs. Wright had little time to be interested in my work, and I had little time to be interested in hers." Further, Catherine was laboring under a misconception. "She thinks I am infatuated with another woman. That isn't the whole of it. I went away because I found my life confused and my situation discordant. To have remained longer in the house in which we had lived was impossible and untrue. . . . [I]f I could have persuaded myself that human beings are benefited by the sacrifices others make for them, if I could have lied to myself, I might have been able to stay. But there has always seemed to me to be something hypocritical in the talk of selfishness. We misuse the word to indicate meanness, [just] as we misuse the noble word *passion* to indicate uncontrolled animalism."

Wright shared a number of other Emersonian truisms with the man from the *Tribune*. "I would be honestly myself first and take care of everything else afterward," he said, sententiously adding, "[N]o man is strong until he is himself." From time to time during the interview, Wright seems to have huddled with Mamah in whispered conversations. "After consulting his companion," the newspaper reports, "he said her opinions were exactly the same as those which he expounded." Here, apparently, was the unanimity of ideals and unstinting support that the architect had failed to find in Oak Park.

And then Wright stumbled badly. Apparently without any baiting on the journalist's part, he volunteered a naked, unnecessary, and potentially incendiary revelation of his *Übermensch* mentality. "As for the general aspect of this thing," he mused, "I want to say this: laws and rules are made for the average. The ordinary man cannot live without rules to guide his conduct. It is infinitely more difficult to live without rules, but that is what the really honest, sincere, thinking man is compelled to do. And I think when a man has displayed some spiritual power, has given concrete evidence of his ability to see and to feel the higher and better things of life, we ought to go slow in deciding he has acted badly."

Elitist pronouncements of this sort would not play well in the Midwest, as the *Tribune* editors well knew. When the interview appeared on page one the next morning, the article was coyly and provocatively headed, "Law for Ordinary Man."

—🔲—

The public's reaction was swift and predictable. One Spring Green farmer gave voice to many of the locals' bewilderment. "[Wright] seems to know a lot about horses," the unnamed citizen purportedly conceded. "But this love affair of his is beyond me. I've only had a common school education, and when he explains why he left his wife and children in Chicago, he gets beyond my depth."

Others were more angry than baffled. On the same day that Wright's interview appeared in print, several Spring Green residents approached Iowa County sheriff W. R. Pengelly, demanding that the lawman evict the errant couple from their hillside retreat. Sheriff Leonard Meyer of neighboring Sauk County even offered to help in the eviction. "Wright in Castle Fearless of Raid," trumpeted the *Tribune*.

But Pengelly was hesitant, casting about for due authorization before taking action against Wright. "I don't know yet just what charge can be brought against him," the sheriff temporized. "If reports are true, there are several charges which might be instituted. I am in doubt, however, whether any of them can be proved. I am ready to act the moment a citizen of Iowa County swears out a warrant for Wright's arrest. I shall act on my own account if I find on consultation with the district attorney that I have the authority." Apparently, at least some local people were prepared to take matters into their own hands. "I told them," said Sheriff Pengelly, "I would do my best to thwart any attempt at tarring and feathering."

Two days later, Pengelly retreated even further from an open confrontation with Wright. Denying rumors that Mamah, fearing violence or arrest, had already left Taliesin and that a warrant against Wright was imminent, the sheriff groused to reporters, "There's nothing going. I haven't seen any complaint yet, and I am not going to monkey with this business until I do. You can say for me that I am in Dodgeville and that I do not expect to go to [Taliesin] or Spring Green. The story that I said Mrs. Cheney had left the bungalow is a canard. I don't know what is going on there."

The press was less reluctant to weigh into the controversy. Within a day of the interview, for example, the *Chicago Record-Herald* published a withering indictment of Wright and his affair with Mamah. But the most telling blow came from closer quarters, when, on December 28, W. R. Purdy, editor of Spring Green's *Weekly Home News,* printed his unsparing jeremiad, "A Prophet Is Not without Honor, Save in His Own Country." It was this editorial that would both reflect and help shape local opinion of Wright for years to come.

After providing his readers with a bare-bones history of Wright's liaison with Mamah, Purdy goes on the attack. Wright's published defense notwithstanding, says Purdy, "no man or woman can live in the relation which these two brazenly flaunt and explain it to law-abiding, God-loving people in a manner that they may see no insult to decency." Fully venting, Purdy contends that a "father who deserts his own offspring and their faithful mother" and a woman "who gives the opportunity to brand her children with this disgrace" together constitute a couple who "are either insane or degenerates." Further, "soul mates" like Wright and Borthwick represent a moral contagion that threatens all of Spring Green: "[A]ny man and woman who live together as man and wife should be legally married . . . otherwise, they are a menace to the morals of a community and an insult to every family therein." Purdy detects a whiff of self-promotion behind the whole affair: "[T]his escapade will give the architect more advertising than his knee panties, long hair and other funny ways ever could." Finally, the most tragic victims of Wright's nonconformity are ultimately his Valley brethren, "who are disgusted, humiliated, and chagrined by his actions. This family contains men and women, good and true, who are giving their lives and brains to the intellectual uplift of mankind, and are doing all in their power to discourage [the sort of] vice and immorality" exemplified by the ongoing adultery at Taliesin.

In sum, what Wright was calling "ideals," provincial Spring Green was more bluntly calling "sin."

—◫—

Wright recognized well enough that his "Christmas message" had not been received as he had hoped. But undaunted by the failure and as rock-solid secure as ever in his own beliefs, he immediately began to churn out further pronouncements for the ravenous Chicago press. Perhaps no longer trusting himself in an interview situation, he next turned to a formal, signed statement, which he issued from Taliesin on December 30 and characterized as revealing the "uttermost depths of his soul."

This somewhat more cautious second statement is often couched in the third person—"as if," says Meryle Secrest, "he were retelling a universal legend"—and in the passive voice, rhetorical devices that serve to deflect personal responsibility. "Here were four people," Wright begins, "a wife and a man [he means Catherine and himself] and a husband and a woman [i.e., Edwin and Mamah] who had each . . . assumed earlier in life the responsibilities of marriage. Then the thing happened which has happened to men and women since time began—the inevitable." The subtext is clear: one can hardly be faulted for succumbing to the ineluctable.

"[A]s soon as the situation developed its inevitable character," Wright continues, tactically maintaining the passive voice, "a frank avowal to those whose lives were to be affected by a readjustment to meet the new conditions which had arisen was made."

According to Wright, Edwin Cheney—the "husband"—gave Mamah a year in which to test the depth of her love for Frank; Wright reached some similar agreement with Catherine. So Wright and Mamah lived with their respective spouses, during which time "the claims of daily companionship with little children were pitted against the integrity of life that is the only real life. All was wretched, all false, all wasted."

At the end of the stipulated year, Wright embarked for Europe with Mamah, a sojourn widely characterized as an "elopement" only because they had not troubled themselves to inform the Chicago newspapers. Finally, after "a year of travel and work and trial," Wright left Mamah in Berlin to return to Oak Park, "not as husband to the wife, but . . . only as the father of his children." Finding his architectural practice in disarray, Wright then determined that "the future of his work must be cared for and some place found or be made for the woman, the work, and himself." Out of this need, "the so-called bungalow grew on the hillside," to which retreat Wright "gathered the remnant of his forces [and, of course, Mamah] to fight for the life of his work."

His flight, Wright maintains, was not only inexorable but also common: "Thus may be written the drama that is played now in countless cases behind the curtain, so that honest souls may profit." To the well-worn charge of selfishness, Wright responds with a weary "I cannot care"; his actions, he claims, perhaps reflect "not much more than the 'selfishness' of nature, when the word is stripped of the meaning with which Christianity has misused it."

Wright fittingly concludes this second effort with an ardent appeal to be left alone: "And now that all have worn their hearts for daws to peck at, may not the matter be left in privacy to those whose concern it chiefly is?" (Possibly Wright could have done better here than to quote from Iago, the arch Machiavellian villain in Shakespeare's *Othello*.)

But Wright was still not done defending himself. One of his more dubious plans toward gaining expiation involved convincing Mamah, Edwin, and Catherine to sign off with him on a "round robin" document, to be released auspiciously on New Year's Day, in which all parties would proclaim in writing that Frank had, in fact, truthfully reported the history of his relationship with Mamah. To no one's surprise, nothing came of this scheme, and there is no evidence that Wright ever followed through with his announced intention of traveling to Chicago in the supremely unlikely hope of collecting the willing signatures of Edwin and Catherine.

Wright's eventual response to the *Weekly Home News* and its hostile editor Purdy was notably (and necessarily) modulated, muted both in diction and tone. He tells his neighbors that he "had no thought of dragging scandal into their midst when [he] built [his] home in their vicinity"; he had been motivated solely by "an honorable spirit and a hope to be something valuable and helpful to the people here in time." Having only narrowly avoided tarring and feathering, he now unctuously lauds Spring Green for its "consideration and courtesy" and for its ability to see "beyond the reach of the yellow press," and he expresses his gratitude and "admiration for the dignity Spring Green has maintained in this onslaught of slanderous intent." He asks only to be permitted to go "about [his] business quietly" until he can "set [his] life in conventional order."

—🔲—

Remarkably, his wish was largely granted. Except for very occasional broadsides in the Chicago newspapers, Frank and Mamah were allowed to settle into Taliesin without much further open opposition from populace or press. Scandal, however initially titillating, enjoys a very short shelf life. Local passions and animosities moderated from full boil to a quiet, acceptable simmer. Calm had descended over Taliesin, Wright said later. Still, given the furor that his several printed "messages"— justification piled atop justification—had initially provoked, one must ask why this most independent-minded of men had bothered to defend himself publicly in the first place.

Various theories are available. For Secrest, the repeated defenses were crafted to appease his Lloyd Jones kin in the Helena Valley, who, as editor Purdy had suggested, were mortified by Wright's abrupt introduction of his mistress into their pious and bucolic midst. Another view suspects a keen awareness on Wright's part of his past peccadilloes and a commensurate willingness to undergo that symbolic public ritual "by which suspect outsiders enter rural communities"; on some level, arguably, Wright craved the town's "approval . . . a reflection of his conflicting allegiances to both artistic and conventional modes of behavior." Or maybe Wright's goal in the statements was ultimately prophetic, an attempt "to set his relationship with Borthwick as a model for others to follow," with the idea that only "by broadcasting insistently his views on marriage . . . [could] his union with Borthwick . . . finally obtain the social sanction he so desperately seemed to need." And on a more practical, dollars-and-cents level, Norris Kelly Smith pointedly observes, "In asserting his freedom to live an unconventional life, Wright had jeopardized his acceptability, especially as a domestic architect." In this view, therefore, the various statements primarily represent an effort toward professional rehabilitation.

But whatever the impulse behind Wright's series of dogged defenses, they all failed miserably. Time proved a more reliable palliative. As the snows of January fell, Frank and Mamah hunkered down snugly at Taliesin, and the locals, however grudgingly, adapted themselves to what the press would call the "peculiar establishment" in the house on the neighboring hill.

"All happy families resemble one another," Tolstoy remarks in *Anna Karenina*. And there is every reason to believe that Wright was supremely happy with Mamah, happier than he had ever been before. Perhaps it is this lack of domestic turmoil that accounts for the fact that not much is known about Frank and Mamah's day-to-day life at Taliesin between 1911 and 1914.

There are other reasons. As the scandal cooled, for example, press coverage of Wright's every move pretty much ceased, as well. And Wright's trade predictably suffered as a result of his "hegira," so that new commissions (and their attendant publicity) were few. From thirteen new commissions back in the palmier days of 1905, Wright's practice could attract a scant three by 1912. Part of the problem was logistical, of course. While Wright maintained an office in Chicago, he seems not to have gone there much during his years at Taliesin with Mamah: now prospective clients had to come to *him.* "Hiring Frank Lloyd Wright after he moved to Wisconsin," notes Twombly, "involved a ritual demonstration of how much he was needed, which is exactly what he wanted to know."

But the scandal played a role, too, in the atrophy of Wright's professional success. While the influential Wasmuth folio was attracting serious admiration in Europe, the "kind of fame [Wright] was getting in his own country," biographer Herbert Jacobs observes, "was not the kind that would bring clients to his door"—certainly not clients for houses, Wright's specialty to this point. Whereas residential designs comprised fully two-thirds of Wright's practice earlier in the century, they made up less than half his output during the "hegira" years of 1910–1914. He did begin work on a few houses—including homes for his lawyer Sherman Booth, for Francis Little in Minnesota, and a fabled playhouse for his early client Avery Coonley—but it was two hefty commissions for commercial buildings that highlight and dominate these years: namely, contracts for the Imperial Hotel in Tokyo and for the lavish Midway Gardens on Chicago's south side.

—🔲—

The Tokyo commission was especially welcome, addressing as it did both Wright's real financial need at the time as well as his passion for all things Japanese. The precise genesis of Wright's involvement is less than clear, chiefly owing to his own obfuscating and self-aggrandizing account. In his *Autobiography,* he suggests that the commission came to him only after the Taliesin tragedy and resulted from a Magi-like pilgrimage by a cohort of Japanese experts who "had gone around the world to find a model building." Only when they finally reached the American Midwest and saw Wright's designs did these wise men from the East discover what they were looking for, and they immediately and eagerly offered him the lucrative job. More likely, Wright got the commission through the earlier intervention of Frederick W. Gookin, a Chicago banker who had bought prints from Wright and who had connections in the upper echelons of the imperial Japanese government. "The glory of Wright's whoppers," Brendan Gill dryly observes, "is that they pay no heed to mere pedestrian verisimilitude."

In any case, Wright and Mamah sailed for Tokyo in January of 1913—at the express invitation of the emperor himself, Wright said, though this claim, too, is unlikely. Baraboo's *Sauk County Democrat* was among the regional newspapers to make note of the trip, not neglecting to remind readers that Wright and his lover had "lived for the past year in defiance of conventionality" and that in "their wake they left the deserted wife of the architect, who still resides at Oak Park with her six children, and Edwin H. Cheney." (The news account overstates the situation; by this time Wright's sons John and Lloyd had joined him in partnership, and, after securing his divorce, Eddie Cheney had promptly married Elsie Mello, an Oak Park school teacher, and had happily begun a new family with her.)

In Tokyo, Wright bought prints, took soil samples, and rendered preliminary designs. When he and Mamah returned to Taliesin in May, he announced triumphantly (and prematurely) to Darwin D. Martin that the commission—worth some $50,000—was his; actually, the agreement would not be finalized until three years later.

But meanwhile, the commission for the Midway Gardens *was* in hand, and Wright set to work on that grandiose project with his customary zest and ingenuity.

—◻—

It is hard for us today to comprehend fully the intentions and vision behind the group of linked buildings that comprised the Midway Gardens; the structure was torn down in 1929, and nothing even remotely like the place exists now in the United States or, probably, anywhere else.

The inspiration had sprung from the brow of Edward C. Waller Jr., a young real estate developer and Wright's friend. In the fall of 1913, he told Wright that he wanted to build a grand-scale, open-air urban resort, a *Biergarten* of the sort then popular in Europe and calculated to attract Chicago's large German population. But Waller was not envisioning polka bands, foaming steins, and lederhosen; rather, he proposed a year-round and decidedly upscale garden of urbane delights, featuring sophisticated, world-class entertainment (Caruso would sing, Pavlova would dance, Max Bendix's popular orchestra would play), dancing, and fine dining. Waller had already found his site, a full city block on the Midway Plaissance, at the intersection of Cottage Grove Avenue and 60th Street, near where the Exposition had held sway back in 1893. Now he needed an architect.

"Frank," Waller said (or so Wright tells us), "you could make it unique."

"I know I could," Wright modestly replied. Then, "Come back Monday."

Wright set quickly to work. "The thing had simply shaken itself out of my sleeve," he reported later. "In a remarkably short time, there it was on paper—in color. Young Ed gloated over it. 'I knew it,' he said. 'You could do it, and *this is it.*'"

Waller may well have gloated: the resulting design was magical, spectacular, "a fantasy on a prodigious scale"—an enormous open court surrounded by a complex of turrets, parapets, loggias, and terraces, "suggesting a movement of space upwards and downwards, as well as parallel to the plane of the earth," so deftly and delicately manipulated that the eventual visitor would be uncertain whether he was outside or in. Recalling Hugo's critique of modernity, Wright had conceived a kind of pre-Renaissance pagan cathedral of Gothic immensity that "sprang up out of its commonplace location like the battlements of some castle in Graustark." And yet at the same time the Gardens, especially in its ornamentation, was stunningly modern, even futuristic; the wonderful abstract figures of chief sculptor Alfonso Ianelli, for instance, reflected the Cubist movement of Picasso and of the pioneering Armory Show that same year, which together with the Gardens "helped move graphic and sculptural art into the twentieth century."

However, the project was beset by two problems: money and time. Waller had budgeted some $350,000 for the Gardens, but he and his associates could raise only $65,000. He took to issuing soon-worthless stock certificates, many of which were unwisely snapped up by Wright himself. And although the blueprints had been rendered only the previous fall, Waller was pressing for a grand opening on May 1, 1914. The result was that everyone involved in the construction, including Wright and his son John, were working nearly around the clock in a furious attempt to get the thing done. Because the cash flow had dried up, Wright had to let go, painfully, of some of his ideas: green and scarlet wall decorations, vine-covered "sky frames," even balloons. And well after the Gardens' opening, Wright and John continued their exhaustive labors deep into the summer, fashioning and executing the final touches.

That is why Wright was still at Midway Gardens on the day in mid-August when he received the worst news of his life.

—🔲—

Despite his concentrated efforts at Midway Gardens, Wright somehow found time to pursue two other projects: one, another Chicago Art Institute exhibition of his recent work, and the other, his endless attempt to extract a divorce from Catherine.

At least the exhibition went well. After the Taliesin scandal, Wright later recalled, "It was imperative that I do something to let people know that I [was] up and doing."

One of the things he was doing was fending off creditors. For instance, a policeman named Bigsby showed up at his Chicago offices during the Midway Gardens project, intent on evicting him because of $1,500 in back-due rent. When his legendary charm failed him for once, Wright diverted Bigsby's attention by referring him to son John, and then he snuck out of the office. He returned soon with a check for $10,000, no doubt the largest check poor Bigsby had ever seen; Wright had hurriedly collected on a sale of Japanese prints to the millionaire William Spaulding. Then Wright, John, and Bigsby walked down to the nearest bank, where Wright cashed the check and handed $1,500 to the befuddled constable. Wright and John spent the rest of the afternoon strolling between the offices of various creditors, paying them all off. Then father and son retired to Marshall Field's department store, where Wright bought a dozen expensive chairs and a dozen Chinese rugs for Taliesin. Finally, he bought three concert grand pianos and took John out to dinner at the most expensive place in town. By the end of the day, he was back in debt and perfectly content.

This, he must have thought, was precisely how life should be lived.

—🔲—

Of course, there was still the nagging problem of Catherine, that persistent cloud on the "hegira's" horizon. In his Christmas apologia of 1911-1912, Wright, parroting the precepts of Ellen Key, had insisted, "The time is coming when people will understand what it means to say a wife is not the property of the husband and that the husband is not the property of the wife." Although vestiges of the old patriarchal order lingered on, he said, the dominance of the husband over wife and children was being replaced in modern times by something equally bad: namely, the dominance of the wife and children over the husband. What was needed, Wright said, was for marriage to be put on a purely "economic basis," although it is decidedly unclear what he meant by that.

Perhaps he meant a sharing of the joint domestic income. At least that was the deal that he dangled before Catherine in a letter dated November 22, 1914, but actually written and mailed the year before (no one knows who later altered the letter's date or why he or she bothered to commit this clumsy forgery). In that missive, Wright, criticizing Kitty's "unfair hold" on him, offers her a share of the money accrued "during the time which our partnership lasted and as much more as I could reasonably make it," and he urges her to discreetly divorce him on the grounds of desertion.

But Catherine, displaying what Meryle Secrest calls her habitual "mixture of sentimentality, unwarranted optimism, and . . . pious resentment," would not budge. She was sorry, she wrote her English friend Janet Ashbee, that Frank was so agitated; but although he was being stubborn right now, he would eventually come back to her, she was sure.

At about the same time that Kitty was writing to Janet Ashbee, Janet's husband, the Arts and Crafts architect C. R. Ashbee, was composing a laudatory article about Frank and his work, the most important piece written about Wright during the years of the first Taliesin. In his monograph, Ashbee sees Wright as the progenitor of "what is equivalent to a new architecture . . . something absolutely new and original . . . a different conception as to what constitutes a modern building." Still, Ashbee has some reservations about his friend's iconoclastic individualism, an extreme self-centeredness that, for Ashbee, has its wellsprings in the historical development of the Republic; he sees Wright as a model of "the Puritan cut adrift from his gods and from his conventions, striving to make new ones out of himself." The results are sometimes unsettling, but Ashbee is anxious to forgive. Echoing Wright's own "Christmas messages," the Englishman allows that "one may pardon in a strong man a display of individualism that one cannot forgive in a weaker."

Wright could not delude himself that his Lloyd Jones brethren in the Valley would be nearly so understanding as Ashbee. Indeed, by the time that Frank moved Mamah into Taliesin, his kinfolk were already closing ranks and were ready, they told the Chicago papers, "to sit in judgment on [their] errant member." The family had been jolted badly by the revelation of James's mismanagement of their assets; nonetheless, as editor Purdy's attack on Wright makes clear, the Lloyd Joneses still carried enormous moral clout in the Helena Valley. And they were prepared to employ it.

"What can I do to help?" asks Uncle Jenk in a despondent letter of December 28, 1911, to his sisters Nell and Jane. "What can we do to save and strengthen all hands—most of all the blinded egoist" who had moved his lover into Taliesin. Things cannot stand as they are, Jenk writes: the scandal is a "cloud-burst," a "real calamity" that threatens them all. For one thing, skittish and scandalized Chicagoans were withdrawing their children from the Aunts' Hillside Home School in droves, despite Frank's attempt to dissociate himself from the place. "I don't know what we ought to do," Jenk at last confesses. "But I think we as a family and as neighbors ought to do something to set ourselves right with the county." The Valley, he says, had received its "deadliest blow."

As with the Oak Park house before, Wright could not leave Taliesin alone; he kept changing it, adjusting it, re-imagining it. It was, after all, his home: in one manifestation or another, Taliesin would shelter Frank Lloyd Wright for forty-eight years. And so he kept tinkering with the place, "building and rebuilding the horizontal limestone and stucco complex," fashioning it into a village of buildings that was at once "a farm, a school, an architecture studio, and an entertainment center."

For her part, Mamah Bouton Borthwick (as she called herself now) seemed perfectly content to leave Frank in charge of such household matters. She herself was busily at work on her translations of Ellen Key, whose books had proved so helpful to her and Frank in justifying their unconventional ways. Shortly after Mamah's return from Europe,

Wright had put her in touch with his Chicago friend, the publisher Ralph Fletcher Seymour, who was impressed by her early submissions. Key's pronouncements, Seymour declared, "appeared to be of a pattern similar to Wright's and dissimilar to the thinking of almost everybody else. . . . Ellen Key's writings marked a step ahead in the matter of sex."

Seymour began publishing Mamah's translations as rapidly as she could produce them. In 1911 came *The Morality of Woman and Other Essays* and *Love and Ethics;* these volumes were followed the next year by *The Torpedo under the Ark* and *The Woman Movement.* Wright himself claimed to have been the co-translator of *Love and Ethics*—a neat trick, since he knew no Swedish. But at least he shared Key's worldview, to the point that he later parroted her ideas about "love-marriage" in his own *Autobiography*'s presentation of the three premises of "an honest life":

> *First:* Marriage not mutual is no better, but is worse than any other form of slavery.
>
> *Second:* Only to the degree that marriage is mutual is it decent. Love is not property. To take it so is barbarous. To protect it as such is barbarism.
>
> *Three:* The child is the pledge of good faith its parents give to the future of the race. There are no illegitimate children. There may be illegitimate parents—legal or illegal. Legal interference has no function whatever in any true Democracy.

Brendan Gill complains that Wright's understanding and use of Key's precepts amounts to philosophical "gibberish" and reveals an alarming "lack of intellectual rigor" on his part. But Wright recognized a kindred spirit when he saw one: any woman who could write (as Key did) that "No individualist persuades himself that he lives for anybody's sake but his own" was Wright's natural ally.

In fact, Wright was so pleased with Mamah's work that he toyed with the idea of a hostile buyout: he seriously considered purchasing Spring Green's *Weekly Home News,* ousting his adversary Purdy, and installing Mamah as the local newspaper's editor.

But nothing came of that scheme, and Mamah labored on as a translator, not a journalist. Ominously, one of her translations—an essay included in Key's *The Morality of Woman*—is entitled "The Woman of the Fire."

—◻—

That is how matters stood in Spring Green by mid-August 1914. Just across the Valley from Taliesin, at Tan-y-Deri ("Under the Oaks," a cottage Wright had designed seven years before), lived Wright's sister Jennie, her husband Andrew Porter, and their two surviving children, Anna and Franklin. (Their son James had died at age thirteen in 1912, a loss that Mamah had openly grieved.) Down the road stood the failing Hillside Home School, administered by the aging Aunts, Nell and Jane. That old patriarch Uncle Jenk had come up from Chicago and had spread his tents at Unity Chapel for the annual Tower Hill assembly, where there would be speeches urging moral uplift, clarifying politics, and explicating science. And throughout the Valley were sprinkled the farms of the still considerable, if buffeted, Lloyd Jones clan. Presiding over it all from the brow of its lofty hill was Taliesin: Frank, Mamah, the workers, the apprentices.

And two newly hired servants, Julian and Gertrude Carlton.

4

"A Summer Day That Changed the World"
Murder at Taliesin

Where shall we find a clue
To solve that crime, after so many years?
If we make enquiry,
We may touch things that otherwise escape us.

Sophocles, *Oedipus Rex*

Nothing lasts like a mystery.

John Fowles

Mamah was the first to die, surely, the insane force of the blow driving through her thick, upswept hair and burying the axe blade deep within her skull, spattering brain matter and bone particulate into the air like a terrible nimbus around her head, that head then falling onto the table's white linen and gushing blood.

And yet . . .

And yet, we finally do not *know*.

When it comes to the murders at Taliesin on Saturday, August 15, 1914, so much remains a mystery. We do not know—at least to the degree that we hungrily want to know—about motive, logistics, time. Some things we think we have right we do not: errors in fact, once reduced to print or circulated in the oral tradition, become picked up by subsequent inquirers and repeated endlessly, accreting layers of undue credibility with each retelling. On some points, moreover, we have been lied to and have swallowed the lie. Sure footing is hard to find.

Still, the stark fact of the murders remains. And simply because they happened (and thereby tilted a bit the world that we ourselves inhabit), those murders stubbornly carry with them, down through the decades, an implicit and insistent obligation to tell them aright, or at least to try. Attention must be paid.

The narrative that follows, then, is an honest and even painstaking attempt — relying largely on a mountain of contemporary accounts — to trace the cartography and chronology of the murders truly, to get the story right. Still, residual errors will no doubt insinuate themselves into any reconstruction, however well intended. Every assumption, every gloss, every assertion made here is intended to be preceded by a silent but implicit "I think," "I believe," or sometimes even "I guess."

—▣—

The clear Saturday sun that rose over Taliesin seemed to promise yet another dry, hot day in a summer that had been marked by dry, hot days. Eleven people were in residence at the house.

As it happened, Frank Lloyd Wright was not at Taliesin that morning. He had left the previous Tuesday evening to go to Chicago to join his son John in putting some finishing touches on Midway Gardens. He was due back the next day, Sunday. But Mamah was there, of course, overseeing the draftsmen's work for Frank's upcoming exhibition in San Francisco and, as always, toiling away dutifully on her translations.

Her children were there, too, for their yearly summertime visit. John was all of twelve now. His sister Martha, proudly sporting a pageboy haircut and a sapphire birthstone ring, was eight, due to turn nine the next month. Neither child was particularly content. In fact, they wanted to go home. Their father Edwin, currently on a business trip, had shipped them off to Mamah two weeks before, and there wasn't much to do at Taliesin, they thought, or many playmates to do things with. Further, the house seemed strange — framed pictures that looked like no recognizable thing, caged birds that talked back, an off-putting bearskin rug. Martha had invited her friend Edna Kritz, a local farm girl, to ride over on horseback for a visit. (Edna much admired Martha's sapphire ring, and they liked to play dolls together in the crooks of a gnarled, triple-trunked oak on the grounds. Way back in the 1880s, Edna's father and Frank Lloyd Wright, as youngsters, had worked adjoining farm fields in the Valley.) Martha had invited another friend, Verna Ross Orndorff, to come, too. But Verna's father, over his wife's protests, had forbidden his daughter to visit Taliesin that day, citing the unconventional lifestyle there, the "goings on" associated with the place. He insisted that Verna would be better off, morally safer, with her parents, who, with the second Mrs. Edwin Cheney, were planning a junket to Lake Delavan. Edna's father, more liberal minded, thought it would be all right for his eight-year-old to visit lonesome Martha. "Are not the children innocent?" he asked.

In addition to the family, six workmen—draftsmen and laborers—were lodged in the sprawling house as well. The oldest was burly Tom Brunker, sixty-six, a widower from the nearby town of Ridgeway. A solid Catholic, he was father to ten children, all surviving, and he would know that this was the church's feast day of the Assumption of the Blessed Virgin Mary. He worked as a general handyman and occasional foreman for Wright.

William ("Billy") Weston, thirty-five, was at Taliesin with his thirteen-year-old son Ernest. Every day, the two of them rode their bicycles four miles to Taliesin and had done so for months. Billy was Wright's favorite carpenter, a tall, lean, and lithe fellow with a sandy moustache. "A natural carpenter," Wright called him. "He was a carpenter such as architects like to stand and watch work. I never saw him make a false or unnecessary movement. His hammer, extra light with a handle fashioned by he himself, flashed to the right spot every time like the rapier of an expert swordsman." Weston, in fact, had built much of Taliesin. "America turns up a good mechanic around in country places every so often," said Wright. "Billy was one of them." And by that afternoon, he would also be the day's most conspicuous hero.

Over in the apprentices' quarters in the north wing, the morning sun woke the two architectural draftsmen, Emil Brodelle and Herbert Fritz. Brodelle, thirty or a bit younger, had every reason to be gratified at this early stage of his career. Like his employer Wright, he had been born in Richland Center, and his masterful aerial drawings for the Midway Gardens and Imperial Hotel projects had won him the great man's applause. Now a Milwaukee resident, he was engaged to his best friend's sister. Life must have looked good.

By the end of the day, Chicagoan Herbert Fritz, a draftsman barely into his twenties, had been set on fire, had broken his arm, and had been knocked unconscious. For all that, he was surely the luckiest of them all.

Swedish-born David Lindblom, who was either forty-five or fifty-five, depending on which source one credits, would run a mile over rough terrain that day at full tilt to summon help and would drag dead and dying people from Taliesin's greedy flames. The middle-aged landscape gardener would perform all of these heroics with much of his flesh burned away and with the back of his head split by an axe. He did not die until he took time to rest.

Finally, there were the servants, Julian and Gertrude Carlton, fairly new to the place, having shown up at Taliesin only in mid-June. They were from Chicago and they were black, probably the only black people for miles around and decidedly the only blacks at Taliesin. Actually, Julian—he was about thirty, and his wife the same—claimed that he was from Barbados, or from the West Indies generally, or perhaps from Cuba. His death certificate suggests he was from Alabama. It is possible that his father was from the Indies. No one knows for sure. One plausible guess is that Julian was one among that great migration of southern blacks who had made their way to the industrialized Midwest in search of work during the latter part of the nineteenth century and the early part of the twentieth. It is also possible, given the endemic racism of the day, that by claiming West Indian ancestry he could hope to win for himself some sad but mitigating cachet.

It was John Vogelsang Jr., a prosperous Chicago caterer and restaurateur, who had recommended the Carltons to Wright. Edward Waller had hired Vogelsang back in May to supply food and drink for Midway Gardens. Vogelsang said that the couple had worked as house servants for his father and had done a good job. He did not know much more about them.

Nor, after all these years, do we. We do know that Julian was on the small side—about five feet eight inches tall and weighing 145 pounds— but that he was strong. The only extant photo of him suggests that he was thin lipped, slender, dark-complexioned, well muscled, and conventionally handsome. He and Gertrude had been married about two years, he said. Before going to work for Vogelsang's father, Julian had been a Pullman porter, headquartered in Chicago. After leaving Vogelsang, the couple had lived for a time at 4733 Evans Avenue in the city, where Julian took on various odd jobs, finally finding some fairly demeaning work, early in 1914, as an assistant janitor at the Frances Willard School. Then the Carltons landed the job at Taliesin. She would cook, and he would serve as a kind of butler-cum-handyman around the place. They caught a train and traveled northwest to isolated Spring Green, almost two hundred lonely miles from home.

Again, this was in mid-June. Within two weeks, Julian wanted to leave.

On June 28, Archduke Franz Ferdinand and his wife were assassinated in Sarajevo, the capital of Bosnia, by a Serbian nationalist.

On July 16, Wright's block-like design for a proposed Spring Green Women's Building and Neighborhood Club was proudly trumpeted on the front page of the *Weekly Home News*. The design, drawn by Herbert Fritz, reflected both Wright's continuing interest in women's issues and his desire to ingratiate himself with the community as a public benefactor. The design was well received.

In late July, Billy Weston and David Lindblom sat in J. M. Reuschlein's Spring Green tavern, saying some ominous things about Julian Carlton, the new butler at Taliesin. Reuschlein overheard them.

At about the same time, Julian was telling his wife Gertrude that he had to go to Madison to see a dentist. But on August 1, she received a mysterious telegram from him. He was in Chicago, not Madison. He never did tell her, she claimed later, what he had been doing there. The next day, Edwin Cheney packed off John and Martha to Taliesin. Julian must have appeared back in Spring Green at about the same time that the children arrived there safely.

A world away, Germany was declaring war on Russia.

Around Friday, August 7, Julian went to Spring Green and bought a bottle of muriatic acid from a druggist. For the farm stores at Taliesin, he said.

England had just declared war on Germany. "All Europe Aflame," blared the *Baraboo Daily News*.

Around August 12, Julian had a nasty confrontation with Emil Brodelle. For some reason, the servant had refused to saddle the draftsman's horse, and Brodelle hotly called him "a black son of a bitch."

Wright had left for Chicago just the day before.

At some point during the torrid morning of Saturday, August 15, Julian approached Billy Weston and asked him where Wright kept his gasoline. A rug had become soiled, Carlton explained, and he needed some gas to clean it. Weston told him that Wright stored a barrel of fuel in the garage for his automobile. Julian went off to get the gasoline.

With the blazing summer sun at its highest, the Taliesin coterie sat down to lunch at two separate sites, in keeping with the custom of the house. The laborers and draftsmen—Tom Brunker, Billy and young Ernest Weston, Emil Brodelle, Herbert Fritz, and David Lindblom— took their meals in the far western room of Taliesin's residential wing; it seems originally to have been intended as a sitting room for Anna. Its southwest wall, featuring three low windows, immediately fronted a walled-in garden, then a steep hill that led precipitously down, over jagged rocks and through straggling trees, to a creek. There was a door near the far corner of the opposite wall, leading out onto a flagstone "yard" and from there into the gardened court. It was the only door in the room that permitted direct access to the outside.

Mamah and the children, meanwhile, had seated themselves on a screened terrace just off the family dining room. From there, they could hope to catch a stray, cooling breeze and could look out on the lovely green swales of the Helena Valley, cut through by the Wisconsin River. Below them, too, was a lovely manmade pool that Frank had built.

The two companies of diners, although more or less sharing the southeastern wing of sprawling Taliesin, were separated from each other—Mamah and the children to the east, the workmen to the west—by some eighty feet. Just to the workmen's north, Gertrude was finishing up her food preparation in the kitchen.

Julian, dressed in a clean white jacket, stood stiffly on the terrace just behind Mamah; Martha and John sat at opposite sides of the small table. Julian expertly served them soup. Then, as the family bent to eat, he produced a hand axe of a type known as a "shingling hatchet," and he set about his murderous business with a terrifying intensity and concentration of purpose.

From behind, he struck Mamah first, with a blow so furious as nearly to cleave her skull in two. She fell forward onto the table, her head belching blood, and then she sank slowly, wearily off her chair and sprawled on the flagstone floor.

Carlton had already turned his attention to John. He killed the boy, we assume, with one swift and horrific blow to the forehead.

Martha ran—screaming, we must imagine—through the dining room and entry, over the flagstone loggia, and into the court, which was really an extension of the driveway that led into the grounds from the north. It was a stunning place, bordered on one side by a massive flower garden in full bloom and anchored at one end by a bubbling fountain and at the other by a stand of fine oaks, just below the crest of the hill into which Taliesin had been built. And it was here that Carlton caught Martha, hammering her repeatedly in the head with the gore-smeared hatchet until she collapsed. He assumed she was dead.

Tragically for her, she was not, quite.

Three miles away, little Edna Kritz had mounted her sun-bleached mare Beauty to ride over to Taliesin and invite Martha and John to watch the threshing at her farm.

It was at about this time that Gertrude hurriedly left the house after (for some reason) first pausing to put on her best hat. She tried initially to escape through the basement but encountered a door there that would not budge. So instead she dove through a window, scrambled down the hill to the road that led to Spring Green, and, like Martha before her, began to run.

She no longer had anything to fear from her husband, however. By now he was entering the workmen's dining room through the door—apparently screened at the top, solid wood beneath—off the court, stepping past the rolled-up rug and the pails of gasoline he had stored there earlier just outside the door. The rug was a subterfuge, of course, in case anyone got suspicious; Julian had no intention of cleaning any rug that day.

The hungry men, chattering away about the day's work, were seated around a table that took up much of the cramped room. One of them later estimated that the room was about twelve feet square. Actually, it was somewhat larger than that, but they were big men, most of them, so the place must have seemed smaller than it was.

Julian went into the kitchen, found the pot of soup that Gertrude had left simmering on the stove, and brought it into the dining area. Silently, gravely, he served each of the men in turn. (Was he still wearing his crisp white jacket? Was it spattered with blood? If so, none of the men noticed. It is unlikely that they were used to taking much notice of the black servant, anyway.) Then Julian left through the door to the court. As the men started to eat, he quietly bolted the door from the outside.

Julian waited for just a moment at the door. He fished his pipe out of his pocket and clamped its stem in his white teeth. Then he bent and started picking up the cans of gasoline, pouring them under the court door so that the fuel glided silently over the floor of the dining room.

Herbert Fritz, who sat—perhaps at a separate table with Emil Brodelle—facing the door and with the low windows just to his back, was among the first to notice the liquid that was streaming now toward the men in broad, flowing sheets under the main dining table. His first assumption, a natural one, was that Carlton was mopping outside and had spilled a pail of soapy water. But almost at once he became aware of the unmistakable smell of gasoline. He was just about to speak a word of warning when they were all shaken by the booming thump of the gas being ignited, and suddenly the whole room was literally filled with fire—blue, searing, lasciviously clinging. Outside, Julian Carlton had lit his pipe and then thrown down the burning match into the fuel.

Inside, terror of the most naked and elemental kind. The men arose as one, howling, staggering, waving their arms madly, living torches. Thought, insofar as thought was possible, had reduced itself to the single, intense passion to escape that place of agony. The three or four men closest to the door crashed headlong against it, but it held. And outside Julian waited, and again he held the hatchet in his hand.

Some primitive synapse closed in Herbert Fritz's brain: there was water, saving water, down the hill in the creek. He threw his flaming body against a low window, bursting through it in a shower of glass and fire and then falling a storey and a half (or so he testified later) onto the rocks below. The seared arm that absorbed the impact snapped like a dry twig, and he began to roll down the steep incline, out of control and shrieking.

On the other side of the house, standing murderous watch at the door, Julian Carlton felt a thrill of alarm—his plan was threatened, falling apart. Central to that plan was the idea that none should escape, that none should live to tell stories and lay blame. He had assumed that all the men would try to flee through the door, but he could see through the screen that Fritz had gone through a back window instead and that Emil Brodelle was even now squeezing himself through that same opening. This was intolerable: Brodelle, of all of Taliesin's residents, must not get away.

Julian ran wildly around the building to the other side and approached the dazed draftsman just after he got through the window and landed on the ground below, his clothes aflame. Julian swung the hatchet at Brodelle's head, the blow catching him at the hairline over his left ear, penetrating into his brain and bringing him, dying, to his knees.

Looking up from halfway down the hill, where his tumble had ended before he reached the creek, Herbert Fritz reportedly witnessed Brodelle's murder. Then he saw Carlton dash back around the house. Fritz, his flesh burned badly but his clothes no longer ablaze, scrambled to his feet and started the tortuous climb back up to flaming Taliesin.

Meanwhile, Carlton reached the door just as the other burning men had managed to break it down. As they came through into the court, Carlton was waiting, but apparently rattled. He hit Billy Weston twice in the head, for example, but clumsily and with the back of the hatchet, not its blade. The carpenter fell, stunned senseless, but alive. Similarly, severely burned Tom Brunker at first sustained only a glancing blow and was able to stagger away. Young Ernest Weston, however, deprived of his father's protection, was not as fortunate. Carlton brained him on the spot, although the boy may somehow have staggered over to the garden's ornamental fountain and collapsed into it, his body a charred ruin. David Lindblom, already grotesquely burned, was struck in the back of his skull and collapsed. Finally, Julian chased down old Tom Brunker in the court and laid him low with a terrific stroke, cracking open his head so that brain matter protruded through the gaping fissure.

Herbert Fritz, his left arm fractured and his body painfully burned, hobbled around the corner of the house in time, he claimed, to witness at least the last part of the slaughter. Then he fainted amid the bodies.

The attack was over, or nearly so.

With no one left standing to oppose him, Carlton grabbed a bucket of gasoline and went back to the terrace off the family quarters and doused the fallen Mamah and young John, still in his chair, with the gas. He tossed a lighted match onto them, and their bodies exploded into flame. The fire spread.

Taliesin was visible from anywhere in the Valley, but Edna Kritz, her little girl legs sticking out on either side of old Beauty's broad back, was probably the first to see the smoke and to hear the shouts and screams. She urged the horse past patches of oxeye daisies and finally she neared the house, her young mind filled with horror and her childhood innocence falling away from her on all sides. "Hail Mary, full of grace!" she kept chanting, over and over again. "The Lord is with thee." Then, seeking comfort, seeking denial, she allowably altered the prayer: "The Lord is with *me*," she murmured. "The Lord is with *me*."

Julian retraced his steps into the court, where six of his victims lay sprawled. He may have doused little Martha there with the last of the gas and set her afire, or it may be that her clothes had been ignited by the burning bodies around her or by a vagrant pool of flaming gasoline. In any case, her clothes were burned away. In addition, she had suffered three hatchet wounds to the back of her head, one of which went clear through her skull. A fourth blow had caught her under her right eye. She was burned on both arms, her shoulders, and left leg.

She was still alive.

Incredibly, contemporary reports imply that *all* of the workers who lay strewn about her in the court may have been alive at that moment. To be sure, most of them would die before long, but probably only Mamah and John, over in the blazing family quarters, and Emil Brodelle, whose smoldering body lay at the far end of the wing, were dead outright at the scene. (And, indeed, even Brodelle may have still been clinging, however tenuously, to life — and in the courtyard, not beneath the windows. One of the first outsiders to arrive at Taliesin after the attacks was a farm laborer named Jake Ferris, who swore that he had found Brodelle crawling on his hands and knees about "half way down the court" and only then falling "prone from that position," presumably dead at last.)

Julian may not have known that so many still lived: save for the crackle of the flames, the place must have seemed eerily quiet to him. Or he may not have cared. After all, by now Taliesin was engulfed in fire, giving fair promise that the inferno would burn away any trace — and any survivors — of his frenzy.

But the columns of smoke were rising, and outsiders would come soon, he knew. He must not be found, a living black man among a host of dead white folks. Checking his pocket for his bottle of muriatic acid, he went off to find somewhere safe to hide.

He had a place in mind.

He was still carrying the axe.

—◈—

This portrayal of how the murders happened varies significantly from versions that have long been accepted and repeatedly parroted. Indeed, the traditional reconstruction of the crime — drawn from very early and often unreliable sources — insists on a quite different chronology from the one argued here. This is how the more conventional view sees the murders playing themselves out:

> Carlton *first* serves luncheon to the workmen and only *then* to Mamah and the children. Next, he returns to the area of the workmen's dining room, bides his time for a while, and then seals the courtside door, pours gasoline into the room, and ignites it. While the fire roars away in the dining room and the workmen lunge desperately against the

locked door, Carlton abandons that site entirely to run back to the terrace off the family quarters, where he kills Mamah and John; he chases down Martha and assaults her in the court. Finally, he takes his stand outside the workmen's dining room door, attacking Billy and Ernest Weston and David Lindblom as they emerge from that hellhole. Rushing around to the other side of the building, he narrowly misses catching Fritz, but arrives in time to deal with Brodelle and, depending on the particular report, perhaps Brunker or the elder Weston, as they, too, seek exit through the window. Fritz, his arm broken by his fall, rolls down the forested hill and witnesses in dismay Brodelle's savage murder.

This received, traditional timetable—namely, that Carlton first set fire to the workmen's dining room, then raced off to kill the family members on the terrace, and then finally returned to the dining area to assault the escaping workers—has become the foundation of all retellings, the standard text relating to the murders. But this orthodox view is mortally flawed in two respects: first, it overlooks the crucial eyewitness testimony of survivor Herbert Fritz; and second, it misconstrues the distance between the two sets of diners who sat down to lunch at Taliesin that day. Both of these errors speak ultimately to the central, informing issue of time, and both grow out of glaring defects in contemporary news reports.

Herbert Fritz was the only survivor of the Taliesin massacre to make a substantial, detailed statement to the press. Accordingly, his eyewitness account—appearing first in the August 16, 1914, edition of the *Chicago Tribune* and transcribed on the very day of the murders—deserves recitation in full:

> I was eating in the small dining room off the kitchen with the other men. The room, I should say, was about twelve by twelve feet in size. There were two doors, one leading to the kitchen and the other opening into the court. *We had just been served by Carlton* and he had left the room *when we noticed something flowing under the screen door from the court.* We thought it was nothing but soap suds spilled outside. The liquid ran under my chair, and I noticed the odor of gasoline. Just as I was about to remark the fact, a streak of flame shot under my chair, and it looked like the whole side of the room was on fire. All of us jumped up, and I first noticed that my clothing was on fire. The window was nearer to me than the other door, and so I jumped through it, intending to run

down the hill to the creek and roll in it. It may be that the other [kitchen?] door was locked. I don't know. I didn't think to try it. My first thought was to save myself. The window was only about half a foot from the floor and three feet wide, and it was the quickest way out. I plunged through and landed on the rocks outside. My arm was broken by the fall, and the flames had eaten through my clothing and were burning me. I rolled over and over down the hill toward the creek, but stopped about half way. The fire in my clothes was out by that time, and I scrambled to my feet and was about to start back up the hill when I saw Carlton come running around the house with the hatchet in his hand and strike Brodelle, *who had followed me through the window.* Then I saw Carlton run back around the house [i.e., back to the *door* side of the wing, next to the court], and I followed in time to see him striking at the others [i.e., the Westons, Lindblom, and Brunker] as they came through the door into the court. He evidently had expected us to come out that way [i.e., through the courtside door, as opposed to through the windows on the other side of the room] and [had been] waiting there, but ran around to the side in which the window was located *when he saw me and Brodelle jump out.* I didn't see which way Carlton went. My arm was paining me, and I was suffering terribly from the burns, and I suppose I must have lost consciousness for a few moments. I remember staggering around the corner of the house and seeing Carlton striking at the other men as they came through the door [i.e., only Fritz and Brodelle had exited through the room's window; all of the other victims among the workmen were attacked as they broke through the door leading onto the court], and when I looked again [i.e., after coming to following his bout of unconsciousness], the negro had gone.

Oddly enough, it is this same *Tribune* article containing Fritz's narrative that first submits what has become, over time, the commonly accepted sequence of the murders, as outlined above. Five days later, that same chronology—shamelessly cribbed, most often verbatim, from the *Tribune* story—resurfaces in the *Dodgeville (Wisconsin) Chronicle* and a host of other regional papers, and thereafter this proffered timetable, a patchwork of preliminary surmises, takes on final authority.

The problem is this: such a sequence cannot be made to correspond—or even to coexist—with Fritz's own testimony.

Again, what is most important about Herbert Fritz's narrative lies in its implications regarding *time*. Note what Fritz says: The workmen *had just been served by Carlton* when they noticed the gasoline flowing from outside the door and across the dining room floor; further, and even more relevantly, *Carlton touched off the fire immediately after he splashed the gasoline.* In fact, in the interval between these two events—the sudden appearance of the gasoline and the eruption of the fire—Fritz could not find an opportunity even to "remark the fact" to his companions. Therefore, how much time can have elapsed between Carlton's departure from the men and the explosion of fire in the room? Clearly, according to Fritz (and who should know better?), not much time at all. And how much time elapsed between the start of the fire and Carlton's appearance at the back window? Again, not much. Fritz, remember, is *on fire*—hardly a circumstance for hesitant, tentative action. "My first thought was to save myself," he says, bespeaking his sense of urgency. He throws himself through the window at once, rolls halfway down the hill, and looks up to see Carlton already running around the house and assaulting Brodelle, who had immediately followed Fritz out of the window. Carlton is already *there*. Accordingly, the time that passes between Carlton's setting the fire on the court side of the room and his appearing at the back or window side of the room must be measured in mere seconds.

Which fact leads to another point, one that also involves time and, once more, that seminal but misleading *Tribune* article.

Specifically, the *Tribune* has this to say about the two discrete sets of Taliesin diners on the day of the murders: "Mamah Borthwick had requested the butler to serve luncheon for herself and the children on an enclosed screened porch which overlooks a little pond and the river beyond. It [the porch] is separated from the main dining room of the low, rambling house by a passage way at least twenty-five feet long."

As was the case with the *Tribune*'s preliminary version of the murders' chronology, this early reference to "twenty-five feet" was repeated by the *Dodgeville Chronicle* in its August 21 edition, by a host of other regional Wisconsin newspapers, and by an unbroken parade of subsequent researchers as well. In short, it has become the separating standard by which we measure the physical distance that obtained between Mamah and the children on the one hand and the workers in their makeshift dining room on the other.

But again, it cannot be true. For one thing, while the "main dining room" to which the *Tribune* refers was indeed situated about twenty-feet from Mamah and her children on the adjacent screened terrace, that "main" dining room, intended solely for the family, was not where the workmen and apprentices took their meals: the workmen ate separately, at the far southeast end of the residential wing—much farther away from the terrace than the *Tribune*'s "twenty-five feet."

Floor plans abound for the 1911–1914 Taliesin—"Taliesin I," as it came to be called—and a glance at any of them immediately discredits the "twenty-five feet" figure by a factor of three or even four. William Storrer, for example, supplies a reconstruction of Wright's original floor plan for Taliesin, and reference to the scale he provides reveals that even the straight-line distance between the screened porch (labeled "Terrace" on Wright's rendering) and the workmen's dining room (labeled "Sitting Room," its intended function within Anna Wright's living quarters until it was pressed into improvised use for the workmen) is no less than eighty to ninety-five feet (depending upon the exact location of the two respective dining tables and Carlton's exact route between those two sites.)

This much enhanced and suddenly significant distance between the two dining parties, coupled with Fritz's testimony, plainly becomes crucial to any proper understanding of the logistics of the murders and stretches the credibility of the conventional chronology to the snapping point.

For if we persist in clinging to that widely accepted timetable, here is what Carlton accomplishes in those few seconds—perhaps, at the outside limit, a minute—between his first setting the fire at the courtside door and his later attacking Brodelle at the back of that same room: specifically, he runs from the far end of the wing, crosses the mouth of the courtyard, veers onto the loggia and then takes a sharp right to pass through the main entryway and the formal family dining room; finally arriving back on the porch, he kills Mamah and John; then, retracing his steps, he chases Martha back through the dining room, past the entry, and across the loggia, before he catches her at last in the court and strikes her four times in the head. He then goes over to the door of the workmen's dining room—a room that has been an oven of flames all this time—expecting the workers to exit there. When the understanding dawns on him that some of the men are escaping through the back windows, he runs around the building in time to confront Brodelle, the second man out.

All this activity in, at the outside, sixty seconds.

It could not have happened that way. There simply was not enough time. Mamah and her children, therefore, must have been served first and killed before the setting of the dining room fire.

But might reasonable objections be raised against the revised chronology as well? Admittedly yes, on at least two grounds. The first has to do with the killing of Martha Cheney. If, in fact, the little girl was murdered in the courtyard after having fled from the butchery she had witnessed on the screened porch, how can it be that the workmen, seated relatively nearby in the dining room, did not hear her screams? It was a warm summer day, after all, so windows and solid doors must have stood open. Accordingly, it is natural to infer that the workers should have been aware that something terrible was happening to Martha.

But perhaps not. Jake Ferris told the *Weekly Home News* that, when he arrived on the scene shortly after the assaults, Martha was not yet fallen but rather was still madly running about the court, "all ablaze, with her clothing practically burned off her body." This testimony, if true, suggests that Martha may have been attacked later than has been generally supposed. Or perhaps Martha had been stunned into mute horror by the murders of her mother and brother, to the point that she did not—could not—cry out, even when Carlton's deadly shadow fell over her there in the court.

Second, the revised chronology assumes a level of self-control in Carlton that is not so much inhuman as superhuman. Namely, according to that timetable, we must imagine that Carlton, having just bludgeoned Mamah, John, and (probably) Martha, somehow summoned up the steely presence of mind and icy resolve to then walk into the dining room and serve luncheon to the workmen. We need not be much concerned with such mere externals as bloodstains on Carlton's white jacket; a jacket is an easy enough thing to dispose of. But it is the psychology of the thing that appalls: a man who has just committed a triple murder leans politely over a table and steadily pours soup into waiting bowls.

And yet it must be true. Or at least something *like* it must be true: as we have seen, the element of time utterly undoes the conventional version of the story. And there is yet another reason to question and finally reject that traditional reconstruction of events—a reason having not to do so much with time as with motive.

Who? how? and why?—the eternal and irreducible triad of questions that attaches itself to any act of homicide, demanding answers.

In terms of the Taliesin murders, the response to the *who?* question has always appeared self-evident. Both surviving witnesses pointed to Julian Carlton as the sole agent of the horror. His own wife concurred, and it is very likely that Carlton himself admitted his guilt from the start. Before they succumbed, both David Lindblom and Tom Brunker named Carlton as the killer. So the servant's culpability can hardly be questioned.

That said, it *has* been questioned—however unconvincingly—from time to time, most often in the oral tradition, in stories handed down through generations of local families and among their friends. Such tales are more frequently libelous than persuasive.

For example, the degree to which so many ordinary people in southwestern Wisconsin are eager to believe the worst about Frank Lloyd Wright comes as a distinct surprise to an inquirer conducting field research in the area. Probably this animosity grows more out of Wright's legendary arrogance and his legacy of financial debts than from his unorthodox love life. But whatever its source, Wright remains a deeply controversial figure on his home turf. "Frank Lloyd Wrong," one repeatedly hears the great man called. A prominent area citizen asserts, "Wright was one of the most despised men in the history of Iowa County." Having learned that an itinerant researcher is looking into the Taliesin murders, a librarian in Sauk Prairie, upriver from Spring Green, sidles up to him and volunteers, "You know Frank did it, don't you?" The charge, while preposterous on its face, in not uncommon in these parts; in Wright's own birthplace, Richland Center (city motto: "From Farming to Frank Lloyd Wright"), another librarian recalls that her parents had confidently assured her throughout her childhood that

Wright had hired Julian Carlton to kill Mamah, of whom the architect had purportedly tired.

None of this is true, of course; what fascinates is the unquestioning rapacity with which it is believed. Noted Wright scholar Bruce Brooks Pfeiffer bitterly remarks, "In the small farming community of nearby Spring Green, the presence of this rebellious architect was something that they found hard to accept. Except for a very few close friends, the townsfolk and other close towns showed, throughout most of his lifetime, utter disdain for him. It was only when he was dead and buried that they all opened their arms and claimed him, now world famous, as 'their son, their neighbor.'" And even that qualified acceptance is often still tainted by scorn.

Or alternately, could Gertrude Carlton have been involved? Shortly after the murders, a party of motorists found Julian's wife hiding in some brush just off the road to Spring Green. She was dressed in a white blouse, blue serge skirt, and her best hat—fancy dress, some thought at the time, for a working woman. She was taken to a lock-up in Spring Green on Saturday, spent the night there, and the next day was transferred to the Iowa County jail in Dodgeville. For a short time, local press reports indicate that she was under suspicion, and in fact she was detained as a material witness under $2,500 bond. But nothing finally came of it: after spending two weeks in the jail, consistently maintaining her innocence, repudiating all past ties to Julian, and providing some fairly useful comments to the police and press, she was released outright on the morning of Saturday, August 29, partly on the grounds of thrift. "As a witness only against her husband," reported the *Dodgeville Chronicle,* "she would not have to testify, and holding her in jail here would only be further cost on the county." Deputies put her on a Chicago-bound Illinois Central train. She had seven dollars in her pocket, the same amount, oddly enough, that Frank Lloyd Wright had on him when he left Wisconsin for Chicago back in 1887. Once she boards that train, Gertrude vanishes from the historical record; we know nothing more of her thereafter. And while the logistics of the Taliesin murders might be simplified by arguing the cooperation of an accomplice, there is no evidence that she directly participated in the crime. It is quite possible, of course, that Gertrude knew more than she told the police; such obfuscation on her part would reflect a natural, even necessary defense mechanism for any black woman caught up, alone and abandoned, in a rural white power structure. But the odds that she engaged herself in the murders in any active way seem remote, at best.

Apparently, at least one prominent Wright biographer interested himself mightily (though off the printed record) in the whereabouts that fatal Saturday of Frank's mother, Anna Lloyd Wright; her conspicuous absence from the scene of slaughter struck him as deeply suspicious. And given Anna's instinctive, lifelong antipathy toward her son's women, the question *Where was Anna?* initially seems suggestive, enticing. But the question itself presupposes that Anna was in residence at Taliesin on August 15 and that therefore her absence was remarkable. In fact, Anna did not move into Taliesin until very late in 1914, not until Taliesin II was under construction and well after the summer murders. Even then, she was there only intermittently; and by no later than December 1915, she was living with Maginel in New York. Finally, while Wright had incorporated living quarters for her in his original plan for Taliesin I, those premises had been taken over by the workmen and draftsmen for their own purposes. Anna's absence seems accounted for.

In sum, no credible case has ever been made that the Taliesin murderer was anyone other than Julian Carlton, and he alone.

Conversely, the *how?* of the crime—its logistics—clearly does pose problems. Questions and nagging doubts persist. Nonetheless, we now think that we have the essence of the thing right and that we understand—at least in its untidy outlines—how Carlton did what he did.

All that remains, then, is the question of motive.

But that is everything. Within days of the murders, the *Dodgeville Chronicle* reported that District Attorney James E. O'Neill, in "the belief that there is a reason for everything . . . is trying to find an answer to the question 'Why?' to explain the murders." At the same time, Spring Green's *Weekly Home News* was already cautioning, "Many theories have been advanced and repeated as truths, growing as they traveled."

So, too, today. After all the intervening decades, we still want to know *why?* and we are still confronted with a daunting variety of ideas on the matter. It is argued here that the question can be answered to a fair degree of certainty. But not until all those alternatives have first been explored: clearly, we shall have to return to the matter of motive.

⎯▣⎯

Meanwhile, in the courtyard at Taliesin on that dreadful Saturday, the flames continued to burn. Carlton had disappeared.

And then, unexpectedly, signs of life began to stir.

Lithe, dexterous Billy Weston—Wright's "natural carpenter" and "good mechanic"—was the first among the victims to rouse himself, collect his senses, and rise unsteadily to his feet. It is hard to imagine his anguish upon finding the body of his son and the bodies of the others. Tom Brunker, badly burned and hatcheted into senselessness. Herb Fritz, unconscious, burned, broken. Little Martha, her head split open and her clothes burned off. David Lindblom, lapped by flames and with a hatchet wound to the back of his head. Perhaps Emil Brodelle was there, too, dead or dying.

Nonetheless, and although himself seared by burns and still dazed from the blows he had taken, Billy Weston understood that the necessity now was to raise the alarm and to save what could be saved of Taliesin.

He cast about for help. Among those still alive, Fritz (if indeed, as he later claimed, he lay there in the courtyard) was certainly the most able-bodied; he alone had avoided Carlton's axe. But Fritz seems to have remained unconscious. David Lindblom, despite his grievous wounds, was the next most promising choice among a decimated lot. Billy dragged the gardener to his feet, and the two men, battered and burned, set off through the cornfields, running as best they could toward the Rieder place, a half mile distant. Rieder, they knew, had a telephone.

Somehow, they accomplished their exhausting quest. Rieder duly sent out word to the police and to neighbors. Then, with Lindblom limping behind, Billy Weston ran resolutely back to Taliesin and found the fire hose in a niche in the garden wall. Although barely able to stand, he began to spray the flames that were eating away at the working quarters northwest of the residential wing. "In thirty minutes the house and all in it had burned to the stone work or to the ground," Wright noted later. "The living half of Taliesin was violently swept down and away in a madman's nightmare of flame and murder. The working half only remained. Will Weston saved that."

Soon he had help. Frank Sliter was the first local to appear on the scene, bringing with him his farmhands Albert Beckley, Fred Hanke, and the aforementioned Jake Ferris. Then neighboring farmers and their wives and children joined them, first by the dozens and then, as reports reached more distant fields and villages, by the hundreds—perhaps as many as seven hundred, all told. They filled the road, and many of them were armed with rifles. Attendants came swiftly from the Hillside Home School to help. The men instinctively formed themselves into impromptu groupings: some established a bucket brigade to fight the fire, while others coalesced into posses—one of them headed up by Civil War veteran Jenkin Lloyd Jones, who had come running from nearby Tower Hill—to scour the fields in a frenetic search for Julian Carlton. A few of the men gently took the fire hose from Billy's charred hands and persuaded him to lie down. He had done enough that day, they told him.

The law showed up in the impressive person of the new Iowa County sheriff, John T. Williams, and several of his men, including Undersheriff W. R. Pengelly and District Attorney James O'Neill. Williams's hurried trip from Dodgeville had not been without incident: on a steep patch of road known as Fann's Hill, the brakes on his Reo automobile had failed while passing through a pool of water that had collected on the road, and the driver was spilled from the car. In the first of several decisive moves he would take that day, Williams leaped to the wheel and applied his full weight to the emergency brake, stopping the vehicle just before it overturned. O'Neill had jumped from the car, injuring his hands and arms.

Williams had already ordered the telegrapher at a local train station to send word down the line for all the countryside to be on the lookout for Carlton. James Sharp's bloodhound was brought in from Richland Center, and the chase was on.

At around 12:45, Wright's brother-in-law, Andrew Porter, found Mamah over in the residential wing, or what was left of it. Her corpse was still on fire, her hair burned away. Near his mother's body, young John Cheney had been completely consumed by the fire. There was simply nothing left of him, save for a handful of ashes, stuck through by a couple of delicate young bones. For all practical purposes, he had vanished, as if he had never lived out his twelve years of joy and pain: no death certificate was ever issued in his name.

About this time—perhaps an hour after the fire first broke out—young Edna Kritz finally rode swaybacked Beauty onto the grounds of

Taliesin. She dismounted and walked over to the big three-hearted oak where she and Martha had liked to play dolls. She saw the flames leaping and heard the cries of the men "in sooty, bloodied clothes, their faces sweat-striped masks barely recognizable." After a while, one of those men found Edna's horse but not her, and a new shiver of terror raced through the house. But then she was found, and relieved "father-arms lift[ed] her from darkness" and carried her into the courtyard, where she saw Martha. *"That is not Martha!"* she screamed in her mind, even as she recognized "the September-sapphires [*sic*] ring on the swollen hand" of her butchered friend. Martha's burned lips seemed silently to mouth Edna's name. In a poem she wrote years later called "A Summer Day That Changed the World," Edna speaks of her subsequent feverish nightmares, in which she would dream of "Julian, liver-color and crouched on all fours . . . his teeth . . . like unbaked ladyfingers."

The fires burned on. In the courtyard, the men laid out the bodies of the dead, the dying, and the two who would survive. Gently, they covered them with towels. Plans were made to take them all, both the quick and the dead, to Tan-y-Deri, the Porters' place across the Valley.

—▣—

At about one o'clock, a phone rang at Midway Gardens and was answered by a staff stenographer. The call was from Frank Roth in Madison, asking to speak to his friend Frank Lloyd Wright. Wright went off to take the call.

His son John—sandwich in one hand, paintbrush in the other—was busily at work on a polychromatic mural that was to decorate a tavern wall. He and his father had been sleeping the last three or four nights on a pile of wood shavings and working furiously during the day to whip the Gardens into its final shape.

Wright returned unnoticed to the room where John was working. John recalled later that "a strange unnatural silence" had abruptly filled the room, followed by sounds of labored breathing and a groan. John looked down at his father. His face had gone white, and he was leaning on a table for support.

"What's happened, Dad?"

"John," Wright gasped, "a taxi. Taliesin is on fire—Mamah, the children, the students, what if they're hurt? Why did I leave them today?"

Then his voice broke. John summoned a taxi. The two of them picked up Sherman Booth, Frank's attorney, and headed at once for the railway station. At the counter, they learned that the next train to Spring Green was a slow local run by the Chicago, Milwaukee and St. Paul line, one that would not depart until early evening and that would take hours to reach its destination.

And then the unthinkable. There on the platform, suitcase in hand and waiting patiently for the same train, was Edwin Cheney.

There was nothing for it but to approach him and offer to shake hands. Edwin responded: he clasped the hand of the man who had run off with his wife and at whose house she and his children lay murdered. This handshake cemented the two men, John thought, in a close bond of "grief-stricken, mute understanding." Perhaps.

As the train pulled in, reporters began to descend on Wright and Cheney. Alarmed, John shoved the two men into the same compartment, and they all huffed out of the station, headed north into the waning day.

John seemed a bit surprised that Edwin had nothing to say to Frank throughout the long, slow trip.

By chance, eighteen-year-old Frances Inglis, the pretty daughter of a prominent Chicago family, was also catching a train for Spring Green that day. Her nephew was a pupil at the Hillside Home School, and he had been bragging for months to the Aunts about Frances's abilities in elocution, costuming, and theatrics, to the point that Jane and Nell had finally invited her to Hillside to demonstrate her skills. As she boarded the train, her mother detained her for a moment. "Remember, Frances," she said, "the wages of sin are death!" Young Frances, oblivious to the events that were transpiring that day in the Valley, found her seat, and the train chugged away.

By mid-afternoon, the dead and injured lay at Tan-y-Deri, the dead now decorously covered with sheets. These included Mamah and Emil Brodelle. Soon other sheets were needed: both young Martha Cheney and Ernest Weston were released at last from their agony at around three o'clock.

Dr. Marcus Bossard, the long-time physician for Taliesin and the Hillside Home School, and his colleague Dr. Frank Nee presided over the victims; both men had arrived early at the scene of the fire. Tom Brunker clung improbably to life, despite "a great hole in his skull and burns covering most of his body." David Lindblom's chances for survival were deemed "excellent" at the time. By the next day, Billy Weston was allowed to go home, but he still was too injured to attend his son's funeral.

Over at Taliesin, amid a protracted atmosphere of barely controlled chaos, the fire had finally been subdued, but fully two-thirds of the house, including the entire residential wing, lay in smoldering ashes. Makeshift posses of farmers and tradesmen—headed up by Uncle Jenk, Sheriff Williams, and a local doctor named Jones—continued to probe the recesses of the house and to beat the surrounding fields in search of Carlton. Smoke rose in ponderous, oily billows above the ruins. Taliesin, the apotheosis of the Prairie house, so long in its loving conception, had been destroyed in three brutally short hours.

And then, around five-thirty, one of the searchers, Charles Burdell, thought to look in the furnace. There was Carlton, crouched on all fours. Burdell ran off to find Sheriff Williams.

By the time Williams reached the furnace, Carlton had drunk his bottle of muriatic (hydrochloric) acid; when precisely he swallowed it is unknown, but it seems likely that he waited until his capture was inevitable. Speculation at the time was that Carlton had hoped to avoid both the fire and detection in the asbestos-lined boiler and then to escape the scene once night had fallen. He had drunk the acid, it was thought, only when it became clear that he was on the point of being captured.

Williams yanked Carlton from his hiding place. The servant seemed only half conscious. He moaned in pain. According to most accounts, he still gripped the shingling hatchet, crusted with gore. Williams wrested it away from him.

"Acid," Carlton murmured. Williams called for some deputies to assist him.

Dr. D. B. Hamilton of Ridgeway was on hand, part of the crowd that one newspaper reported was steadily "growing both in number and in feeling." Hamilton thereby became the first in a series of physicians to examine Carlton. He took a cursory glance at the servant's throat and found it swollen, but attributed that symptom to the fire and smoke. There seemed to be no medical reason why Carlton could not be taken into custody and jailed.

But by then word that the murderer had been found was already filtering out to the milling, angry crowd. Men looked to their rifles, and some of them produced coils of rope. Threats were spoken, then yelled. Their blood lust up, the bucket brigade was turning into a lynch mob.

"They'd better let me live," Carlton croaked hoarsely, "if they expect to find out something."

Williams understood that he had a dangerous situation on his hands, and he took decisive action. He had a police car brought around to the back of the building; then he and his deputies dragged Carlton through a rear window near the car. Shoving Carlton into the vehicle, Williams tried to drive away from Taliesin with his prisoner.

Immediately, however, he found himself hemmed in by three carloads of volatile men from Ridgeway, old Tom Brunker's hometown. The Ridgeway men brandished their guns and rope, demanding that Williams stop and turn Carlton over to them. The sheriff coolly pulled his service revolver and leveled it in their direction. After a moment of charged hesitation, the cars reluctantly made room, and Williams, his gun still drawn, dashed by them, heading south down to the road that would take them to Dodgeville, the county seat, eighteen miles away. According to many accounts, the Ridgeway vigilantes followed the speeding patrol car for several miles before finally giving up the chase.

Carlton, for now, was safe. Deputies even gave him some milk for his throat and whisky for his pain.

At Taliesin, storm clouds congregated to the west, and it was suppertime: the crowd began to disperse, although some die-hard gawkers lingered on well into the night. Six armed men were put on patrol around the ruined house to guard against looters and against the chance—this was much feared—that Carlton had confederates who were still lurking in the nearby fields and woods.

—🔲—

Jennie Porter, Wright's sister, was shopping in Madison that day with at least one of the Aunts from the Hillside Home School. While waiting for the 4:40 p.m. train home, she was informed of the murders at Taliesin by a *Wisconsin State Journal* correspondent, quite possibly Uncle Jenk's son Richard. Jennie could not bring herself to believe the story. Carlton, she said, was such "a mild-mannered man."

When the news reached Lake Delavan, the parents of Verna Ross Orndorff—the little girl whose father had forbidden her to go Taliesin that Saturday—were stunned with both horror and relief. Verna's mother collapsed, and Edwin Cheney's new wife stayed up, wide-eyed, all night.

At 3015 Gladys Avenue, Chicago, *Tribune* reporters were informing Herb Fritz's parents that their son had conducted himself in all ways as a hero. His mother had already received a spare telegram from him: "Dear Mother: Our house burned. Am all right. Don't worry. Herbert."

Even as the smoke still poured from Taliesin, Uncle Enos, a justice of the peace, summoned Iowa County district attorney James E. O'Neill to convene a coroner's inquest. Professor J. E. Rohr served as clerk; the five local jurors included a man with the wonderful name of Hannibal Hatch. The finding was predictable: the victims had met violent death "at the hands of one Julian Carlton."

At Tan-y-Deri, Franklin Porter, Jennie's son, was bewildered by all the sound and fury—horses racing down the road from the Hillside Home School, black billows of smoke dominating the sky. As an elderly man, he recalled for Meryle Secrest, "Those who had been burned fighting the fire were brought over to Tan-y-Deri and laid on improvised beds on the porch, right below the room in which I slept. Mingled with the memory of intense excitement of the fire is that of men moaning in the night with pain, and of a whippoorwill singing during moments of quiet. For ever after, the song of a whippoorwill at night at Tan-Y-Deri seems infinitely sad."

—◻—

Frances Inglis, the young elocutionist from Chicago, arrived at the Spring Green station by early evening. She saw two women there; both were sobbing. A train porter informed her that there had been murders and a fire at Taliesin. Then the train left the station, stranding the bewildered Frances on the platform. Night folded in around her. Heat lightning flashed on the horizon.

—◻—

At 10:10 p.m., the slow train bearing Wright and the others reached Madison, where his sister Jennie and the Aunts awaited him. But he stayed in his compartment and would not speak with the press. His gloomy reticence is understandable: all along the sluggish route from Chicago to southern Wisconsin, at one milk stop after another, Wright's party had been pelted by unwanted news. Wright's son John comments dolefully, "I have often tried to erase from my mind the anguish that was in Dad's face in that feebly lighted compartment when he learned the ghastly details from the reporters and heard them shouted from the throats of newsboys along the way: *'Taliesin Burning to the Ground, Seven Slain.'*"

When he finally arrived at the Spring Green station around midnight, however, Frank did give a brief statement to reporters and law enforcement officials. "The Carltons—Julian and his wife—were the best servants I have ever seen," he said, according to the *Chicago Tribune*. "The wife cooked and Julian was a general handy man. They were Cuban negroes, and Julian especially seemed to have an intelligence above the average and a good education for one of his class. They had not been engaged permanently and were to have quit our employ today [Saturday]. The train [from Spring Green] would have reached [Chicago] shortly after one o'clock, and he was to have visited my offices to get his wages. Three days ago, when I last saw him, he seemed perfectly normal. He must have lost his mind—and yet I cannot believe that the news is true. The fact that the telegram signed M. B. B. was received after the alleged murders buoys my hopes."

Much matter for reflection is contained in those brief remarks, assuming (a largish assumption) that they were transcribed accurately—versions of the statement vary significantly from source to source. For one thing, Wright indicates that Carlton was to have come to Wright's "offices to get his wages" on that same Saturday afternoon; but, of course, Wright would not have been in his "offices"—he was at Midway Gardens constantly, day and night. (Wright cannot have meant Sunday, for he was due to leave the city for Spring Green that day.) Further, it had been four or five days since Wright had seen Carlton, not the three he mentions. And finally, whether or not the Carltons actually "were to have quit [Wright's] employ" is in some ways an open question, one that implicitly speaks to the crucial issue of Carlton's motive, as discussed below.

But surely the most troublesome aspect of Wright's purported testimony is contained in its last sentence, the one about the "telegram signed M. B. B. [i.e., Mamah Bouton Borthwick]" that apparently had given Wright some desperate hope for his lover's survival.

What does Wright mean by "the telegram"? Well, in the same article containing his statement, the *Tribune* insists that shortly after Roth's phone call, "Wright received a telegram [at Midway Gardens] from Spring Lake [*sic*] signed with the initials of Mrs. Cheney—or Mamah Borthwick, as she now calls herself. 'Come as fast as possible—serious trouble,' was her message." Wright then supposedly called the Spring Green telegraph office, where he learned that "The message signed M. B. B. was filed at 2 o'clock."

Two days later, this story gets picked up by the *Wisconsin State Journal*, with a few variations on the theme: "One of the unexplained incidents of the tragedy is a telegram that Wright is said to have received from Mamah Borthwick Saturday afternoon at 2 o'clock. It was signed 'Mamah' and read: 'Come as quickly as you possibly can. Something terrible has happened.'" (It is this latter version of the alleged telegram that one hears repeated most often these days—not least by docents at Taliesin itself.) The Madison reporter then quotes Wright on the subject: "Either Mamah had an intimation of something dreadful or someone signed her name to the wire."

A third alternative is more probable: namely, that the whole business about the telegram is apocryphal, woven out of whole cloth by a *Tribune* copy writer. There are a number of solid reasons to question the existence of the telegram. First, the document itself has never surfaced. Second, whether the message was *received* at two o'clock (as the *State Journal* suggests) or *sent* at that time (the *Tribune*'s reading), the fact remains that Mamah Borthwick had already been dead for two hours and could hardly have been dispatching urgent communications by wire to Wright in Chicago. Of course, it is vaguely possible that some Spring Green resident wanted to notify Wright of the catastrophe while hiding (for some reason) behind Mamah's name; but any such speculation strains credulity. Moreover, no further reference to the telegram appears in the popular press after August 18, and Wright nowhere mentions it in his autobiographical writings. Accordingly, the possibility seems remote that any such telegram was ever sent.

Still, we are left with the fact that Wright is quoted at least twice — once by the *Tribune,* once by the *State Journal*— to the effect that he received the telegram. The story has proved durable and is endlessly repeated. This puzzling and irksome missive, therefore, must finally be filed vaguely under the heading "Who Knows?"

—◩—

A large crowd of curious farmers and townsfolk had gathered at the station to greet Wright and the others. In his biography *My Father Who Is on Earth,* son John uncharitably calls those in the assembly "morbid . . . ghouls," "Pharisees," "Sadducees," and, finally, "sadists." Of course, many in that lantern-bearing throng had labored energetically that day, often at considerable peril, to save Wright's house and to find Mamah's killer. Further, John did not know these people well; he had spent some time in his boyhood at the Hillside Home School but confesses that he had never been to Taliesin in his life. Accordingly, his overt contempt for the people of Spring Green seems notably misplaced and ungrateful. What could have prompted his vicious enmity?

In this context, it is helpful to remember that John's biography of his father is an exercise, almost, in slapstick. At one point, for example, John wonders in print (he often wonders about things) why his mother so resisted granting Frank a divorce and why so many of his siblings remained bitter over their father's desertion. He offers a festive alternative: "I wonder what would have been the result had we all gotten together to sing: 'Papa has fallen in love again, let's all be merry and gay.'"

Presumably Kitty and Mamah would have stood side by side in the performance of this hallelujah chorus in praise of desertion and adultery, so that everyone could be, in John's words, "happy about the whole thing."

This, then, is what John has against the good people of Spring Green—namely, the fact that, like Catherine, many of them harbored old-fashioned prejudices against his father's open infidelity and Mamah's promotion of free love. Worse yet, those prejudices sprang from religion: "There were those [in the crowd] of the clergy, too, who later from their pulpits used this tragedy as a moral lesson. . . . I wonder if their previous criticism and prophecy of evil could have influenced the Barbados [i.e., Carlton], who may have seen the possibilities for future glory in his warped mind."

So while others might search tediously after Carlton's motive, John has already found it: the poor man had heard a sermon. Finally, John recoils at the crowd's presumed hypocrisy: "I wonder how many of the critics do not envy the man who has had courage to love and risk all, while they in their cowardice only yearn and refrain!" To resist an illicit impulse, therefore, is pharisaical and ghoulish; to indulge in it constitutes genius and courage. This is how John's mind works in his biography of a father whom, philosophically, he strikingly resembles.

One man strode forth from that crowd and grabbed Frank by the collar. It was his cousin Richard, Jenk's son, the *State Journal* writer who had hustled over to Spring Green when news of the tragedy crossed his desk in Madison. "Stand up, Frank!" he cried, pounding the dazed, bewildered Wright on the back and shaking him. "It couldn't be worse, get hold of yourself!"

Wright seemed to revive a bit. John, Edwin Cheney, Sherman Booth, and Frank then clambered into a car and drove off across the river to Taliesin, where Wright first caught an agonized glimpse of what he later called a "scene of devastating horror."

Richard had been accurate: it could not have been worse.

Wright stared blankly from the car at Taliesin's smoldering shell. "From the window," John later recalled, "I could see great clouds of smoke curling upward toward the heaven, shrouding the hill upon which Taliesin once stood." His father's assessment was similarly gloomy: "Thirty-six hours earlier I had left Taliesin leaving all living, friendly, and happy. Now the blow had fallen like a lightning stroke . . . violently

swept down and away in a madman's nightmare of flame and murder. . . . The great stone chimneys stood black and tall on the hillside,
their fireplaces now gaping holes. They stood there above the Valley
against the sky, themselves tragic."

At the Porters' Tan-y-Deri, "the charred and axed remains of the
victims" lay strewn about under sheets. Wright recoiled instinctively
from the bloodied cloth draped over Mamah Borthwick's corpse. Jennie
Porter gave her brother and Cheney rooms for the night.

After weeks of dry weather, rain began to fall. Not far off, a brief
hailstorm shredded much of the area's corn crop.

—◩—

Young Frances Inglis had somehow made her way from the train station
to Tan-y-Deri. On her first night in the Helena Valley, therefore, she
found herself in a house filled with dead bodies, injured firefighters, and
the cloying smell of scorched flesh. Candles burned everywhere. She was
there when Wright arrived. For the rest of her life, she remembered the
howls of his unrestrained sobbing. A trained actress, she would later im-
itate those miserable sounds for the chilling entertainment of her family.

—◩—

The next morning, Sunday, Wright and Edwin Cheney breakfasted together at Tan-y-Deri, Edwin exhibiting his customary decorum under
even these most extraordinary and excruciating circumstances. (Frances
Inglis thought him a "dullard.") The two men spoke few words. After
breakfast, they wandered separately over to Taliesin to survey the damage by daylight. Wright was trailed by a *Chicago Tribune* reporter, probably the celebrated Walter Noble Burns, who watched the architect sift
through the ruins of his dreams, what Burns would poignantly call "his
inventory of loss."

At one point, Wright bent to pull a broken shard of a porcelain vase
from the smoking ashes. "Satsuma, $250 in Japan," he murmured. Then
he found a crisply burned sheaf of his priceless Japanese prints. "He fin-
gered them over," the reporter recalled, "and then let them flutter away
in the breeze."

The *Tribune* man did manage to garner a few stray remarks from the
stunned and otherwise mute Wright:

"I will rebuild it all, every line of it, as it was before when she—"

His voice died and he stood musing. "This is home." A broken dahlia stem at the edge of a flower border attracted his attention. He lifted the crushed flower, pinched the earth about it, and gave it a new lease of life. He cast a glance at the ugly rust-red stains in the path and strode away.

Back at Tan-y-Deri, young Frances Inglis was in the kitchen, helping the women to clean. A man came in, carrying a large wash basin covered with a piece of cloth.

"Where do you want to put this?" he asked Frances.

She asked what it was.

"Well," the man replied, "it's what is left of the little girl—you know, one of the kids."

Wright himself headed back to Tan-y-Deri, where that afternoon he and Edwin held a whispered conference on the delicate subject of the disposition of the bodies.

"Once, years ago," Edwin reportedly told Frank, "[Mamah] said that if anything ever happen[ed] to the children, [she wanted] their bodies cremated. I will take the bodies to Chicago to fulfill that wish." Then a pause. It became clear that Edwin had formulated no intentions regarding Mamah's own burial.

Frank filled the breach. "We will bury her here," he announced, and he sent someone off to notify the sexton at Unity Chapel.

Later that afternoon, two cars pulled into the drive at Tan-y-Deri. One contained a man named Clarence Boettcher, Emil Brodelle's prospective brother-in-law, who was there to carry Brodelle's body home to Milwaukee for burial. The second car had been hired to take Edwin Cheney back to the station in Spring Green to catch the Chicago train. There was a wooden box in the back seat; it held the mingled remains of Cheney's children, Martha and John. It was a painfully small box, easily carried in one hand.

The time had come for Wright and Cheney to take their final farewells. This almost surreal social ceremony was played out on the lawn at Tan-y-Deri.

Edwin said, "I'm going now."

"Good-bye, Ed," Wright replied, looking him in the eye.

Then the two men shook hands. The *Tribune* reports, "There was no trouble in their voices at the farewell. They spoke as men with an understanding. Cheney stepped into his automobile beside the small wooden box that held the bodies of his children and rolled away without a glance back at the place where the woman who was once his wife lay dead."

At the station, Edwin found telegraphed notes of condolence from his Oak Park neighbors. Also awaiting him was a horde of insistent reporters.

"You are not remaining for the burial of Mrs. Borthwick?" one newsman asked him bluntly.

"No," Edwin replied. "I am only here to take the bodies of my children home for cremation. You may say, however, there will be no funeral, either here or in Chicago. Concerning Mrs. Borthwick you must talk to—to someone else."

It was clear to the reporters who that "someone else" was. So they asked another question: "Will you take any part in the prosecution of Carlton?"

Edwin pleaded ignorance of the details of the crime and said that he would not be further involved. Then he had a question for the press: What had been Carlton's motive, did they suppose?

The journalists informed him that insanity was the prevailing—but not the exclusive—view. Then one asked, "Do you believe there could have been any other explanation of the crime? There have been rumors, you know."

The reporter who asked the question—and his contemporary audience—must have known what he meant by his provocative statement. But displaced from the scene by so many years, we do not understand what he meant, exactly. What were the "rumors" that were flying around Spring Green immediately after the murders? That Carlton had been given cause for his actions by reason of mistreatment of some kind at Taliesin? That Wright himself was somehow involved? That someone else was?

Edwin replied with characteristic diplomacy. "I am sure that he was insane and that there was no other reason," he said.

And then, offering nothing more, he carried the box containing his children onto the train and rode with them slowly out of the station, off to Oak Park, little John and Martha bound for the near redundancy of cremation at the upscale Graceland Cemetery.

—🔲—

Frank Lloyd Wright spent a good part of the afternoon cutting down the flowers—bright zinnias, dahlias, and nasturtiums—that Mamah had planted in the courtyard garden and all around the grounds of Taliesin. Finally he had collected great fragrant heaps of them. He sent a couple of men down to the grounds of Unity Chapel with instructions to dig a deep grave near the burial sites of Grandfather Richard and Grandmother Mallie; Uncle Enos had said it would be all right. He instructed some of his carpenters to build a simple, unadorned casket out of fresh white pine. Wright filled the casket with flowers.

Then he and his son John—along with two of Wright's young cousins, Orin and Ralph Lloyd Jones—went over to Tan-y-Deri. They lifted Mamah's body into the spare casket, the weight of her corpse crushing the flowers beneath her. Wright sprinkled more flowers on top of his dead lover; then they nailed the lid shut and placed the casket on the bed of a plain farm wagon drawn by two sorrel horses, Darby and Joan. Wright filled the wagon with the remaining flowers. "It helped a little," he wrote later.

In the gloom of approaching nightfall and gathering rain, Wright walked alongside the wheels of the wagon, slowly leading the horses toward the deserted chapel. The other three walked behind him. When they reached the freshly dug grave, Frank and John lifted the casket from the wagon and set it down at the bottom of the excavation. "The box was lowered," John wrote, "but [Frank] neither wept nor prayed. His face bore the expression of one not on earth. . . . I watched him, but he made no sound." Then Wright signaled the others to leave. He wanted to fill the grave himself, alone.

"The August sun was setting I remember on the familiar range of hills," he later recalled. "Dimly, I felt coming in far-off shadows of the ages struggling to escape from subconsciousness and utter themselves . . . Then slowly came darkness . . . I filled the grave, staying there in the dark. It was friendly."

Toward the end, the night sky clouded over and rain spattered down on Wright's lone figure. His job was done: no gravestone or monument of any kind capped the grave.

Wright walked up the dark path from the graveyard to the studio workshop where John awaited him. The "spiritual hegira" was over.

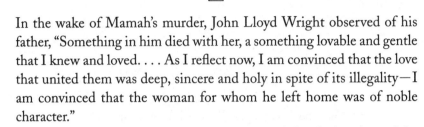

In the wake of Mamah's murder, John Lloyd Wright observed of his father, "Something in him died with her, a something lovable and gentle that I knew and loved. . . . As I reflect now, I am convinced that the love that united them was deep, sincere and holy in spite of its illegality—I am convinced that the woman for whom he left home was of noble character."

John is anxious to let his father off the hook for the breakup of the Oak Park family. "What is it that wants the heart fixed and placed by law or else crucified?" he asks indignantly. "I thank God that when [Frank's] heart left he was courageous enough to make his home elsewhere." One might be forgivably bemused by John's thanking God for his father's adultery and by his blinking the suggestion that his mother Catherine had, in some ways, been "crucified" by Frank's desertion. But that point aside, John's eulogizing of Mamah as "noble" seems heartfelt, especially given the discord she had sown in the life of his family: John had every reason to detest Mamah, but he did not—in life or death.

As for Frank, he was devastated. Like Job, he broke out in boils. He took to sleeping on a cot in the back of his studio workshop. During the fire, his piano had been thrown out of the living room and onto the lawn. Its legs had broken off in the fall, but Wright had the instrument propped up on top of the studio vault, and, like his father before him, he thundered away at its keys from time to time. Then he would pace restlessly or would ride his horse to some high ridge and stare hollow-eyed down into the ruined Valley below. Years later he wrote, "After the first terrible anguish, a kind of black despair seemed to paralyze my imagination in [Mamah's] direction and numbed my sensibilities. The blow was too severe. I got no relief in any faith nor yet any in hope."

Faith and hope, of course, are cardinal virtues in a tradition of belief that Wright had consciously discarded; it is not surprising, therefore, that these consolations were unavailable to him. As a merciful alternative, some part of him, oddly, began to forget Mamah almost at once. "Something strange had happened to me," he said. "Instead of feeling that she, whose life had joined mine there at Taliesin, was a spirit near, she was utterly gone." A further consolation, as always for Wright, was work. "Except repulsion, I could feel now only in terms of rebuilding. I could get relief only by looking forward toward rebuilding—get relief from a kind of continuous nausea, by work. . . . In action, there is release from anguish of mind."

As John had feared, many among the press and clergy immediately began to portray Wright's tragedy as a moral object lesson. Some of the criticism was reasonably muted. The *Chicago Tribune* ("Rituals Ignored as Nephews and Son Help Carry Coffin"), for example, adopted an arch but fairly restrained tone in noting the stark austerity of Mamah's internment: "The burial of Mrs. Borthwick was marked by the same disregard of the canons as her life. She went to the grave under the code she and the man she loved had made for themselves. . . . There was no spoken prayer, no word as he stood in the night." Back in Oak Park, the local editor suggested that the community could only "bow its head in silence" out of respect for the dead.

Other voices were more sententious, however, especially among regional Wisconsin papers. For instance, the *Mineral Point Tribune* (motto: "Home First, the World After"), even in its earliest dispatches, discerned the relentless wages of sin at work behind the murders: "All the farmers and their families for miles around were acquainted with the story of the Wright 'spiritual hegira,' and the 'love bungalow' was a show place, a beauty spot by nature and made more attractive by the skill of flower cultivation, etc. But the unrighteousness associated with it was unconcealed—a brazen violation of both moral and statute law. It should have been nipped in the bud. Then innocent lives would have been spared and the state free of disgrace." As Bruce Pfeiffer puts it, "When Taliesin was burned in 1914, many felt that a holy vengeance was being levied upon [Wright]. The fact that he was living not with his wife but with his client Mamah Borthwick Cheney, and that her two children visiting her at Taliesin were slain with her, was further fuel for some neighbors and the press to point to him and accuse him of receiving punishment for his life and life style."

Not surprisingly, Wright—in print, at least—contemptuously dismissed any attempt to link the murders to his unconventionality. "Waves of unkind, stupid publicity had broken over Taliesin again," he grumbles in his memoirs. "The human sacrifices at Taliesin seemed in vain. Its heroism was ridiculed, its love mocked. Its very heart [he means, of course, Mamah], struck from it at a blow, was profaned by a public sympathy harder to bear even than public curiosity had been. 'Tried and condemned,' some said. Well . . . was this trial for heresy too? Was this trial, like Grandfather's, at some judgment seat, to quell the spirit that would not be quelled?"

In self-defense, Wright offers up an analogy that one might wish he had avoided. Some months before the murders, it seems, he had been looking out at three of his cows grazing beneath an oak tree. One of the cows was Taliesin's prize Holstein, Maplecroft, "a thoroughbred worth several hundred ordinary cows" and marked somehow by "unconventionality," Wright asserts, in terms of her bovine virtues. Abruptly, lightning struck the tree, killing Maplecroft but sparing her "comparatively worthless" companions. "Why peerless Maplecroft?" Wright then asks. "Why Taliesin?"

Wright's point is sound enough. Truly, the rain falls indiscriminately on the just and the unjust. For that reason, he argues, his neighbors should have been slow in presuming that his troubles reflected any edifying sign of divine disfavor. Good women are killed and good houses burn in the same way that good cows are unaccountably struck down by lightning: mere catastrophe, by itself, implies no moral design. Still, the trope is unfortunate: to compare Taliesin—and therefore Mamah, its "very heart"—with a Holstein, however accomplished, seems reductive at best and insulting at worst, both to "peerless" Mamah and especially to her implicitly "worthless" Spring Green neighbors.

But if Wright did not intend, at least in print, to accept the town's censorious assessment of the murders, he was more forthcoming about his culpability in private. His sister Maginel came out from the East to comfort him; Jennie Porter had told her that Frank, just after the fire, was "at the mercy of his personal and unremitting torment. . . . numbed, paralyzed. . . . But then the numbness wore off and the pain came." In that frame of mind, he said to Maginel, just before her departure back to New York, "You know, you told me once, when I was reaching so high, that someday I would pull something down that would destroy me."

The comment seems almost Sophoclean in its resonance: one thinks of Oedipus, blameless in a sense for his catastrophe, but guilty at least of hubris, of overweening pride. Vincent Scully Jr., in fact, likens Wright's tragedy to that of the Theban king, pursued by inexorable nemesis. The fire and murders at Taliesin, "democratically recognized by various persons of the region as the inevitable punishment for differentness and sin," seemed destined to destroy him. His "refuge upon the Jeffersonian farm had proved illusory." Even in secluded Taliesin, Wright felt he could not escape punishment at "that same hand he had always feared, the wrathful God of [Grandfather Richard's] Isaiah."

But any such misgivings or breast beatings were stuff for personal contemplation and for sharing with intimates, not for public consumption. The villagers would be given a quite different vision. Despite the disaster of the "Christmas message" of three years before, Wright characteristically set about preparing a press release.

——▣——

In the meantime, Wright's despair was so complete that it may have spurred him to a suicide attempt, at least a half-hearted one. Meryle Secrest, citing a "small item" in the local press, notes that—on the Tuesday following the murders—the prior weekend's rains breached the dam of Wright's artificial lake at Taliesin. For some reason, Wright was there when the break occurred, and he got caught up in the flood. "But then the shock of finding himself in actual physical danger," Secrest speculates, "brought about the moment of truth he had, perhaps unconsciously, courted." Remarkably, Billy Weston was on hand again to help in a rescue, pulling Wright onto the bank. "He still, it seemed, wanted to live."

At least Wright had a choice. That same Tuesday, August 18, Tom Brunker finally died, followed shortly by David Lindblom, whose prognosis had once seemed so hopeful. And over in Milwaukee, Emil Brodelle was being buried. Brunker was buried Thursday afternoon at St. Regis Catholic Church in Ridgeway, while Lindblom, who had no area relatives other than a sister in Chicago, was interred at Unity Chapel, just a few steps from Mamah's grave.

Now the death count stood at seven.

——▣——

Wright managed to get his "To My Neighbors" statement printed in the August 20 issue of Spring Green's *Weekly Home News,* the same edition that covered the murders and fire. It is hard to know exactly how

Wright's carefully crafted letter went down with the villagers, but it is clear that subsequent readers have disagreed fundamentally over the statement's *tone*—that is, over the attitude that Wright brought to his subject and to his intended audience. Robert C. Twombly, for example, reads Wright straight, taking his words at face value and finding in them little more than a properly grateful "memorial sermon," prompted by his new appreciation for the town's "inchoate friendliness, dormant during the quiet years." For Brendan Gill, conversely, the statement is nothing less than an outright "war cry thinly disguised" as an expression of appreciation.

Gill's cynical view is more on target. True, Wright begins his long letter amicably enough, lauding all "who have rallied so bravely and well to our assistance" and to the defense of "a brave and lovely woman" from slanderous assaults. But even in his opening remarks, Wright is disingenuous. For instance, he early on thanks the townsfolk for being so "invariably kind" toward Mamah: "No community anywhere could have received the trying circumstances of her life among you in a more high-minded way. I believe at no time has anything been shown her as she moved in your midst but courtesy and sympathy." Generous words, indeed, but words that conveniently overlook the fact that a fair share of those villagers, only three years before, had tried to have Mamah and Wright forcibly evicted from their hilltop hideaway. For the moment, however, Wright is anxious to put all that unpleasantness behind him, clearing the rhetorical decks for his real purpose in the letter—an attack on the press generally and on the *Chicago Tribune* specifically.

Wright was enraged by the *Tribune*'s Sunday coverage of the Taliesin tragedy. He cannot, in fairness, have objected much to the paper's generally straightforward recounting of the murders themselves. Rather, what seems to have riled him was the lengthy background material appended to the cover story, a detailed retrospective of the Wright-Borthwick saga that harkened all the way back to Mamah's college days, her subsequent marriage to Edwin, her two elopements with Wright (along with Wright's published defenses of them), the sorrows of faithful Catherine, the construction of Taliesin, and Mamah's approving translations of Ellen Key's "commentaries on free love." On the same page, a three-column-wide photo montage displayed Taliesin, Frank, and Edwin under the heading, "The Rivals and the Love Bungalow."

It is this dredging up and sensationalistic treatment of his past to which Wright reacts so violently in his *Home News* statement. He flatly calls the account "a lie—the work of an assassin that in malice belongs with the mad black except that he [i.e., Carlton] struck in the heat of madness, and this assassin [i.e., Noble Burns?] strikes the living and the dead in cool malice. It leaves me with the same sense of outrage to the dead that the black, cunning face of the negro wears as it comes before me in my dreams."

Mamah had been misunderstood, Wright maintains, both in the press and among the public. Hers was a soul that pursued "a higher, more difficult ideal [Wright is enamored of the word *ideal*] of the white flame of chastity" than is generally considered "moral or expedient" and "that valued womanhood above wifehood or motherhood." For this supposed crime—and for the titillation of "the man in the street"—Mamah had been molested in life and now in death by "the pestilential touch" of newsmen, likened here to gluttonous "birds of prey."

Of course, Wright's implicit challenge to women to learn from Mamah's example in rejecting "the matrimonial trap," "motherhood," and conventional "chastity" seems ill-calculated to win the admiration of his provincial *Home News* readers, especially the married men among them. And certainly he was worldly enough not to have been truly surprised by the public's appetite for scandal or by the fourth estate's eagerness to sate that hunger. Nonetheless, he plunges ahead.

Mamah was actually a wonderful mother, he asserts, one who "did more for her children in holding high above them the womanhood of their mother than by sacrificing it to them." Ultimately, she was a victim of society's straitened norms: her "tragedy was that it became necessary to choose the one or the other"—motherhood or full womanhood. Wright concedes that he and Mamah had "struggles" and "differences" in their relationship—"our moments of jealous fear for our ideals of each other"—but he insists that they were essentially very happy in their unsanctioned union. Their supreme contentment might have exasperated some of their less enlightened neighbors—a "peculiarly 'Christian'" reaction, he dryly observes—but in the end, as Ellen Key argues, "only true love is free love [he probably means the obverse]—no other kind is or ever can be free." Such sexual freedom, while not for ordinary folk or the faint of heart, finally ennobles the society it only seems to threaten.

"You wives with your certificates for loving," Wright cautions pointedly, "pray that you may love as much and be loved as well as was Mamah Borthwick!"

Wright closes his letter with touching words in memory of Mamah, but his elegy is also driven by a note of defiance and resolve: "She is dead. I have buried her in the little Chapel burying ground of my people — beside the little son of my sister, a beautiful boy of ten, who loved her and whom she loved much — and while the place where she lived with me is a charred and blackened ruin, the little things of our daily life gone, I shall replace it all little by little as nearly as it may be done. I shall set it all up again for the spirit of the mortal that lived in it and loved it — will live in it still. My home will still be there." In other words, those who had hoped, silently or otherwise, that the Taliesin massacre and fire would spell the end of Frank Lloyd Wright in their presence were to be disappointed.

Wright intended to stay.

—┐▣┌—

But first he needed to rest. With the dead buried and the statement made, Wright fled to Chicago, to the little house he kept at 25 Cedar Street. He lived alone there for a while, tended to by his Irish caretaker, Nellie Breen. He was still plagued by boils and had lost weight. He had never needed glasses before, but discovered that now he did. He walked the city streets aimlessly. He would not see his children and refused even Anna, who pouted.

"I do not understand this any better now than I did then," he confided much later. "Whatever the truth may be, the fact remains — until many years afterward, to turn my thoughts backward to what had transpired in the life Mamah and I had lived together at Taliesin was like trying to see into a dark room in which terror lurked, strange shadows moved — and I would do well to turn away in time. I could see forward only. I could not see backward. The pain was too great."

But in time, a matter of months, a "green shoot" began to grow from the wreckage's "charred and blackened stump" in the form of Taliesin II. A "memory temple," Wright called it, dedicated to Mamah Borthwick.

August 16, 1914: The outbreak of war and the Taliesin murder vie for attention on the *Tribune*'s front page

NEGRO MURDERS SIX IN WRIGHT'S RURAL BUNGALOW

Mamah Borthwick and Children Killed with Hatchet.

SLAYER HIDES IN RUINS

The Rivals and the Love Bungalow.

The *Tribune*'s coverage on August 16 pits mild Edwin Cheney and Wright as Mamah's rivals and depicts Taliesin as "Wright's 300-foot House of Happiness"

August 17: patient Catherine, Mamah's children, and (purportedly) the awful hatchet

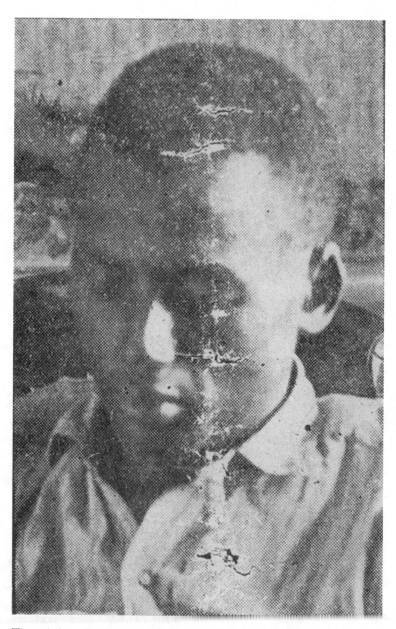

The only known photo of Julian Carlton, Wisconsin's greatest mass murderer
(Dodgeville Chronicle)

5

"I Guess You Solved the Question"

The Motives, Trials, and Lonesome Death of Julian Carlton

Tyger! Tyger! burning bright
In the forests of the night,
What immortal hand or eye
Could frame thy fearful symmetry?

William Blake

What happens to a dream deferred?
. . . .
Maybe it just sags
like a heavy load.
Or does it explode?

Langston Hughes

Will you, I pray, demand that demidevil
Why he hath thus ensnared my soul and body?

Shakespeare, *Othello*

Julian Carlton, one of the greatest mass murderers of civilians in Wisconsin history, lived for about seven and a half weeks after his arrest. Except for three brief court appearances, he spent his fitful, pain-wracked days and nights in the Dodgeville jail, and it is conventionally assumed that he said nothing germane about the crimes in all that time. Even Wright reports in his memoirs that Carlton, once locked up in Dodgeville, refused "meantime to utter a word, [and] he died there." A usually reliable Wright biographer goes so far as to claim that Carlton was physically incapable of speech, that the acid he had drunk "had burned his throat so badly that he was unable to eat or speak; he [therefore] left no explanation of his crimes."

Actually, Carlton could eat—a little, anyway—and he said any number of things after his arrest, all of them touching upon why he had conducted his appalling and apparently senseless rampage at Taliesin. Much of what he said was lies, of course: for someone in his situation, no other course could have seemed available. And he was the victim of lies, as well—or at least of utterly unfounded assertions. But he also said true things, and much of the most essential information told about him by others seems perfectly credible and persuasive. Although Carlton's motives, as with those of most murderers, may elude rational comprehension, they are at least straightforward enough in a starkly literal sense. In sum, District Attorney James E. O'Neill's early question "Why?"—echoed repeatedly by researchers and biographers down through the intervening decades—perhaps proves, upon investigation, to be not so very hard a question to answer after all.

—🔲—

In the immediate aftermath of the murders, two potential reasons for the crime are mentioned most frequently and insistently in contemporary press accounts. The first is the natural one, that Carlton was emotionally deranged. Within a week of the crime, District Attorney O'Neill was commenting, "There are a half dozen hypotheses and only one answer tenable . . . and that is 'insanity.'" And clearly, there is an indisputable sense in which the Taliesin murders exhibit a kind of madness or frenzy on Carlton's part. The horrific nature of the crime speaks for itself: no stable person could have done the things that Carlton did. The real question therefore becomes whether or not outside events at Taliesin drove Carlton mad in the two short months he was in residence there, events that in some way explain, if never justify, his deadly eruption.

A source for this second possible motive — some external force acting upon and influencing the murderer — grows out of Carlton's raspy
warning to Sheriff Williams at the time of the killer's capture. "They'd
better let me live," he had said, "if they expect to find out something."
As we have seen, however, Carlton's remark — much circulated in the
press — was made in the context of a direct threat on his life: many in
the restless crowd surrounding Taliesin were intent on lynching him on
the spot. Most likely, therefore, Carlton was merely playing a card that
he hoped would buy him some time and save him from an imminent
rope. Indeed, once he was safely ensconced in the Dodgeville jail, he
immediately backed away from the more sinister implications of his
earlier comment and started talking instead about a less ambiguous
motive of "self-defense," a tactic that must have struck him as more
promising for the long legal haul.

But Carlton's statement to Williams was just enigmatic, suggestive,
and evocative enough to touch off a fury of theory building among the
locals and the press — suspicions, as the *Wisconsin State Journal* put it,
that Julian "had been influenced by an outside source." Almost certainly, it is this idea of an "outside source" as a motive for murder that
prompted the journalist who questioned Edwin Cheney at his departure from Spring Green to remark, "There have been rumors, you
know." But what could that external force have been?

Chief among the "outside source" theories is the persistent idea that
Carlton had become enraged when he and Gertrude were suddenly
fired from their employment at Taliesin, probably by Mamah during
Wright's brief stay at Midway Gardens on the week of the murders. As
early as the day after the crimes, the *Chicago Tribune* speculated that
between Tuesday, August 11, when Wright left Taliesin, and the fateful
August 15, "something caused Mamah Borthwick to dislike Carlton.
What it was may never be known." The *Tribune* sought credence for its
own speculation by citing the uncorroborated testimony of "one of the
survivors" to the effect that "whatever had happened had led Mamah
Borthwick to tell the negro and his wife their time would be up on Saturday [August 15] night." The "survivor" is not identified, nor does his
alleged testimony appear again in print, except in those regional press
accounts (there were many) that parroted the *Tribune's* original line,
often verbatim and always without any independent verification at all.

Nonetheless, this notion of the Carltons' sudden firing endures, often couched in language that itself recalls the *Tribune*'s early account. In a very recent article, for example, filmmaker Ken Burns remarks, "[S]omething went wrong [at Taliesin during Wright's absence]; no one would ever know precisely what. Mamah may have told [Julian and Gertrude] they would have to leave." It is likely that Burns is in turn indebted to Meryle Secrest, who surmises, "Perhaps Mamah Borthwick sensed that something was going very wrong, that August Saturday morning."

But whatever premonitions Mamah may have been entertaining on August 15, they could not have involved the abrupt firing of Julian and his wife. Indeed, Mamah had told friends that the Carltons were "ideal servants . . . too good to be true." Her lover was of the same mind: although he called Julian a "madman" after the fact of the murders, Wright had spoken positively of him up to that time—even, as we have seen, in his comments to the press upon his arrival in Spring Green on the night of the fire. One contemporary source in fact implies that Julian and Gertrude had been urged to stay beyond August 15 and had agreed to do so. In short, there is no evidence of ill will between either Wright or Mamah and the Carltons before the horrors of August 15.

More to the point, the Carltons had not been fired at all—they had quit. "We were well treated and liked the place," Gertrude told authorities during the three weeks of her imprisonment. But she was speaking mostly of herself: Julian seems to have felt psychologically threatened by the rustic isolation of Taliesin almost from the beginning of their employment there in mid-June. Gertrude testified that sometime near the beginning of August, "[Julian] forced me to tell Mrs. Borthwick that we were going to quit because I was lonesome." Contrary to many press reports of the time, therefore, it was Julian, not Gertrude, who felt alienated at Taliesin and homesick for Chicago. Julian had used his wife in a campaign to get out of their obligation to the Wrights. And the tactic worked. Ron McCrea of Madison's *Capital Times* has found classified advertisements that Wright took out in the *Wisconsin State Journal*, appearing on August 12 and 13, 1914, and seeking "two girls or married couple" to perform housekeeping duties for a "country house and kitchen. . . . Wages forty dollars per month for two. Increase if satisfactory." Clearly, this ad was placed to fill the vacancy that would open once the Carltons made their announced departure from Taliesin on or immediately after August 15. All of this is perfectly in keeping with Wright's muddled comment upon his painful return from Midway Gardens: "[Julian and Gertrude] had not been engaged permanently and were to have quit our employ today." Therefore, as McCrea rightly concludes, "The Carletons [*sic*] may have given notice or been dismissed, but there was no sudden firing."

An alternate "outside source" theory mimics John Lloyd Wright's speculation that Julian had become a religious zealot, bent on eradicating an unrighteous house of open adultery. This theory found fertile ground among the religiously liberal Wright clan. Sister Maginel, for example, was quick to embrace her nephew John's unfounded surmises and to proclaim them as fact, asserting that Julian "considered himself a servant of the Lord." Subsequent Wright loyalists picked up this dubious spoor and followed it. In his fawning biography of Wright, for instance, Herbert Jacobs offers the following: "An ignorant handyman at Taliesin [note that Wright himself assessed Julian as unusually intelligent] who had become a religious fanatic, took it into his head that the Lord had commanded him to do something about the unconventional household in which he worked." Echoing Jacobs, another chronicler has it that Julian had been "driven mad by the unconventional lovers" at the house on the hill.

The chief difficulty with these various assertions is that there is no evidence whatever to support them. None of the contemporary news accounts cites religion as a motive lurking behind Carlton's crimes. Rather, the unfounded charge grows directly out of John Lloyd Wright's elitist predisposition to view the good people of Spring Green as witless, slack-jawed religious fanatics, a prejudice that does not carry much clout. Among other considerations, as Robert C. Twombly points out, "the rumor that the superstitious Barbadian émigré had taken it upon himself to punish Wright's 'immorality,' prodded by vindictive preaching at a local evangelical church, does not explain why he acted in the architect's absence." Further, McCrea notes that Julian had been "a worldly Chicagoan and former Pullman porter," someone unlikely to have been theologically affronted by the sleeping arrangements of his employers. And finally, Carlton, as part of a deathbed confession in the Dodgeville jail, seems to have told Sheriff Williams that he and

Gertrude themselves were not legally married but that rather, much like Wright and Mamah, they had been living together for the past two years in a common-law arrangement. Accordingly, Julian Carlton was in no position to assume the moral high ground when it came to the issue of fornication. Despite John Lloyd Wright's rabid anticlericalism (a sentiment he shared with his father), the "religious zealot" construct therefore doesn't hold.

A third theory, this one growing out of the area's endemic dislike and mistrust of Wright, sought to tie Wright himself to the crime, if not as conspirator, then perhaps as the intended victim. For example, one newspaper article at the time, subheaded "Think Carlton Was a Tool," makes much of Carlton's mysterious and unannounced trip to Chicago on the week before the murders. "Whether Julian Carlton while insane was alone responsible for the awful crime or whether the negro cook was the tool of enemies of Frank Lloyd Wright is a question that is puzzling authorities here [in Dodgeville]," the reporter asserts. In the abundant light of other evidence, however, it is unlikely that the authorities were puzzled much. No doubt many townsfolk harbored the notion that Wright, the local renegade, was either a hidden hand behind the massacre or had at least prompted it by having alienated shadowy, powerful gray eminences in the metropolis beyond. But as with the "religious zealotry" theory, this conspiratorial idea founders on the fact of Wright's absence from Taliesin, and speculation of this sort enjoyed, mercifully, only a brief shelf life in the press.

A final "outside source" motive is occasionally suggested—namely, that Carlton was having financial problems with Wright. This theory at least rests upon established patterns of personal behavior—namely, Carlton's habitual money worries in his Chicago days (about which more later) on the one hand and Wright's notoriously cavalier treatment of money on the other. Apprentices, draftsmen, laborers, contractors, suppliers, creditors, clients, merchants—pretty much everyone who did business with Wright ended up waiting to be paid, and many never were. Owen King, a Spring Green lumberyard owner, is an all-too-typical case in point. He once telephoned Wright, informing him that the great man owed him money. "Are you worried about it?" Wright asked. "Yes, I am," King replied. "Well, then, why should *both* of us worry?" Wright said brightly, and he hung up.

Wright failed to pay even his own son John on a regular basis. An architectural historian observes, "[T]he attrition rate [of the apprentices at the Studio] was rather high, due partly to Wright's callousness concerning pay." And certainly Wright's explanation at the Spring Green train station about how Carlton was to collect his final wages comes across as unconvincing and evasive, at best. One online source claims that money was an issue for the "Barbados servant who, they said, was underpaid" and who "exacted a revenge" by burning down Taliesin. But no one specifically identifies the nameless "they"—local gossips, no doubt—who speculated about the money motive; in fact, that motive is nowhere reflected in press accounts, in the testimony of the Carltons, in the police and court transcripts (such as they are), or in the recorded commentary of Julian's friends and neighbors.

Once again, therefore, another attempt at explaining away the Taliesin murders in some manner that approaches the rational is found to be shaky: no evidence exists that Carlton had ever feuded with Wright or with Mamah over money, much less that such a feud spilled over into arson and murder.

—◉—

Carlton's "fiendish acts," says McCrea, "were either insane or prompted by a desperate motivation." But even McCrea, who seems to favor some unidentified "outside source" or "desperate motivation" for the crimes, is forced in fairness to concede that "no evidence of a rational intention or motive, including a conspiracy, has ever come to light." As District Attorney O'Neill suggested long ago, therefore, only one tenable motive for the crimes remains: namely that Carlton had gone mad, berserk.

This is not to suggest that the fact of Carlton's insanity struck everyone as an open-and-shut matter at the time. Indeed, McCrea insists (hyperbolically, perhaps) that "the idea that he was actually mad seemed unbelievable—radically out of character—to nearly all who were acquainted with him." As noted above, John Vogelsang Jr., the Chicago restaurateur and caterer who had referred Carlton to Wright as "an excellent and honest workman," remarked defensively after the murders that the butler "was highly thought of by my father. He was a good, honest servant and seemed rational at all times." Similarly, Jennie Porter, Wright's sister, could not at first bring herself to believe that the "mild mannered" Carlton was a mass killer, declaring the whole idea an absurd mistake. Again, both Wright and Mamah had praised Carlton, emphasizing his education and self-evident intelligence. The arresting deputies who accompanied Carlton on the perilous car ride from Taliesin to Dodgeville later testified that the prisoner "talked intelligently to them." Immediately after the murders, their boss, Sheriff Williams, flatly told the papers, "I do not believe the negro is insane." Some press accounts at the time portray Carlton as a man of a "jovial" and "mild disposition," addicted neither to drugs nor drink and "never giving evidence of his fiendish propensities." And even Billy Weston, one of the two survivors of the slaughter, apparently told the *Wisconsin State Journal*, "Carlton had been here about two months, [and] he had been pleasant."

But, in fact, Carlton's deeply troubled psyche had made itself evident long before the volcanic eruption of his madness on that awful Saturday at Taliesin. Back in his hometown of Chicago, for example, Julian had already established a disturbing reputation among his African American neighbors. Mrs. Maurice Dorsey lived at 4782 South Wabash Avenue and had befriended the Carltons when she worked with Julian at the Vogelsang catering enterprise. A day after the murders, she told a *Tribune* reporter that Julian had acted erratically, bizarrely, ever since she had known him and that he had worried constantly about money matters. "He seemed to be nervous and quivering all the time," she said. "He'd fly off the handle at the slightest provocation. I remember one time when I gave a whist party and he was playing. All of a sudden he jumped up and let out a yell that scared us all nearly to death. All of the women started to run out, thinking he had gone crazy. But [then] he sat down, trembling, and mumbled a few words of apology. His mind always seemed to be wandering away from what he was doing, and what little talking he did was about his poor circumstances and how afraid he was that he wasn't going to get along [financially]."

After Julian left the Vogelsangs' employ and moved to Evans Avenue, his neighbor was Mrs. Harry Long, with whom Gertrude sought refuge whenever Julian terrified her. "As far as I could learn," Mrs. Long told the *Tribune*, "they had been married two years. I didn't like [Julian] and was afraid of him. He always did look queer to me. I thought he was 'off' all along. His wife was afraid of him, too. She'd come here often all trembling and nervous and say he had tried to frighten her. She said he'd get spells when he was wild eyed and do such strange things that she feared for her life."

If anything, Julian became even more emotionally volatile after the move to rural Wisconsin. At some point late in July, for example, Spring Green barkeep J. M. Reuschlein overheard Billy Weston and David Lindblom talking about Carlton. "He's polite and smart," one of the Taliesin men said, "but he's the most desperate, hotheaded fellow I ever saw. Don't ever contradict him; he'll fly off the handle any minute." Certainly Lindblom had reason to fear Carlton. At some point that summer, Lindblom told Taliesin farmhand Joseph Grauvogl that the servant had given him "an awful calling-down, telling him that the whole bunch [of apprentices and workmen] kept running to Mr. Wright with stories about him." According to Lindblom, Carlton had threatened that "if anyone around [Taliesin] ever did him any dirt, he would send him to hell in a minute." Further, Grauvogl told the *Weekly Home News* that the night before the murders, Carlton had entered Lindblom's room "with a large butcher knife in his hand"; Carlton, Grauvogl, and Lindblom "talked awhile and then Carlton left." And as we have seen, Carlton—probably on August 13, two days before the murders—had a decisive confrontation with draftsman Emil Brodelle, during which Brodelle called him a "black son of a bitch"; it is likely that the two had a subsequent contretemps that ended with Brodelle's striking Carlton. So while Wright and Mamah may have thought well of Julian, it is clear, as a local newspaper reported at the time, that he had been "disliked and mistrusted by most of the Taliesin staff" from the start of his service there.

Of course, the person who knew Carlton best was Gertrude, and in all of her statements she is adamantly consistent in her depiction of him as utterly deranged. "[M]y husband had the notion that he was being pursued," she told Iowa County deputies. "He recently got to waking me up in the night at our quarters in the bungalow to listen for noises. 'They're trying to get me,' he kept saying. Then sometimes he would choke me and threaten to knock my brains out. He took that hatchet to bed with him. Two weeks ago, he forced me to tell Mrs. Borthwick that we were going to quit because I was lonesome. Then a week ago he kept saying he was going to Madison to see a dentist. The next day I got a message from him in Chicago, but he would not tell me why he went there. Saturday he served lunch and went into the court with a pail of gasoline. I saw him start to dip a rug in the gasoline. Then he struck a match and lighted his pipe. I went into the kitchen, and a minute later the whole place was afire. I saw Julian running toward the barn with the hatchet in his hand. I ran into the basement, tried a door, then jumped out a window and ran down the road toward Spring Green. I didn't see my husband hit anybody, and I did not know anything until I was arrested on the road to town." Further, Gertrude apparently testified to Julian's "hallucinations of persecution which drove him to frequent threats of violence" and to the fact that "her husband had been entertaining queer notions for several days prior to Saturday." According to Gertrude, Julian kept insisting "that certain people were picking on him. Sometimes at night [I] would start up suddenly . . . to find Julian sitting at the window, staring into the darkness with wakeful eyes."

If Gertrude's testimony often betrays evidence of a subsequent editor's pen, her formally recorded statements are at least consistent in tone with the spontaneous testimony originally attributed to her, cast by newsmen in the skewed Steppin Fetchit diction of the day: "I dunno what took him [Julian]. 'Dis noon he was all upset. De las' I seen, he was runnin' round de house, actin' crazy and talkin' 'bout killin' folks." Therefore, whichever version of Gertrude's declaration one credits, the conclusion to be drawn remains the same: namely, that Julian Carlton's most intimate companion considered him psychotically paranoid and, at least on occasion, an outright madman.

And while Sheriff Williams initially expressed confidence in the prisoner's sanity, he may well have changed his mind when, on Wednesday, August 26, Carlton attacked him in the corridor of the jail, throwing first a drinking cup and then a pail containing water at the lawman. It took two deputies to wrestle Carlton back into his cell.

— 🔲 —

In his three brief appearances before the bar of Iowa County justice, Carlton certainly struck most observers as obviously unbalanced.

Actually, the first of those appearances did not take place in a courtroom at all. On the night of August 16, Carlton seems to have become violently ill in his jail cell. The next day, Sheriff Williams hurriedly scribbled a handwritten note on the front of a blank warrant form to Justice of the Peace Thomas H. Arthur, advising him that Carlton's condition was such "as to make it almost impossible to produce him in court." In response, Dr. Wallis G. Lincoln was dispatched to Carlton's cell and, after examining the murderer, apparently informed him that he would die from the acid he had swallowed. Confronted with this unhappy news, Carlton, by one report, offered the doctor an unsolicited, spontaneous confession, declaring "that he had planned the murders, had secreted a bundle of clothing in nearby woods and intended to escape, but . . . men came running from the whole neighborhood so fast that he did not have time to get away. He hid in the big heating plant boiler for hours, but finally concluded that escape was impossible. So he drank the acid and gave himself up."

Lincoln's examination having confirmed Sheriff Williams's concern, Justice Arthur decided to hold Carlton's preliminary arraignment hearing that afternoon in the hallway of the jail. Carlton was "carried from his cell to a chair outside the grated door" of his cell. There, in the presence of District Attorney O'Neill, Arthur formally charged Carlton with the murder of draftsman Emil Brodelle. Carlton, apparently in a state of near unconsciousness, mumbled a few words that no one could understand and either could not reply audibly or feigned that he could not.

In light of the prisoner's lack of cooperation, Arthur immediately filed a "Complaint for Murder" statement with O'Neill: "John T. Williams complains in writing on oath charging Julian Carlton with the murder of Emil Brodelle at this county [on] August 15, 1914. . . . The sheriff having advised the court that the accused is not in condition to be moved, the court adjourned to the jail where the prisoner is confined; complaint read to him and a plea of not guilty entered. On account of the physical condition of the accused and the absence of material witnesses, an adjournment of ten days is taken. . . . This case is therefore adjourned until August 27." Carlton remained jailed. No attorney was appointed to represent him.

At that August 27 hearing—a continuance of Carlton's arraignment—the defendant suddenly found himself charged with ten felonies, not one. A mere day before the hearing, in a flurry of judicial activity, Iowa County for the first time charged Carlton, in separate warrants, with, respectively, the murders of Mamah Borthwick, Tom

Brunker, John Cheney (despite the lack of a death certificate in his case), Martha Cheney, Ernest Weston, and David Lindblom; on that same date, the prisoner was additionally charged with arson and with assaults upon Billy Weston and Herbert Fritz "with a dangerous weapon, to-wit: a hatchet."

But the important factor here is that this hasty, last-minute litany of charges constitutes mere legal window dressing: a full nine days earlier, the first working day after the tragedy, the county had already quite specifically determined that "Emil Brodelle came to his death by being hit on the head with a hatchet in the hands on Julian Carlton." Going into the hearing, therefore, it is clear that the prosecution had one particular murder in mind—that of Emil Brodelle.

More than a week before the August 27 hearing, the *Baraboo Daily News* records, "Although he killed five [only five had died by that time], Carleton [*sic*] was charged formally with only one murder, that of Emil Brodell [*sic*], draftsman, with whom he had had words a few days ago and against whom he admits he was enraged." Even after the hearing, the *Mineral Point Tribune* specifies, "The Negro will be tried [solely] for the murder of Emil Brodelle of Milwaukee [and only] then for the murder of Mrs. Mamah Borthwick and the other victims." Similarly, the *Grant County Herald* notes, "The first trial of the negro will be for the murder of Emil Bourdelle [*sic*] of Milwaukee."

In cases of multiple homicide, it is, of course, common for the state to limit the initial charge against the defendant. Still, the parameters of this particular charge are suggestive and revealing. For a variety of reasons, prosecutor O'Neill accurately sensed that Brodelle's murder presented him with his best, most transparently provable case. He could count, for example, on the eyewitness testimony of survivor Herb Fritz, who claimed to have seen Carlton hatchet Brodelle to death beneath the dining room's rear window. Further, there was good reason for O'Neill to suppose that Brodelle's death reflected the state's most promising opportunity to clarify once and for all the key element of *motive*.

At the August 27 hearing, Harper Harrison, a Spring Green harness maker, took the stand and testified to this crucial point. Harrison had gained entry to Carlton's jail cell on the day of the murder; probably he was a part-time Sauk County deputy or was part of one of the impromptu posses that had assembled to look for the fugitive servant, and it is likely that he was among those who had transported Carlton to Dodgeville, pursued by the Ridgeway vigilantes. Harrison informed the packed courtroom that Carlton, when pressed for a reason for the crimes, had told him that Brodelle had grossly insulted him during a confrontation on August 13 and had actually struck him during another altercation the following day. It was at that point, Carlton told Harrison, that "he made up his mind [that] he would 'get' [Brodelle]." Carlton then improbably related that he had killed Mamah Borthwick only because he mistook her for a man who had come to Brodelle's aid. At that point, he would give Harrison no reason for slaying the five other victims and then burning down the house.

But again, this revelation, although varying in its particulars from conversations Carlton had with others, was in some ways old news: Iowa County officials had already determined to their satisfaction that Carlton's overriding motive for the Taliesin murders grew out of an obsessive desire on his part to kill Emil Brodelle, specifically. As part of his jailhouse confession to Dr. Lincoln, Carlton seems to have freely admitted that he and Brodelle "had an altercation on Saturday [August 15] morning, during which Brodelle abused me for more than a half hour. I told him I would 'get him,' and I waited for my chances." According to at least one local newspaper, Carlton "insisted that it was because of the [insults that] the Milwaukee man heaped upon his head that he decided to end the lives of the party living in the bungalow." Carlton told Lincoln that he had killed the others and set fire to the house only to eliminate witnesses and evidence; he may even have signed a statement to that effect.

And right up to the point of his death, Carlton apparently made several similar confessions to Sheriff Williams, admitting the murder of Brodelle but telling the lawman that he could not recall killing the others. In fact, during Carlton's last days in the jail, Williams urgently solicited yet another ante-mortem confession, demanding from him directly "whether he killed Brodelle because he was angry with him, whereupon the negro said, 'I guess you solved the question.'"

Sometimes Carlton offered variations on this established theme, suggesting, for example, that he had acted in self-defense, out of fear of Brodelle and the others. "They all imposed upon me," he groused during the early days of his incarceration. "They were all picking on me, and I had to fight for my life. I took the acid and tried to burn myself up in the furnace." According to Spring Green's weekly newspaper, "Carlton claimed that in wielding the deadly hatchet he had acted in self-defense, admitting that he had struck Brodelle, but that it was while defending himself from the men, who, he said, had attacked him. The fire, Carlton said, was an accident and was caused by his 'lighting a pipe while cleaning a rug with gasoline.'"

But despite Carlton's differing and often contradictory statements, a common thread evolves from them, quite in keeping with the confessions he variously made to Harrison, Lincoln, and Williams: namely, that Carlton had one main target in his conducting of the murders and the fire—the Milwaukee draftsman Emil Brodelle.

And this fact, most often overlooked in reviews of the Taliesin murders, is centrally important: it speaks not only to motive but also to the most likely logistics of Carlton's crime. Specifically, if Brodelle was Carlton's chief intended victim, then even more doubt is cast upon the most usual reconstruction of the slaughter. Again, according to that received scenario, Carlton sets fire to the workmen's dining room harboring Brodelle and then unaccountably abandons that locale to run off and kill Mamah and her children in a fairly remote part of the house, thereby allowing Brodelle enough time to escape from the dining room and nearly to avoid his fate beneath the rear window. Given Carlton's virulent hatred for Brodelle, it is hard to imagine that he would have left the scene of the initial fire before he was convinced that the hated draftsman—if no one else—was dead.

—┐▣┌—

Ever since Carlton's imprisonment in the Dodgeville jail, the Iowa County courthouse—which contained the jail, the courtroom, and Sheriff Williams's residence—had been besieged by armies of the curious, to the point that Williams, on August 19, banned access to the jail to anyone not there on official business. Small wonder, then, that the long-anticipated August 27 preliminary hearing attracted what was deemed "the largest crowd that court has ever held." "Long before ten o'clock," the local *Sun-Republic* reports, "every seat in the gallery at the court room was filled, and the aisle [was] crowded with people," all intent on catching a glimpse of the "colored slayer."

Justice Arthur again presided as magistrate, with District Attorney O'Neill representing the state. Arthur duly recited the complaint, spelling out all ten daunting charges. The prisoner, who had been carried into the courtroom by no fewer than seven deputies, responded with little more than unintelligible grunts and mumbles. In fact, it was widely charged in the press that Carlton "feigned insanity" at the hearing, "seeming to try to make his hearers believe he had not understood the charges."

The state paraded ten witnesses to the stand, including Billy Weston and Herbert Fritz, the massacre's only survivors and therefore the two men who could speak directly to Carlton's self-evident guilt. Sheriff Williams testified about Carlton's capture and the prisoner's assault on him in the jail just the night before. Harper Harrison related the story of Carlton's confession and his desire for vengeance against Brodelle. Further testimony was elicited from Dr. Bossard, Dr. Nee, Frank Sliter, Andrew Porter, and Jake Ferris.

Arthur finally closed the proceedings, routinely entering a "not guilty" plea in the mute Carlton's behalf, remanding him to the next sitting of the Circuit Court without bail on the murder charges, and setting bail at $5,000 on the assault and arson complaints.

During all the testimony from the cloud of witnesses that Arthur called to the stand, we are told that Carlton "sat at a small table, eating in turn from some bananas and apples which had been given him and toying with a glass of water. He seemed to pay no special attention to the proceedings." Another account has it that Carlton "incessantly chewed orange peel and made faces," behavior that must have incensed the large, revenge-minded coterie of Ridgeway residents who attended the hearing. In fact, Carlton's demeanor struck most observers as madness— whether genuine or feigned. "A personified enigma," one paper had already dubbed him.

But in fairness to Carlton, it should be pointed out that by the time of the August 27 hearing, and doubtlessly well before that, he was a profoundly injured, sick man—a dying man, in fact. As soon as the day after Carlton's capture, Dr. Lincoln was publicly predicting the prisoner's impending death, and a few days later he pronounced specifically that the servant was "dying of strangulation," caused by his ingestion of the acid. Indeed, from the earliest hours of his confinement, Carlton was most often judged to be in "serious condition" and was said to be tossing and groaning on his cot and taking little nourishment.

Throughout his incarceration, however, county officials and the regional press adopted a maddening practice of issuing utterly contradictory statements—both to the public and (apparently) to Carlton himself—on the status of the prisoner's health. The August 18 edition of the *Wisconsin State Journal*, for example, confidently reports that Carlton had been told that he was in no real danger of dying; on the very next day that same newspaper headlines, "[Carlton] Is Slowly Starving to Death." In the same issue of the *Dodgeville Chronicle* in which Dr. Lincoln diagnoses Carlton's condition as "serious," he also predicts his recovery, this just three days after Lincoln had foreseen the inevitability of the servant's death. And only two weeks before Carlton in fact died, the *Chronicle* unaccountably portrays him as "eating better . . . and . . . gaining strength."

What really was the state of Julian Carlton's health?

—🔲—

On the morning of October 1, 1914, the date set for Carlton's actual trial, Circuit Court judge George Clementson, a thoroughly decent jurist from the village of Lancaster, took decisive action in an effort to clear up this whole muddled matter of Carlton's physical condition. First, he ordered Dr. Lincoln and his Dodgeville colleague Dr. William Pierce to conduct a thorough physical examination of the prisoner in his jail cell and then to report back to him. Later that same day, Judge Clementson entered these comments into the official record: "I was informed this morning that the defendant was physically weak. Whether this was simulation or reality I could not tell. I deemed it advisable to appoint two physicians to carefully examine the defendant and to determine whether he was in a condition physically to endure a trial of this case. . . . They examined him and later reported to me that he was not in a condition to be tried at this time, that he was weak. I asked them whether in their judgment he could be brought into the court room to plead to the information filed against him, and they reported that he could endure that."

But just barely. When later that morning Carlton finally appeared in court, he had to be carried in by two deputies. "He feigned unconsciousness," a local newspaper opined, although by this time his semi-conscious state may well have been quite genuine. "The court room was filled with people, and all eyes rested upon the prisoner, who kept slipping off his chair, being prevented from doing so by the sheriffs." Later, in deference to his weakened state, they laid him on a makeshift cot.

Clementson first read the charge against Carlton—still, at this point, it was only for "the murder of Emil Brodelle," and Carlton again stood mute—and then announced that the prisoner had finally been accorded legal representation. "Yesterday," said Clementson, "I was informed that the defendant had no attorney and had no means to employ one, and thereupon I appointed Mr. E. C. Fiedler as his attorney in the case."

Clementson turned to Fiedler. "Mr. Fiedler, I understand, has had conferences with the defendant, and I ask him now if he has anything to say in reference to the arraignment of the defendant at this time."

Understandably, the freshly appointed counsel for the defense temporized a bit, seeking to buy some more time for his new and obviously ill client. "If your honor please," said Fiedler, "I think it would be my duty to say at this time that I do not believe this defendant is physically in such condition that he should be tried." Recalling the testimony of physicians Lincoln and Pierce, Fiedler argued that while Carlton was marginally strong enough to attend this plea hearing, he plainly could in no way withstand a full trial. Besides, given the desperate state of Carlton's health, staying the trial might spare the state some embarrassment and criticism: "Under the circumstances, I am inclined to think it would be my duty to enter for the present a plea of 'not guilty' for him. . . . I cannot help but think that a short postponement of the case would be advisable. . . . I think it would look better and be creditable to the courts and our American court procedure if a short postponement were to be had, and the defendant tried just as any other man charged with murder should be tried."

Clementson had anticipated such a plea and, within limits, was prepared to accept it. More than that, he had actually orchestrated it. It is here that Clementson enters a remarkable statement into the record: not only had he sent physicians that morning into Carlton's jail cell, but he had also gone there himself, at the request of the prisoner. "Later [after hearing the report from Lincoln and Pierce], I was informed that the defendant wanted to speak with me," Clementson remarked, "and upon that statement I went to the jail to see him. He did not say anything to me while others were present, but when all [the others] had withdrawn, he then talked with me. I saw he was weak, but that he could comprehend the situation, and I therefore determined that he should be arraigned this afternoon. . . . I say this now, because in my conference with him in the jail, when he thoroughly understood what I was saying to him and I put the question to him whether his plea would be guilty or not guilty and explained how he might be benefited by a certain plea in the case in his now physical condition, he told me that he would plea 'not guilty.' So let that plea be entered."

Given current standards of judicial ethics, Clementson's actions cannot fail to surprise and perhaps even to disturb: here we have a judge — on the very day of a trial over which he would preside and in which his word would determine the defendant's fate — chatting amiably with his prisoner about the charges against him and what sort of plea he ought to make in his own best interest.

But present-day notions of judicial conduct aside, Clementson, in all his dealings with Carlton, impresses one as being wise, humane, and enlightened. It was he, after all, who first secured Carlton legal representation and a thorough physical examination. And while he seems, like everyone else involved, to have wanted a quick trial and an end to all this unsettling business, he was nonetheless notably sensitive about and attentive to his prisoner's deteriorating health.

Certainly he shared Fiedler's concern that a trial at this point would leave the state open to public censure — how else to account for his advising Carlton to plead not guilty? Local newspapers had long forecast that a guilty plea on Carlton's part would have led to immediate sentencing, no doubt to life imprisonment. And in Carlton's "now physical condition," such a step might be construed in some quarters as draconian. Carlton, doomed though he was from the start, could not have drawn a better, more eminently fair-minded arbiter than the aptly named George Clementson.

The "not guilty" charge having been entered, the judge shut down the proceedings. "Well," he said, "that is all we can do today. . . . However, I will say again that the trial ought not be long delayed. I will say this for the benefit of the defendant as he comprehends what I am saying; and he ought to be eating, [in order] to place himself in a physical condition so he can stand a trial; because to try him in his present weakened condition would be rather shocking; but we will have to do what under the circumstances we are compelled to do. That is all we will do here today."

But Clementson's hope for a speedy trial was frustrated. Carlton was led back to his jail cell, and within a week he was dead.

—▣—

When, at about one o'clock on the afternoon of Wednesday, October 7, Carlton finally succumbed in his jail cell, there was not much left of him; his body weight had shrunk to about ninety pounds. The reaction of the local press ranged from the faintly irritated (the *Dodgeville Chronicle,* for example, headlined a peevish "Negro Slayer Succeeds in Starving Self") to the frankly pedantic. "It is well that [Carlton's death in jail] is so," moralized the *Dodgeville Sun-Republic.* "The county has been saved further expense on the case and the ends of Justice have been fully met. . . . No doubt he has paid the penalty for his crime many times during the past few weeks. All that is left now of his trail of blood is a sad memory. . . . The end of this unfortunate emphasizes the fact of scripture: 'The way of the transgressor is hard.'" Other regional papers simply ignored his passing. Even Wright's hometown *Weekly Home News* afforded the death remarkably short shrift: "Julian Carlton, who on August 15th murdered seven people at Frank Lloyd Wright's country home, died in jail at Dodgeville Wednesday. He has refused food, except at rare intervals, when he would gorge himself, ever since his confinement, and starved himself to death." Two further sentences make brief reference to Carlton's hearing of the previous week; thereafter, the *Home News* has nothing to say. The story is on page one, but it is buried there amid a host of competing articles. The town seems somehow to have lost interest.

The official cause of death was recorded as "Starvation—following attempt at suicide with hydrochloric acid poisoning." His death certificate is signed by Dr. Lincoln, who notes on the form that he had not even seen or treated his patient since September 29.

Carlton was not accorded the dignity of a burial, nor does any attempt seem to have been made to turn his body over either to Gertrude or any of his kin. Rather, on October 8, the day after his death, his emaciated remains were packed in a seven-by-eight-foot wooden crate, without benefit of embalming, and shipped by rail off to the University of Wisconsin at Madison. His corpse arrived there the next day and was taken to Room O of Science Hall, the same red stone building on which Wright had worked as a laborer some twenty-eight years before. There, Carlton's body was divided into three parts for purposes of dissection by faculty members and student physicians; Drs. Trusolt and Ruehl received the head, Drs. Simonds and Youmans the thorax, and Drs. Driver and Diederich the "lowers." Although the *Dodgeville Chronicle* speculated, in a brief story headlined "Negro's Brain May Prove to Be Abnormal," that the purpose of the dissection was to further the phrenological notion that "the brain offers an interesting and instructive study on the relation of crime to mentality," there is no evidence that Carlton's brain was in fact "examined . . . for [any] abnormalities" that could account for his crimes.

—◻—

On October 12, Judge Clementson ordered that E. C. Fielder, Esq., be paid fifty dollars "as reasonable compensation for his services to counsel for the said Julian Carlton . . . for days actually occupied in the preparation for . . . trial."

Earlier, Sheriff Williams had billed the county twenty-five cents, plus seventy cents mileage, for the cost of Carlton's arrest.

—◻—

What finally can be said, then, about the motives behind the massacre at Taliesin?

As both Carlton's own behavior and the testimony of his wife, coworkers, and Chicago neighbors make clear, the primary impetus behind the murders was most likely the servant's mental and emotional instability, a paranoia marked by delusions and by abrupt outbursts of violence. But there is more to the story, of course; even insane actions are often prompted by some sort of stimulus.

At Taliesin, such prompts abounded for Carlton. He hated the isolation, for one thing. And during that long, hot summer marked by war and rumors of war, he, of course, chafed under the racial slurs heaped on him by apprentices and staff. "Race may have been a factor," Ron McCrea observes; "there had been flare-ups."

Indeed there had, and not just Emil Brodelle's "black son of a bitch" retort, either: a general miasma of casual, unthinking racism hung in the air, attitudes to which Carlton must have been sensitive and that are reflected everywhere in the press coverage of his case, especially in the immediate aftermath of the murders. The *Mineral Point Tribune*, for example, felt it ran no risk of alienating its readership when it called Carlton a "devilish nigger" in print. Elsewhere, regional papers routinely referred to Carlton as a "black demon," "black beast," "black brute," "negro fiend," and "negro maniac."

On the death certificates of, respectively, Mamah Borthwick, Emil Brodelle, and Martha Cheney, the official cause of death is listed simply as "Killed by a Negro"; Tom Brunker's death is more amply attributed to "a fracture of [the] skull caused by a hatchet in the hands of a Negro." It is as if Julian Carlton, as an African American, was perceived more nearly as a contagion or simple force of nature than as a man.

And, in fact, that is certainly how he was seen. A close literary treatment of this tendency is found in Thomas Wolfe's short story "The Child by Tiger," published twenty-three years after the Taliesin murders but set in the same era. In that story, Dick Prosser is a troubled but gifted and devout black man who mysteriously appears in Asheville, North Carolina—Wolfe's "Libya Hill"—around 1912 and takes up the only job available to him, that of chauffeur and servant for the white, middle-class Shepperton family. They are pleased with him: "Mr. Shepperton himself declared that Dick was the best man he'd ever had," reports the narrator, "the smartest darky he'd ever known."

But like drops of water gradually eroding sandstone, racial slights wear away insistently at Dick's tenuous self-control: he feels compelled to address white children by such honorary titles as "Mr." and "Cap'n"; he stoically withstands a beating from a thuggish white drunk; and he must loiter outside the white folks' church on Sunday mornings, chauffeur's cap politely in his hand, hoping to catch stray snatches of the sermon. Finally Prosser can stand these indignities no longer, and he erupts in a homicidal frenzy—a fury equaled only by that of the white mob that pursues him to his own bloody death.

Thematically, Wolfe's tale finally speaks to the enigma of the evil that lies hidden on "the other side of man's dark soul" and that, at any moment, may suddenly and destructively pounce, like the powerful, menacing "tyger" in the poem by William Blake that gives Wolfe's story its title. The tiger metaphor for such potential violence is a natural one: in its coverage of the Taliesin murders, the *Iowa County Democrat* remarks that, in his attack, Julian Carlton "was upon [Tom Brunker] like an infuriated tiger."

But this view demonizes and reifies Carlton even more, further diminishing his humanity. There was a kind of innocence, local folks believed, in the horrible fact of his rampage. He was not so much evil, they thought—only those who are fully people can be fully evil—as he was bestial; he was as elemental as the fire that swept away Taliesin, the house built in the name of love and in the doubtful conviction that the sheer will of a man can suffice to draft and design a destiny.

A truer literary parallel is Shakespeare's *Othello*, a tragedy that Wright knew well enough to quote from in one of his 1911 statements to the press. At the end of that play, the murderous Iago, his crimes revealed at last, is led in chains to the great general he has so sorely wronged. Othello's first impulse is to look down at Iago's feet, half expecting to find there the cloven hooves of Satan himself. "What you know, you know," says Iago, then falls silent. And what we know is that evil, however mad, ultimately wears a human face and walks on human feet.

—◻—

By September 7, barely three weeks after the murders, amid the ashes and burnt timbers of Taliesin, the ever-resilient Wright was hosting the semi-annual picnic of Sauk County rural mail carriers, who had arrived there by car. "We are told," reports the *Weekly Home News*, "that this was one of the most successful and enjoyable meetings the assembly has held."

—◻—

Once the physicians and anatomy students at the University of Wisconsin were finished examining Julian Carlton's trisected body, they burned up what was left of him in a crude Science Hall crematory that they called the "human incinerator," this to distinguish it from a similar-looking "animal incinerator" used to cremate beasts. Carlton's ashes were then disposed of on one of several sites located on the Madison campus for such purposes.

So no physical trace of him remains.

Epilogue
The Legacy of Fire

One can look at [Wright] and be awed by the dimensions of . . . the achievement. . . . On the other hand, when you look at who he was as a human being, he was so incredibly at the mercy of his emotions, he's at the other end of the spectrum. He's barely a human being.

Meryle Secrest

At some point, you have to forgive Frank Lloyd Wright for his excesses, his ego, his sensitivities, his horrible relations with his kids, and realize, on balance, that here was an extraordinary contribution to human history.

Ken Burns

As the critic Paul Fussell so hauntingly records, the summer of 1914 is etched in the West's "modern memory" as the ironically benign prelude to our loss of cultural innocence, of any grounds for rational optimism. In England, of course, that particularly glorious summer offered up little hint of what would follow: the Somme, Passchendaele, the Ypres Salient, Verdun. Recalling the hordes of men who flocked so eagerly to London recruiting stations in 1914, poet Philip Larkin can only wonder at it all:

> Never before or since,
> As changed itself to past

Without a word—the men
Leaving the gardens tidy,
The thousands of marriages
Lasting a little while longer:
Never such innocence again.

And in Wisconsin, Taliesin, the apotheosis of the Prairie house, so long in its loving conception, was destroyed in three brutally short hours. So for Frank Lloyd Wright, too, "never such innocence again."

One marker of Wright's loss, in the wake of his desertion of Catherine and elopement with Mamah, was the brochure he published in connection with his 1914 exhibition at the Chicago Art Institute, a bully pulpit from which he could complain publicly (and violently) about the decline of his reputation since his flight to Europe. The brochure includes Wright's essay "In the Cause of Architecture." He had written a treatise with the same title back in 1908, just before the "hegira" and his subsequent exile at Taliesin. That one, however, had been marked throughout by a happy optimism about the capacity of democracy and the American suburb to reconcile the competing demands of societal norms on the one hand with the imperatives of the individual on the other. All that optimism is renounced in the 1914 "In the Cause," an essay that has been characterized as "an unrelievedly morose diatribe" against the new architecture, by which Wright primarily meant the work of his host of imitators, parasitical hacks (in his view) who had stolen his ideas without attribution or due reverence. The problem at the time with "the prairie house bandwagon," says Twombly, was that "everyone was climbing on board, but few recognized Wright as the driver." And Wright was infuriated. Back in the 1890s, he himself had entered into the profession "alone, absolutely alone," he said, and he expected similar individuality from his competitors or, failing that, full credit for his trailblazing efforts in organic architecture. And Wright never relinquished this bitter animosity toward his ostensible colleagues; he railed at them for the next forty-five years. Wright's "belief in the existence of a conspiracy to exploit and discredit him," Twombly speculates, "may have been a manifestation of mild paranoia. Certainly he displayed suspicious symptoms. . . . [U]nless Wright received unqualified praise and total credit for the prairie movement, he suspected treachery and evil intent."

Gone, too, was his former Whitmanesque confidence in democracy, a faith that had always sustained him, his father, and his Lloyd Jones kin. As a result of his experience with the popular uproar over his taking a mistress and the heavy professional price he had paid for it, democracy for Wright was now no more than "the Gospel of Mediocrity," a social construct designed to crush the iconoclast by failing to ground itself in "the absolute individualist as the unit of its structure." In democracy's place, Wright seemed to call for a kind of wild, anarchic libertarianism, in which such an "individualist" would be freed from the constraints of all lawyers, creditors, politicians, and moralizers — specifically, the kinds of people who sought to restrain him and Mamah.

And when Taliesin burned, Wright suffered a loss of a more tangible kind: the five hundred copies of the great Wasmuth monograph that had been reserved for American distribution also burned, delaying full recognition of Wright's accomplishment in his native land for years to come.

Wright justified his placing no headstone on Mamah's grave in this way: "All I had left to show for the struggle for freedom of the five years past that had swept most of my former life away, had now [itself] been swept away," Wright said. "Why mark the spot where desolation ended and began?"

—◻—

Wright appends to his 1914 "In the Cause" statement a poem, Goethe's "Hymn to Nature." According to Wright, he and Mamah had found the piece, "unknown to us in the works of Goethe" (actually, the poem is quite famous), in a Berlin bookshop and had translated it "from the German — together" at Fiesole. This is mere grandstanding: Wright knew no German beyond *lieber Meister;* almost certainly Mamah translated it on her own, although Gill suggests that Wright may have supplied the poem's Whitmanesque tone. If so, it hardly required the contribution. Any man who could write "Surely no divine worship is more beautiful than that which needs no image, which issues purely from a dialogue in our bosom with nature" does not need to have his words twisted into conformity with Transcendentalist dogma.

The poem itself, in this translation, seems little more than an exercise in overstrung high Romanticism, an endless litany apostrophizing an impossibly idealized nature ("She") as the source—for its properly attuned initiates—of all love. Structured loosely along a series of coy oxymorons and generalizations so universal as to be essentially meaningless (e.g., "She is Everything"; "Mankind is all in her and she in all"), the poem closes—or nearly does—with the existential pronouncement that "Past and Future she knows not—The Present is her Eternity."

At least Frank and Mamah liked the poem. "It comforted us," Wright says, adding that the translation was saved from the flames at Taliesin only because he habitually carried a copy in his pocket. Its destruction would have pained Wright, no doubt; his audience, however, might have tolerated the loss pretty well.

Maybe what is most pertinent about the poem is its authorship. Again, Wright had reminded Maginel that once, long ago, she had warned him against "reaching so high" in his ambitions, lest he someday "pull something down that would destroy" him. In the West, the archetype of such an overreacher is Faust, who, in Marlowe's treatment of the story, is consigned to damnation. In Goethe's famed closet drama, however, Faust stands redeemed at the end, largely through his commitment to work.

Wright knew something about work and clearly preferred Goethe's handling of the Faust theme to Marlowe's. Half of Wright's life—astonishingly, his more productive half—lay ahead of him. Despite all the losses, he thought, like Goethe's Faust, he could find some redemption in labor.

—◙—

But the fruit of that labor would prove to be remarkably different from the designs and buildings he had produced before the Taliesin tragedy.

For one thing, there were fewer of them: over the next seventeen years, Wright completed just thirty-three commissions, scarcely two a year. And all those designs, Twombly observes, clearly "reflected the frustration, suspicion, and reversals" that had grown out of the catastrophe that had befallen him at Taliesin. The first casualty of that calamity was the Prairie house itself. "Wright's prairie period ended," says Twombly, "in 1914 with the death of Mamah Borthwick."

Gone, for example, was the happy consanguinity between structure and site that had informed Taliesin and Wright's other Prairie-style homes. Starting in 1915, his new designs betrayed an infinitely more somber, more cautious, and less illusioned worldview.

The differences are easy to trace. Back in 1911, for instance, Wright had sketched out a wonderful Prairie home for his lawyer, Sherman Booth. In its original conception, the projected residence constitutes nothing short of a domestic masterpiece, marrying itself organically to the craggy, rolling lakeshore at Glencoe, Illinois, and featuring a series of dramatic, horizontal modules, poised "like a whirling cross, with wings and bridges shooting out over the ravines."

But then, after the Taliesin fires, Wright's vision changed, and the actual house that he built for Booth in 1915–1916 is nothing like that at all. Rather, the Booth House became a sort of cube, quite isolated from and oblivious to the powerful possibilities of the land on which it sat.

Similarly, the celebrated La Miniatura, a house built by Wright in 1923 for Mrs. George Madison Millard in Pasadena, California, bears no likeness whatever to the Prairie-style home he had had designed for the same family seventeen years before back in Highland Park. Rather, La Miniatura is an unapologetic square box. It is made out of patterned cement blocks—"textile blocks," Wright called them—a material that the architect favored at the time. When selling Mrs. Millard on the concept, Wright, with a probable glance back at Taliesin's fate, stressed that such blocks were fireproof.

These are typical of Wright's designs after the Taliesin fire and for years to come—for example, the Ravine Bluffs Development in Glencoe (1915) and houses built for Emil Bach in Chicago (1916) and for F. C. Bogk in Milwaukee (1916). The Bogk House, like the others, incorporates some superficial Prairie-style elements, but descriptions of the place routinely resort to adjectives such as "heavy" and "massive." As Twombly notes, "Not the environment-embracing but the fortress-like aspects of Taliesin characterized Wright's newest efforts."

What had been broad windows, open to the natural world all around, become slits; slab roofs most often replace low-hipped ones; horizontal line becomes vertical blocks of poured concrete. In most of these post-Taliesin homes, "their relatively few windows pierce the upper stories, usually facing the rear of the lot. Entrances are turned from the street. The houses encourage interior isolation and solitude; they appear to be secluded sanctuaries. Real and symbolic barriers between inside and outside discourage penetration." The tan brick Bach House (1915), for instance, features an entrance that is entirely hidden from the road on which it sits; the Barnsdale "Hollyhock" House (1917) hides its east entrance at the end of a long, protective forecourt.

The house in the Hollywood Hills that Wright built for dentist John Storer in 1923 has a back door but no front one. And in stark contrast to Wright's earlier practice, Storer's house has absolutely nothing in common with its natural surroundings. It looks like a fortress, and an arrogant one, at that. Even Wright conceded that it was "lacking [in] joy."

So, too, with the Ennis House (1924), which approximates a Mayan temple and would seem more plausible surrounded by miles of Central American rain forest than by a few acres of Los Angeles lawn. Unlike Taliesin, it is not built into a hill; it sits jauntily atop one. And the nearby concrete block Freeman House (1924) is aggressively vertical, thumbing its nose at Emerson's old hunger for the horizontal line.

In the wake of the Taliesin murders, all these latter-day houses have one overriding aim in common: they are meant to shield and protect. "By 1923," Twombly writes, "Wright had worked out a more complete statement . . . of seclusion and withdrawal. The concrete houses expanded the fortress-like aspects of Taliesin. They were defense mechanisms made necessary by Mamah Borthwick's death."

—◩—

In any event, Wright was back to work, and he was granted many years. Born just two years after the close of the Civil War, he lived on until the advent of the Kennedy administration. Born into a time and place in which horses provided transportation and kerosene provided light, he was interviewed on television by Mike Wallace. His grandfather was born when Washington and Jefferson still lived; Frank Wright missed seeing men walk on the moon by scarcely a decade.

But he never got over the murders; he certainly never got over Mamah. A long-time apprentice recalls, "In the nine years I lived and worked with Mr. Wright, he never mentioned the name of this extraordinary woman. And I never had the courage to ask about her. I suspect he might have wanted to talk, if I had known how to phrase the questions, but he kept the memory of her far within his own thoughts."

In the wake of the blood and the fires of Taliesin, Wright performed, says Peter Blake, "a supreme act of courage: he went on living."

After Taliesin burned to its foundations in 1914, Wright, true to his word, immediately began rebuilding it as Taliesin II. "Where scenes of horror had identified the structure with ugly memories," he wrote, "I changed it all. Where tragedy had been most obvious, an open stone-floored loggia looked up the valley toward the Lloyd Jones family Chapel."

But this Taliesin burned down, too—due to faulty wiring—and the physical result was much the same as before: the residential wing was destroyed, while the working quarters were spared.

Wright took this as a sign. He later told docent Lori Moon that "God was testing his character by burning his house, but approving his work by letting the studio stand."

So Wright built yet again on the hillside's "shining brow." The result is Taliesin III, the crumbling but still remarkable avatar that tourists visit today. After both fires, Wright kept building along the lines of the unconsumed masonry, so that the current Taliesin, for all the intervening changes, is at least ancestrally similar to the house in which Mamah Borthwick and the others lived and died.

——◻——

Wright endured and achieved mighty things for forty-five years after the Taliesin fire and murders of 1914. His endurance, indeed, is legendary.

Way back in 1896, he had designed and built a windmill for the Aunts' Hillside School. As with Taliesin later, there was nothing else like it in the world. He called it "Romeo and Juliet," because it suggested lovers standing "tall against the storms."

"Folly," everyone else called it. It was sixty feet high and constructed (initially, at least) only out of boards, a kind of octagonal barrel married to a diamond-shaped brace. Wright's bearded Welsh uncles all predicted that it would come tumbling down in the first strong wind. Wright said it would outlive them all.

He was right. This windmill stood until 1990, long after the Valley uncles and all their works had vanished.

Frank Lloyd Wright endured, too.

And in truth he had much to endure. Miriam Noel, for example.

This flamboyant doyenne, a divorced sculptress of uncertain history, showed up at his Chicago studio in December 1914, having written him a sympathy note after the murders. She had seen troubles of her own, her note said. Among the troubles she failed to mention was that she was delusional and a morphine addict.

Surviving photos of her are not flattering, but she must have been impressive in the flesh. That first day, she plopped herself down on the other side of Wright's desk.

"How do you like me?" she candidly asked.

"I've never seen anyone like you," Wright candidly replied.

Within days, they were sleeping together. And by the following August—a scant year after Mamah's murder—she was living at Taliesin. She called Wright "the lord of my waking dreams."

But for the next fifteen years, she made Wright's life a purgatory. There was a brush with a prosecution for white slavery; and there were foreclosures, lawsuits, arrests, and endless battles. She threatened Wright with a knife, then with a gun. Wright, in turn, probably beat her black and blue. Perhaps her chief sin in Wright's eyes was that she "refused to be happy" at Taliesin.

He had at least one golden chance to divest himself of what he called his "entanglement" with her, but he failed to seize it. Instead, unaccountably, he married her in November 1923, exactly a year after he finally acquired a divorce from Catherine.

The ceremony took place on a bridge spanning the Wisconsin River. Within six months, Miriam left him. In 1925, he filed for divorce; by then, he had installed a third woman, dark and beautiful Olgivanna, at Taliesin.

When Miriam Noel learned of Olgivanna, she lay siege to the place and dragged out the divorce proceedings for two turbulent years. She tried to get both Wright and his new mate arrested. She filed a $100,000 suit against Olgivanna, charging alienation of affection. Long-suffering Spring Green had been scandalized by Wright's doings yet again; yet again, he took to composing apologies for readers of the *Weekly Home News.*

One of Noel's most disturbing tactics during this tumultuous time was her threat to reopen an investigation into the 1914 fire and murders.

Wracked by neuroses and drug addiction, Miriam Noel died in Milwaukee in January 1930. But even in death, she continued open warfare against Wright: the executors of her miniscule estate had him arrested for a $7,000 trust deficiency.

—▣—

Meryle Secrest points out that, for all her limitations, Miriam Noel Wright nonetheless succeeded in one area where both Catherine and Mamah had miserably failed: "she had defeated Anna."

Wright's aged mother had uncharacteristically warmed to Miriam at first, but then was stung by a letter from her and found herself alienated from both Miriam and the Aunts. As early as May 4, 1916, Anna wrote from Oak Park, "I do not intend to come to Taliesin never [*sic*] again."

But she did return, and by the summer of 1922 Miriam was issuing Frank an ultimatum: either she or Anna would have to go. Compelled into unwilling action, Wright tried to pawn Anna off on Jennie at Tan-y-Deri, but Anna would not budge. He confessed to his sister that only chloroform would get their mother into an asylum. But finally he summoned the gumption that September to pack eighty-year-old Anna off into exile. She ended up in a sanitarium in rural Oconomowoc, Wisconsin, where she died, feeling betrayed and sad, the next February. She was buried two days later at Unity Chapel, but Frank Lloyd Wright is not listed among those in attendance; he seems to have taken off for Los Angeles.

The long, bitter saga of Anna Lloyd Wright had finally ended in a way far more arid than she could have foreseen back in the days when it had seemed that it was she and Frank alone against a disapproving world.

—▣—

It would have been natural for Frances Inglis, the young girl who had inadvertently wandered into the Taliesin murders, to have fled back to her safe Chicago home at the earliest opportunity. Instead, she actually stayed on in the Helena Valley for about a month. In fact, she met her future husband there. Her grandson is now a Minneapolis-based actor, restaurateur, and property manager.

Carpenter Billy Weston lost one son in the Taliesin massacre, but his wife bore him another one five months later. This son, Marcus, joined Frank Lloyd Wright's Taliesin Fellowship in 1938 and ultimately became a prominent Madison architect, a disciple of Wright's "organic" style. Wright's "natural carpenter," Taliesin's chief builder, had sired a Wrightian acolyte.

Having lost one family to the murders at Taliesin, Edwin Cheney immediately began another one with his new wife Elsie. They had three children, and Edwin thrived. "It was said of him," notes Brendan Gill, "that he never missed a college reunion" at the University of Michigan, where he had first met and pursued Mamah back around 1890. He died in St. Louis after a long, productive, and prosperous life.

W. R. Purdy, the crusty editor of Spring Green's *Weekly Home News* and Wright's old nemesis, died in 1927. Wright was remarkably conciliatory to the memory of the man who, sixteen years before, had called Wright and Mamah "insane" and "degenerate." Purdy, Wright eulogized, "belonged to an old school that was humane and valuable to the lives of others." Spring Green was favorably impressed by this show of magnanimity on Wright's part.

As America prepared to enter World War I, Jenkin Lloyd Jones, who had overseen the rescue efforts during the fire and murders, joined a steamboat full of like-minded idealists and sailed directly into the war zone to protest and to negotiate for peace. The effort—an initiative called the Henry Ford Peace Expedition—failed, of course, and Uncle Jenk ended up criticized and investigated by his own government.

It was the old pacifist's last battle. He died on September 12, 1918. C. R. Ashbee observed, "The puritan chapel in the valley is now empty and the voice of 'the Lord' no longer heard there."

—▣—

In keeping with Uncle Jenk's established model, Frank Lloyd Wright's own spiritual sensibilities continued to become ever more liberal, misty, and ecumenical throughout the remainder of his life. For example, his third wife Olgivanna introduced him to the teachings of the bizarre guru Georgei Ivanovitch Gurdjieff, her long-time spiritual mentor. Gurdjieff showed up at Taliesin in 1934, and as late as 1954, F.B.I. director J. Edgar Hoover—the bureau kept a lengthy file on Wright—censoriously alleged in a memo that the Taliesin Fellowship was conducting "'dances to the moon' and regularly [was] brainwashed by a bald-headed Soviet mystic . . . at the Scottsdale center."

—▣—

As Uncle Jenk had forecast in his despairing December 1911 letter to his sisters Nell and Jane, the scandal in the Valley, culminating in the Taliesin murders, spelled the end for the Hillside Home School. "Old and worn out by debt," writes Edgar Tafel, "the [A]unts retired," donating the school buildings and 160 more acres of Valley land to Frank, "their favorite nephew." Their lifelong commitment to progressive education now in ashes, they soon died. Wright had promised them that he would pick up that torch; but he "remembered the promise [only] later, when the Depression and ill fortune had cancelled all his projects."

On August 4, 1917, Wright bought out the two remaining shareholders in the school for $25,000 and then promptly mortgaged the place for $5,000 in ready cash. In the demise of the Hillside Home School, it could be argued that the Taliesin murders had claimed yet another victim.

—▣—

The Midway Gardens, on which Wright had been working so intensely at the time of the tragedy, did not last long, either. The place opened in August 1914, with its decorations still incomplete, and by that October the owners were already facing bankruptcy.

The problem was not architectural: Robert C. Twombly points out, "Most observers were awe-struck by its immensity, beauty, and grandeur." Rather, a combination of meager financing, changing public tastes, Prohibition, and anti-German sentiment sealed the Gardens' fate.

It was razed in 1929 and was replaced by what Wright called an "auto-laundry." Much of the rubble was dumped into Lake Michigan to serve as a breakwater for a railroad line. Years later, Wright's son-in-law Wesley Peters "remembers having glimpsed, from a train window, a twisted pylon finial [from the Gardens] rising grotesquely out of the waters of the lake."

—◻—

Sadly, in 1968 the Imperial Hotel in Tokyo was torn down, too—a casualty over the years of floods, earthquakes, pollution, and American bombing raids. The management preserved some remnants of the hotel at Meijimura, an architectural park near Nagoya. And a one-ton carved stone urn from the Imperial was donated to Paul Hanna, where today it ornaments his Wright-designed house in Palo Alto, California. Otherwise, this grandest of hotels is gone, replaced by an infinitely more conventional, practical, and less compelling structure.

Edgar Tafel has it that Wright "spent his entire fee from the Imperial Hotel . . . on Oriental art. The collection, which arrived in Spring Green by train, was a full carload."

—◻—

Wright was not alone in his abandonment of the happy vision that had informed the Prairie style. The Taliesin fire and murders coincide (though, as we have seen, it may have been no coincidence at all) with the decline and fall of the Prairie house phenomenon in the United States generally. In that sense, the destruction of Taliesin serves as a requiem for a movement, an understanding, an aesthetic and philosophic sensibility. Norris Kelly Smith provides a fitting eulogy: "[World War I] was followed by a quick, fierce reaction against the mores with which we associate the Gibson Girl, Chautauqua, Arts and Crafts, Mission furniture, and the Prairie House."

House Beautiful published its last review of a Prairie house in 1914.

Gustav Stickley's Arts and Crafts magazine, once so influential, ceased publication two years later. "Each year prior to 1914 the Prairie School had been gaining strength," observes H. Allen Brooks. "Thereafter, house commissions fell off sharply." The 1920s may have roared, but not for Prairie house architects. Wright follower William Gray Purcell retreated into early retirement; Wright disciple George Maher committed suicide. Others caved in and bowed to the public's taste for Cape Cod colonial and Tudor Gothic. Louis Sullivan died penniless in 1924. Wright himself went bankrupt, and Taliesin was seized for a time by creditors. Like the Transcendentalism of Wright's beloved Emerson and Whitman, the "organic" house was perceived by the Jazz Age as hopelessly quaint, outmoded, irrelevant, and passé. Its end came in a rush, like a fire on the prairie.

—▣—

Fire stalked and bedeviled Wright throughout the years, to the extent, says one observer, that "the theme of conflagration is almost a leitmotif of his life."

Way back in 1903, Wright's sons John and Lloyd, accompanied by Catherine's mother, attended a Christmas season play, *Mr. Blue Beard Jr.*, at Chicago's Iroquois Theater. Just as an octet took up the first strains of "In the Pale Moonlight," a calcium lamp exploded, engulfing the whole stage in flame. The fire spread everywhere. In the ensuing panic, more than six hundred men, women, and children died horribly, including everyone in the balcony. Mrs. Tobin was barely able to save herself and her two grandsons. John wrote, "I shall always remember the expression on Dad's face when he learned that we, all three, were safe and unharmed."

Then came the Taliesin fires in 1914 and again in 1925. Wright was there for the second one and did his best to put it out himself. "I was on the smoking roofs," he recalled, "feet burned, lungs seared, hair and eyebrows gone, thunder rolling as the lightning flashed over the lurid scene." Wright as Ahab or as Lear. But much of Taliesin burned down again.

After that fire, says Tafel, "We apprentices shared Mr. Wright's fear of fire. We were repeatedly instructed in what to do should one start: the exterior dinner bell would be rung constantly and a bucket brigade was immediately put into action." That brigade was needed when, in 1932, a fire broke out within a two-by-four stud wall in the apprentices' quarters at Taliesin. The fire was quickly extinguished, but the experience confirmed Wright's suspicion that a hollow stud wall was "the invention of the devil," and he determined never to design such a wall again.

Later, Wright himself accidentally burned down the south wing of the theater at Hillside when he set a brush fire too close to the building. And an explosion in a gasoline drum burned the roof off the garage at Taliesin. "Something always happens in the country," Wright philosophized.

The River Forest Tennis Club and the Nathan Moore house, both early Wright designs, burned to the ground in his lifetime. The fire in the tennis clubhouse, in fact, may have been his fault: he had designed the rafters too near the chimney flue. In Japan once, when fire broke out in his hotel, Wright was able to save his valuable prints and other possessions only by throwing them out the window to a waiting chauffeur below.

When Iovanna, Wright's last child, decided to marry in a Greek Orthodox church in Chicago, she was paying homage to both her parents: Olgivanna (however much she subsequently had strayed) had been raised Orthodox, and the church itself had been designed long ago by Louis Sullivan, Frank's *lieber Meister*. During the wedding ceremony, the attending priest's censer got too close to Iovanna's veil, and it caught fire. Wright's apprentices rushed forward and extinguished the bride, so the wedding went on. Later, Wright, an old man now, "was seen walking up and down along the outer wall of the sanctuary, cane in hand, muttering over and over, 'All my life I have been plagued by fire. All my life I have been plagued by fire.'"

———◙———

Wright was powerless to avoid one last confrontation with fire.

He died quietly in his sleep at a Scottsdale hospital on April 9, 1959. Just fifteen days before, on March 24, his first wife, Kitty—the once-golden girl who waited for him so long—had died in a Santa Monica sanitarium, where she had been cared for since suffering a fall ten years earlier.

The next day, son David, who had been at her bedside until the end, brought the news to Wright; it would have been Kitty's eighty-eighth birthday. Wright's eyes watered. "Why didn't you tell me as soon as you knew?" he demanded.

"Why should I have bothered?" David asked. "You never gave a god-damn for her when she was alive."

Wright had never lost his interest in Mamah, however. In a funeral that eerily mirrored Mamah's own some forty-five years before, Wright was buried beside her back in the Valley at Unity Chapel; like her, he was carried to the grave by a horse-drawn wagon, strewn with flowers. He was finally with Mamah again, on the hallowed grounds of Taliesin.

His grave is still there. His body is not.

Twenty-six years later—March 1, 1985—Olgivanna died. The very next day, her daughter Iovanna, setting in motion an act some thought tantamount to grave robbing, contacted a Spring Green funeral parlor and made arrangements for the exhumation of Wright's body. In the early morning hours of Wednesday, March 21, the funeral director, Bradley Richardson, accompanied by two gravediggers, duly set out for the Unity Chapel cemetery, where they dug up the casket. Coroners in both Iowa and Dane Counties inspected the body, which was then cremated in Madison. The cremains were flown by Richardson and his family to Arizona on March 31 and handed over to a representative from Taliesin West.

Edgar Tafel was among many who thought this a sacrilege. After all, Wright "was a man of his selected base, Wisconsin, deeply rooted in the traditions of his beloved mid-America. It seemed outrageous to me to disturb his body, for it was resting among his family in their own cemetery in the Valley of the Lloyd Joneses, near his mother, in those green Wisconsin hills." From the point of view of Iovanna, it was more important, perhaps, that he had been resting near Mamah.

Iovanna had Wright's newly cremated remains placed next to Olgivanna's dust.

"Yes," notes Tafel, "even after death, he was plagued by fire."

NOTES

SELECTED BIBLIOGRAPHY

INDEX

Notes

Prologue: The House across the River

4 Chicago suburb of Oak Park: The *Examiner* report is discussed in Secrest, 212. Three months later (24 December 1911), the *Chicago Tribune* specifically identified Mamah Cheney as Wright's lover; see Secrest, ibid. For the early suggestion that Taliesin was a mere "cottage" intended solely for Anna Lloyd Jones Wright, see Lind, *Lost Wright*, 21.

4 the most horrific single act of mass murder in Wisconsin history: At least this was true until March 12, 2005, when Terry Tratzman killed seven people, then himself, at the Living Church of God in Brookfield. Thanks to (Mary) Keiran Murphy, researcher for Taliesin Preservation, Inc., for this (unhappy) reminder.

Chapter 1. Prelude to Murder

5 Milwaukee cannibal Jeff Dahmer: On the notorious Gein, see Harold Schecter, *Deviant: The Shocking True Story of the Original "Psycho"* (New York: Pocket Books, 1998).

6 mystery, debate, and evasion: For the (legitimate) "crime of the century" designation, see Ron McCrea, "Murders at Taliesin."

6 the remainder of the twentieth century: On the loss of the folio copies, see Sweeney, 107, and Wright, *Autobiography*, 192. On the influence of the fire and murders on Wright's subsequent residential design, see, e.g., Twombly, *FLLW in Spring Green*, 14–17, and Hurder, 3–4.

6 figure since Michelangelo: *International Dictionary of Architects and Architecture: Architects*, Randall J. Van Vynckt, ed., Detroit: St. James Press, 1993; "in a single paragraph": N. Smith, 107. Of the human cost of the murders, Smith, ibid., says only that the disaster "postponed for many years a fulfillment of the promise that was contained in the new house [i.e., Taliesin] Wright had built"; "a rupture in Wright's career": Hans De Backer, "Life [of FLLW]," http://millennium.arts.kuleuven .ac.be/amsite/Hans_DeBacker/life.htm (1999–2000): 1 (accessed 24 January 2001).

8 "performed by St. Joseph": Gill, 26.

8   "no financial sense whatever": Qtd. in Secrest, 55; also see Twombly, *FLLW: His Life,* 5–6.

8   "who did not like him": Secrest, 49.

9   distinctive extended family: Researcher Georgia Snoke asserts that the Lloyd Jones clan did not settle in the Helena (or Wyoming) Valley per se until the 1860s, purchasing land there first in 1863; Uncle Jenkin, for example, apparently had not seen the Valley homesteads until he came home from the Civil War in 1864.

9   "lion maned and mercury tongued": Edna Meudt, "No One Sings Face Down," 1970; see the William C. Marlin papers (4103.287), Frank Lloyd Wright Archives, Taliesin West.

10   calumny of spinsterhood: Secrest, 49–50; also see Gill, 31.

10   "drearily self-righteous": Gill, 39.

11   ennobled by that contact: Gill, 37; "untoward circumstance": Qtd. in Gill, 50; and see Wright, *Autobiography,* 49.

11   entirely too "Lincolnesque": Qtd. in Secrest, 383; see a reprint of Woollcott's touching tribute to his friend in *The Portable Woollcott* (New York: Viking, 1946), 210–18. Woollcott concludes his essay with the remark that "[If] I were suffered to apply the word 'genius' to only one living American, I would have to save it up for Frank Lloyd Wright." On Wright's notably oracular prose style—in the tradition of Lincoln, Whitman, Sullivan, and Sandburg—see Gill, 43.

12   but turning a profit: Twombly, *FLLW: Interpretive,* 7.

13   "and I would have peace": Qtd. from Lizzie's unpublished memoir in Gill, 41–42; also see Secrest, 57–58, where Lizzie's portrait of Anna is seen as that of "a hateful, vengeful, almost demonic stepmother."

13   "a most tremendous temper": Gill 53, 33.

13   only genuine Lloyd Jones young ones at home: Gill, 33; cf. Secrest, 71–72.

13   took all the credit: Gill, 30.

13   "only for him": Twombly, *FLLW: Interpretive,* 34.

13   a seismic shift: Jacobs, 22.

13   starved emotional needs: Secrest, 57–58.

14   between her and father widened: Barney, 64.

14   "lived much in [me]": Qtd. in Cronon, 10.

14   "hemmed in all her life": Secrest, 46.

14   "something that refused to take shape": Qtd. in Secrest, 48. Actually, Maginel justly applied this comment to *both* her parents; see Barney, 64.

14   "fundamental to art": Thurman, "Siren Songs," *New Yorker,* 3 September 2001, 86.

15   decent home-grown food: On young Frank's room and Uncle James's journey, see Secrest, 72.

16   "make a farmer": Jacobs, 24.

16   "snowy fleece on every breeze": Qtd. in Secrest, 68.

16 "and shoveling shit": Qtd. in Gill, 47–48. The confession was made to Wright's apprentice—and later his biographer—Edgar Tafel.

16 "the coldest room in the house": Qtd. in Gill, 53.

17 calculated campaign on Anna's part: Secrest, 75; cf. Gill, 53.

17 "Say he's dead": Qtd. in Secrest, 77.

17 her funeral, either: on the deaths of Wright's parents, see Gill, 38, 51, and Secrest, 278. Anna was buried on the grounds of Unity Chapel on February 12, 1923, two days after her lonely death in an Oconomowoc, Wisconsin, sanitarium.

17 broods over his own culpability: Wright, *Autobiography*, 49, 51. But Gill, 50, cautions that Wright commits "a feat of calculated misrepresentation" regarding his own role in the breakup; elsewhere, Gill, 24, calls Wright "a virtuoso at bearing false witness. . . . [Sometimes] he seems to have lied simply for the pleasure it gave him."

17 A kind of tragic pattern: Twombly, *FLLW: Interpretive*, 13.

18 psychological blackmail: Gill, 110; also see Farr, 115.

18 "a little money between friends?": personal interview with Joe Wankerl of Plain, WI, 2000. For a discussion of Wright's disregard for money—except as a means toward an artistic end—see Cronon, 25–27. "Given his own perennial indifference to money," writes Cronon, 27, "one can almost imagine that he literally had trouble regarding it as real."

18 two further commissions: Secrest, 442–46. These included Wingspread, the Johnson family home (1937), and the S. C. Johnson Research Tower (1944).

18 "Do you hypnotize your clients?": Qtd. in Farr, 77.

18 to pay off an old debt: Burns, 308. Also see Secrest, 56, 148, and Jacobs, 51.

18 even evangelical, natures: Alofsin, *FLLW: Lost Years*, 100; also see Gill, 35.

19 beat up his father in a fistfight: Wright, *Autobiography*, 12, 48–49.

19 "why he didn't leave sooner": On Wright's difficulties as both son and father, see Secrest, 77; Burns, 311; and Alofsin, *FLLW: Lost Years*, 94. For Wright's disdain for the word "Papa," see Gill, 105.

19 "the imperial self": Anderson, passim.

19 "personal architectural expression": Steiner, 9.

19 "integrity of your own mind": Qtd. in Burns, 318; also see N. K. Smith, 98, and Cronon, 13.

19 "an Edifice—of sound!": Wright, *Testament*, 19; also see Jacobs, 23; Gill, 35; Twombly, *FLLW: Interpretive*, 5, 16; and Secrest, 67. Cronon, 27, observes, "No matter how radically [Wright's] individual buildings may differ from each other, they all express his struggle for aesthetic consistency, his habit of seizing a single abstract theme and recapitulating it with endless variations as if in a Beethoven symphony."

20 not a Lloyd Jones: Gill, 35. For a similarly emphatic assertion of Frank's debt to his father, see Twombly, *FLLW: Interpretive*, 6. Wright's younger

sister, predictably perhaps, demurs: "More than any other thing, Frank is a Lloyd Jones"; see Barney, 13.

20   Anna had been the defendant: Twombly, *FLLW: Interpretive*, 14.

21   According to this credible view: Twombly, *FLLW: Interpretive*, 15; cf. Gill, 54–55.

21   Just as Anna had suffered: Twombly, *FLLW: Interpretive*, 15.

21   not architecture: Gill, 55; Gill took the trouble to examine Wright's official academic transcript; "foundation of shoddy materials": For a perhaps inflated and romanticized portrayal of Wright's contribution to Science Hall, see Jacobs, 16–17; on the collapse of the State Capitol building, see Jacobs, 14–15, and Secrest, 87; "resisted the wrecking ball": For the Tokyo earthquakes of 1922 and 1923, see Secrest, 255, 272–73; for the resistance of Midway Gardens to destruction, see Wright, *Testament*, 118; also see Secrest, 87, and Gill, 173.

22   spent on James's farm: Twombly, *FLLW: Interpretive*, 17–18; Secrest, 82–83.

22   a flock of Madison creditors: Secrest, 83–85.

22   fine clothes and girls: Qtd. in Gill, 56.

23   a woman at the time: Wright, *Autobiography*, 79; also see Steiner, 5, and Gill, 88.

23   "to go to school to Cecil": Qtd. in Twombly, *FLLW: Interpretive*, 23; also see Jacobs, 34.

24   to whom he would ever defer: Jacobs, 38.

24   only to learn architectural design: Gill, 63, 75–79. For more on Wright's sexual purity at the time, see Gill, 46, 88.

24   "and yet nobody laughs": Qtd. in Jacobs, 54.

24   Sullivan's inchoate vision: Brooks, *FLLW and the Prairie School*, 14. In his *Prairie School Architecture*, ix, Brooks observes of Sullivan's pioneering vision that finally "a form-giver, not a philosopher, was needed" and that Wright was the first to achieve "a viable synthesis" of Sullivan's ideas in concrete forms.

25   "small ships in a grand pageant": Qtd. in Secrest, 107; also see Jacobs, 43–44.

25   and classic arches: Jacobs, 45. The most readable history of the Columbian Exposition is Erik Larson's wonderful *The Devil in the White City*.

25   "half a century from its date, if not longer": Qtd. in Jacobs, 45; also see Wright, *Testament*, 37: "The Chicago World's Fair became the occasion of modern architecture's grand relapse."

25   "about to go Pseudo-Classic in Architecture": Qtd. in McCarter, 23.

25   "a lover's quarrel": Gill, 99.

25   "I am surely living in Hell": Qtd. in Secrest, 301.

25   begging handouts: Gill, 80.

26   from the ashes of Sullivan's ruin: Blake, 28–29; also see Cronon, 21–23, on the Japanese influence that Wright "tried hard to hide and for which we therefore have the least documentation."

26   a veritable Gibson Girl in the flesh: Secrest, 96.

26   the perfect Victorian wife: Twombly, *FLLW: Interpretive,* 99; Secrest, 96–100.

26   were scarcely seen apart: Jacobs, 38; Gill, 89; Secrest, 100–101.

27   with any other woman: cf. Gill, 89.

27   on to professional glory: Wright, *Autobiography,* 86; cf. Secrest, 96.

27   "Have you thought of the consequences . . . ?": Qtd. in Jacobs, 39.

27   Michigan for several months: Wright, *Autobiography,* 85–89; also see Jacobs, 39.

28   "so forcible an adversary as my mother": Qtd. in Secrest, 111.

28   took to hiding in closets: Secrest, 111.

28   after he was established and successful: Twombly, *FLLW: Interpretive,* 27–28.

28   "So many churches": Wright, *Autobiography,* 79.

29   "experiments in domestic architecture": Hurder, 2.

29   "It is like living within a work of art": Qtd. in Jacobs, 63. On Wright's disregard for budgets, see Cronon, 25–26.

29   museum of Wright's architecture: Twombly, *FLLW: Interpretive,* 27.

29   promptly Frank bought his Forest Avenue lot: *Guide to Oak Park's FLLW,* 10–12; cf. Secrest, 135.

29   "any woman perceived as a rival": Secrest, 139.

29   "with remarkable competence": Gill, 105.

30   penury, emotional chilliness, and want: See, e.g., N. K. Smith, 66.

30   "fun just to have him about": Qtd. in N. K. Smith, 64; for Maginel's remark, see Barney, 133.

30   "he'll overcrowd this town": Qtd. in Farr, 60.

30   "Mr. Wright is held in high esteem": Qtd. in Twombly, *FLLW: Interpretive,* 29.

31   founding the Guild of Handicrafts: Secrest, 159–61. In 1903, Wright built a sideboard for Stickley; singer Barbra Streisand bought it in 1989 for a staggering $363,000.

31   Hubbard's shaggy hairstyle: For Hubbard's influence on Wright, see Secrest, 158–61, and Farr, 87–88. Hubbard and his wife went down with the *Lusitania* in 1915; "colossus in the life of Frank Lloyd Wright": Secrest, 171; for more on Larkin, see Secrest, 177–79, and Gill, 140–41; "that had so brutally wrecked Sullivan": McCarter, 23; also see Brooks, *FLLW and the Prairie School,* 11.

32   "were competing to invent": Secrest, 129.

32   "work, nature, [and] the home": Alan Crawford, qtd. in Secrest, 127–28. Emphasis added.

33 "the thrill of ideality—A SOUL!": Excerpts from Wright's speech qtd. in Farr, 74–76, and Blake, 58.

33 architecture itself crumbled into ruin: Wright, *Autobiography*, 78, and *Testament*, 17, 37–38; also see Connors, 10–12, and McCarter, 23–25. In his introduction to the Wasmuth folios, Wright rhetorically asks, "Whence came corrupt styles like the Renaissance? From false education, from confusion of the curious with the beautiful"; see Alofsin, "Taliesin," 54.

33 "faint copies of an invisible archetype": Ralph Waldo Emerson, "Nature," in *Selections from Ralph Waldo Emerson*, ed. Stephen E. Whicher (Boston: Houghton Mifflin, 1957), 52.

34 architecture's savior was already standing: see McCarter, 24–25, especially for Wright's pointed emendation to Hugo's text.

34 mainly of houses: Twombly, *FLLW: Interpretive*, 77, 33; Secrest, 112–14.

34 his own boyhood years: Twombly, *FLLW: Interpretive*, 35.

34 an idealized domesticity: Secrest, 199.

35 in a hidden paradise: Secrest, 113. On Wright and *House Beautiful*, see Secrest, 193; Twombly, *FLLW: Interpretive*, 38–39; Steiner, 7; and Sweeney, 1, 4. Back in 1886, Gannett, a Unitarian divine and family friend, had credited Frank ("a boy architect belonging to the family") with the interior design of Silsbee's Unity Chapel. If so, this activity would have marked Wright's first professional work of any kind; see Twombly, *FLLW: Interpretive*, 18.

35 "Was just that we two were together": Qtd. in N. K. Smith, 109.

35 "rewards are peace and contentment": Ernest Newton, qtd. in Secrest, 130.

36 "that his fortunes might change": Twombly, *FLLW: Interpretive*, 89.

36 "the first modern house in America": "Charnley-Persky House Tours, The First Modern House in America." Online, www.sah.org (accessed February 2001). Also see Morgan, 1–3. The extent of Wright's contribution to the Charnley's design remains a matter of academic debate; but Wright himself always claimed that the design was his alone, and Sweeney, 2, submits that the house is "now acknowledged to have been designed by Wright." Assuming the truth of all this, here is one measure of Wright's genius: within five years of leaving Madison for Chicago, he designed the Charnley house. (But cf. Storrer, *FLLW Companion*, 10; and see Burns, 308, who repeats the often-heard charge that Wright "took credit for work his mentor Louis Sullivan had done with his partner, Dankmar Adler." On this point, see Secrest, 177.)

36 "the sacramental nature of . . . marriage": Qtd. in Twombly, *FLLW: Interpretive*, 36; also see Farr, 77; Steiner, 9; and Morgan, 1.

36 if so vaguely, in *The House Beautiful*: N. K. Smith, 70–71.

36 twenty-five designs: Twombly, *FLLW: Interpretive*, 22.

36 "a perpetual inspiration": Qtd. in Twombly, *FLLW: Interpretive*, 31.

37 "strengthen proper family living": Twombly, *FLLW: Interpretive*, 32. Also see Jacobs, 66–67, and G. Wright, 83–84. For a general overview of the growing influence of the various "homemaker magazines," see Brooks, *FLLW and the Prairie School*, 12.

37 decade of prodigious creativity: Secrest, 164.

37 the acknowledged leader: Jacobs, 67.

37 "first masterpiece": Henry-Russell Hitchcock, qtd. in Gill, 135.

37 "image of modern times . . . great original interpreter": Scully, 17–18.

37 one-man exhibition: Twombly, *FLLW: Interpretive*, 90.

37 a 1908 full-issue review: N. K. Smith, 82–83.

37 "hunger of the eye for length of line": Qtd. in Farr, 79; on the Emerson-Greenough connection, see Farr, 79n–80n. Echoing Emerson, Wright wrote, "The horizontal line is the line of domesticity," permitting the house to "lie serene beneath a wonderful sweep of sky"; see G. Wright, 81.

38 into the landscape itself: Farr, 79; Steiner, 7. For a good, brief overview of Wright's conception of "organic" architecture at the time, see Twombly, *FLLW: Interpretive*, 84–89. Wright spells all this out in his seminal essay "In the Cause of Architecture," appearing in the March 1908 issue of *Architectural Record* and featuring some fifty-six pages of illustrations of his work to that point; see Sweeney, 15.

38 "spiritually organic": Qtd. in Steiner, 9.

38 wilderness painters and romantic poets: Steiner, 9; also see Gill, 192–93.

38 unrestrained by considerations of budget: On the Coonleys and their house, see, inter alia, Secrest, 233, 236; Jacobs, 73; Gill, 191–92; and Farr, 99–100.

39 the palazzo among Prairie houses: Manson, 188; and see Gill, 190–92.

39 "cramped and confining": N. K. Smith, 93.

39 "Destruction of something or other": Wright, *Autobiography*, 111.

39 of the imperial self: On the souring of Wright's suburban experience, see Twombly, *FLLW: Interpretive*, 98.

40 for thirty-eight years: Tafel, *About Wright*, 85.

40 hardly someone to introduce: On Wright's Oak Park guest list, see Jacobs, 68, and Twombly, *FLLW: Interpretive*, 98.

40 "church built in twentieth-century America": Scully, 20–21.

40 "What is it—a library?": Qtd. in Farr, 96–97. Similarly, Wright worked five years on a design for Uncle Jenkin's Abraham Lincoln Center at All Souls, and "There would be little or nothing about it to suggest religion in the usually accepted sense." Wright seems willing to have put in all this fruitless effort—his plan was ultimately rejected—because "he was anxious to do a big church, especially so if it did not look like a church"; see Farr, 95.

40   "I wanted to build a building like that": Qtd. in Gill, 183.

40   "Why not build a temple to man": Qtd. in Gill, 174–75. Just after Wright's death, his third wife urged the idea that "His love of man was undeniable, as was his love of God. But when he spoke of man and God, he had them [so] intertwined, especially when he added his love of Nature, that it is difficult for anyone to express [i.e., to comprehend] his innermost faith and vision"; see Olgivanna Lloyd Wright, *The Shining Brow,* 300.

40   "I have heard it enough": Qtd. in Farr, 99.

40   "a good-time place": Wright, *Autobiography,* 154, 160; and see Gill, 174–75.

41   "as clean as my baby": Qtd. in Twombly, *FLLW: Interpretive,* 100.

41   "the tragic lines round her mouth": Qtd. in Gill, 202.

41   "more independent-minded than the average person": Brooks, *FLLW and the Prairie School,* 12.

42   loyal, dogged Edwin: On Mamah's background and courtship, see Gill, 199–200, and Secrest, 193.

Chapter 2. Scandal in Oak Park

43   more resembled Frank's two future wives: See, e.g., Twombly, *FLLW: Interpretive,* 99–100, and Secrest, 201. Cronon, 10, quotes Maginel, who observed that Anna Wright "made the mistake of failing to mask her disapproval of the women to whom [Frank] was attracted, though sometimes they were strikingly like her in looks and in spirit"; see Barney, 150.

43   both members of Oak Park's Nineteenth Century Women's Club: Secrest, 193–94. Interestingly, Anna had helped to found the club; see Secrest, 225.

44   among the best of Wright's small designs: Farr, 94. Mamah and Edwin were moving into their new house at about the time that William Carey Wright was dying in Pennsylvania; see Secrest, 193. Wright, in his *Testament,* 52, claims to have designed the house back in 1893, when he was still with Adler and Sullivan.

44   children reported spying: Gill, 200.

44   centered in the domestic hearth: Steiner, 40. On this same page, Steiner provides a floor plan of the Cheney House.

44   potentially ruinous liaison: Copplestone, 37. Although Copplestone does not attribute his source, confirmation for this version of the early genesis of the romance can be found in Tafel, *About Wright,* 85–87. And see Wright's March 1910 letter to C. R. Ashbee, in which he confesses, "I have for some years past loved another [i.e., Mamah]"; qtd. in Gill, 210.

44   not just a casual pleasure cruise: Gill, 185, has Wright borrowing the money for the Tokyo trip from Walter Burley Griffin, with whom he

later quarreled over the debt and whom he repaid in the form of Japanese prints; other sources give Ward Willets himself as the source of the loan. It is quite conceivable that Wright borrowed from both men.

44 "gains a certain distinction": Gill, 200–202.

45 "a buccaneering type": Qtd. in Secrest, 194.

45 asked Frank for one year of grace: Wright, *Autobiography*, 163.

45 "a conundrum": Secrest, 198. Similarly, see Twombly, *FLLW in Spring Green*, 2: "Why Wright deserted his family and his lucrative practice has intrigued historians." More economically, N. K. Smith, 2, simply asks, "Why did he flee?"

45 lumbered by an unwanted wife: Manson, 211–12.

45 parroted by his sympathizers: See, e.g., Gill, 204.

45 neglect or rejection seems absurd: See, e.g., N. K. Smith, 83.

45 a "nervous breakdown": Farr, 104.

46 the custom of marriage itself: Twombly, *FLLW: Interpretive*, 94–98. In his *FLLW: His Life*, 163, 165, Twombly proposes that Wright may have been suffering from "mild paranoia," convinced of a "conspiracy to exploit and discredit him"; the lifelong evidence, says Twombly, "suggests that unless Wright received unqualified praise and total credit for the Prairie movement, he suspected treachery and evil intent."

46 of their own accord: See, e.g., Gill, 189. Gill observes that Wright "felt so good on the edge, the edge is . . . what gave him the stimulus. Plainly his adrenaline was filling him up to the brim when he was in desperate trouble"; qtd. in Burns, 310.

46 Wright's determination to fly away: See, e.g., Scully, 21. Scully (ibid.) also calls the Robie "a kind of terminal point for the first phase of Wright's career." N. K. Smith, 63, finds evidence of Wright's new commitment to individual privacy and freedom—as opposed to family unity—in the Robie design. Yale's Carroll L. V. Meeks calls the Robie House "one of the great monuments of American architectural history," and the journal *Architectural Record* styles it "one of the seven most notable residences ever built in America"; see Farr, 100–102. And for a residential design as a metaphor for flight, compare Wright's Gilmore House (1908), aptly nicknamed "Airplane House"; see Storrer, *FLLW Companion*, 149.

46 he "could not go on": N. K. Smith, 83–98.

47 to leaf through some Whitman: Wright, *Autobiography*, 162–63. Cf. N. K. Smith, 97, and Twombly, *FLLW: Interpretive*, 98.

47 a less than "mutual" relationship: Wright, *Autobiography*, 163; and see Farr, 108. On Key's influence on Wright's apologia, see Alofsin, *FLLW: Lost Years*, 93.

47 "ended by mutual consent": Secrest, 25. For an enlightening explication of Luther's—and other early Protestant reformers'—views on the issue

of the sacramental or contractual nature of marriage, see N. K. Smith, 69–70.

47 "Transcendentalists and beyond": Cronon, 10. It is in this sense, Cronon suggests (ibid.), that one should understand architect Philip Johnson's provocative remark that Wright was "America's greatest nineteenth-century architect."

48 "a serious encounter with Ralph Waldo Emerson": Cronon, 12.

48 "in the way of his higher truths": Cronon, 26.

48 "quite literally his religion": Cronon, 14.

48 freely exhorted from the pulpit: Gill, 122; Secrest, 142.

48 "for the likes of Frank Lloyd Wright": Cronon, 12. For Wright, the his-torical Jesus was merely the "greatest of all poetic students of human na-ture"; qtd. in Gill, 22.

49 "far from being a monster": Gill, 207–8.

50 "I go to the cross": Qtd. in Secrest, 200.

50 a "hurly-burly flight from Oak Park": Gill, 208; for competing views, cf. Secrest, 203, and Manson, 212.

50 "a hundred years longer": Wright, *Autobiography*, 162, qtd. in N. K. Smith, 1. Gill, 201, is deeply suspicious of this account of the exchange.

50 his doctorate in aesthetics: Farr, 104; also see Secrest, 202.

50 "primer for a new American architecture": Alofsin, *FLLW: Lost Years*, 92. On the Wasmuth invitation, see, e.g., Jacobs, 73–74; Manson, 212; Gill, 201; and Farr, 104. For some years, Wright had been receiving invitations from his friend C. R. Ashbee, the English architect and designer, to visit him at his place in Chipping Campden, Gloucestershire, further whet-ting Wright's desire for a European junket; see Gill, 201.

51 "forced to make an irrevocable choice": Gill, 204. This chronology is offered by Gill, 203–4. Compare the "official" version of these events in Manson, 211–12, in which the flight is characterized as "an overnight decision," one conditioned, in large part, by professional rather than personal considerations. In either case, following Mamah's desertion, Edwin's mother Arilla moved into the Oak Park house to supervise the children; see Alofsin, *FLLW: Lost Years*, 349.

51 "not a day for rational decisions": Manson, 212. On von Holst, see Man-son, 212–13; Gill, 208; Brooks, *FLLW and the Prairie School*, 25; and N. K. Smith, 100.

51 David was still indignant: Secrest, 204.

51 "his son fled to escape them": Twombly, *FLLW: Interpretive*, 102.

51 "he was not asked to leave": J. L. Wright, 54.

52 for seducing Thaw's wife: For this historical precedent, see Secrest, 203.

52 Frank's own Unity Temple: Farr, 117; Catherine's letter is also quoted in Gill, 204. An intriguing question, of course, is who tipped off the *Tribune*'s correspondent. Edwin? Catherine? Anna? A disgruntled

employee or disenchanted client? As with so many Wrightian mysteries, we simply do not know; see Secrest, 203.

52 "the checkered history of soul-mating": Qtd. in Twombly, *FLLW: Interpretive*, 91.

52 "all will be as it has been": Qtd. in Farr, 117–18.

53 "a case of a vampire": Qtd. in Farr, 119.

53 "I don't care to talk": Qtd. in Farr, 119.

53 "affinity fools unmasked": Qtd. in Farr, 119–20.

53 the two worked together: Sweeney, 16; Secrest, 204–5. One account (see the *Chicago Sunday Tribune*, 16 August 1914, p. 6, col. 5) has it that Catherine had dispatched son Lloyd as an emissary to Europe to convince Frank to return to his own fireside. If so, the plan was unsuccessful; Lloyd seems to have worked happily with his father there in compiling the folio. More dubiously, the same source avers that Lloyd physically attacked his father when the latter showed up with Mamah in the fall of 1910 at the New York offices of an architectural publishing firm with which Lloyd was attached; "I've waited for just such a chance to pay you back for the way you have treated mother," Lloyd is reported to have said, at which point he blackened both of Frank's eyes. This unsupported story seems apocryphal and calculated to appeal to the conventional sensibilities of the *Tribune*'s more conversational readers; Lloyd, of course, had had plenty of opportunities to express his outrage back in Europe and appears never to have done so.

54 a formal portrait photo: That photo is reproduced in Secrest, 99.

54 illustrating seventy buildings: Sweeney, 15–18. In addition to the two-folio monograph, Wright also prepared a booklet, *Frank Lloyd Wright: Ausgeführte Bauten*, for Wasmuth; see Alofsin, "Taliesin," 50.

54 "modified the course of architecture": Brooks, *FLLW and the Prairie School*, 16.

54 "His influence was strongly felt": Qtd. in Brooks, *FLLW and the Prairie School*, 17; also see Scully, 23.

54 were similarly affected: Scully, 23. Wright would later break with the "International School" architects he had so influenced, seeing the Europeans as having taken his ideas too far; see Connors, 13.

55 "the song in the deeps of life": Wright, *Autobiography*, 164–65. On one of his visits to Berlin, Wright had a brief (and disappointing) interview with Johannes Brahms; see Twombly, *FLLW: Interpretive*, 93.

55 settling down with Mamah: Wright, *Testament*, 119.

55 a view of green and golden fields: Secrest, 209. For a photo of the Villa Medici, see Levine, 32; for a fascinating comparison of Taliesin I and its setting with the Villa Medici and with the "contoured tillage [of] Japan's steep hillsides," see Aguar and Aguar, 151–53.

56 "I have tried to do this thing": Qtd. in Gill, 210. Wright could be relatively

sure of a consolatory reply from Ashbee, who had assumed the mantle of leadership of the British Arts and Crafts Movement after William Morris retired from the fray. Ashbee was a homosexual who had not shared that fact with his wife Janet until after they had married. Janet, in her letters, reveals an enormous admiration and sympathy for Catherine Wright. See Gill, 202, and Secrest, 159-61, 193.

56 "putting better things in their place": Qtd. in Gill, 211.

57 "he would grow to loathe her": Catherine Wright, in a letter to Janet Ashbee; qtd. in Gill, 213. Secrest, 206-7, comments, "The reason Wright gave for leaving Mamah, that he did not want the beauty of their relationship soiled by too much daily contact, sounds like a rationalization and a grossly unkind one at that."

57 "in his time of need": Secrest, 205.

57 "you should know of it": From the "Typed FLLW/Porter/ALLW 4016" folder, Frank Lloyd Wright Archives, Taliesin West. The letter is dated 4 July 1910.

57 and sailed for home: During her time alone in Europe, Mamah paid a pilgrimage to Ellen Key in Sweden and then tutored students in English in Leipzig; thereafter, she returned to Fiesole to begin her translations of Key's radical books; see Alofsin, "Taliesin," 51.

57 "no mercy except from outsiders": Qtd. in Gill, 213.

58 "damnably to be blamed": Qtd. in Secrest, 206. Mrs. George W. Trout, president of the Chicago Equal Suffrage League, took a more charitable stance, allowing that a "fallen and repentant man should be welcomed back to the community"; see Alofsin, "Taliesin," 63.

58 "any humble pie": Qtd. in Gill, 212.

58 than his own brother: Secrest, 207-9. Wright had a tumultuous relationship with W. E. Martin, for whom he designed an Oak Park house in 1903 and a manufacturing plant. Martin, a maker of stove polish, had begun their connection by calling Wright "one of nature's noblemen," but ended up asserting that "he is not worth a dollar and probably never will be"; see Gill, 140-41, 157.

58 a primitive air conditioning system: Farr, 86.

58 almost brotherly affection: Secrest, 172.

59 "is commonly termed 'sucker'": Qtd. in Secrest, 208; for the Wright–Darwin Martin correspondence, see Secrest, 206-9. Much of the correspondence among Wright, Catherine, Darwin Martin, and W. E. Martin is archived at the State University of New York, Buffalo.

59 scalded to death in the same mishap: Secrest, 194-95; for a fuller account, see Barney, 110-11.

60 "see about building a small house": Qtd. in Secrest, 209.

60 admirable and compelling: Twombly, *FLLW: Interpretive*, 101; also see Gill, 100-101. In October 2001, the present author received a call from

Chicago-based writer Nancy Drew, who is preparing a fictionalized account of the Taliesin murders; she, for one, seems to dispute this conventional portrayal of Mamah as a distant, abstracted mother. But the *Chicago Tribune* for 16 August 1914 (p. 6) reports that "Mrs. Cheney saw little of her children . . . when she was at home with them, employing a governess who had almost entire charge of them."

61   "to instruct the whole universe": Joseph Campbell, *The Hero with a Thousand Faces* (Princeton: Princeton University Press, 1968), 242. For a thorough examination of the wellsprings of the house's name—and especially of Wright's debt in this regard to the Whitmanesque poet Richard Hovey (1864-1900) and the Belgian playwright and philosopher Maurice Maeterlinck—see Alofsin, "Taliesin," 44-48.

61   "his alter ego": K. Smith, *FLLW's Taliesin*, 48. Twombly, *FLLW: Interpretive*, 105, deems Taliesin "as much an autobiography as the book [i.e., *Autobiography*] he later published" and sees the house as providing "an index to Wright's psychological and intellectual attitudes in 1911." Alofsin, "Taliesin," 56, 60, calls the house the embodiment of the "spiritual goals of the artist" and "Wright's image of himself as poet, priest, prophet."

61   "fight for what I saw I had to fight": Wright, *Autobiography*, 167.

61   without being observed: Twombly, *FLLW in Spring Green*, 5; also see Twombly, *FLLW: Interpretive*, 106; Lind, *Lost Wright*, 21; and K. Smith, *FLLW's Taliesin*, 48. Ken Burns, 315, calls Taliesin "a fortress sequestered from the storms of [Wright's] own making."

61   "Nothing . . . I had ever seen would do": Wright, *Autobiography*, 168.

61   "gray tree-trunks in violet light": Wright, *Autobiography*, 170-71.

61   "part of the hill on which it stands": Qtd. in Burns, 311. Of course, descriptions of this famous house and its "organic" nature strain many a groaning bookshelf; among such treatments, see Blake, 62-63; Lind, *Lost Wright*, 21; Scully, 21; McCarter, 119-20; Hitchcock, 64-66; and especially Levine, 32-39. For a contemporary description of the place, see *Spring Green Weekly Home News*, 20 August 1914.

61   "the direct imitation of nature": Levine, 34.

62   of morality derived from the soil: Scully, 22.

62   "as I laid the foundation of the house": Wright, *Autobiography*, 170.

62   "And he didn't have any money": Qtd. in "Taliesin, 1911-1925." Online, www.pbs.org/flw/buildings/taliesin/taliesin_drawings.html (accessed June 2002).

62   "happily with ever after": Wright, *Autobiography*, 168-69.

62   "Taliesin had first taken form": Wright, *Autobiography*, 185; also see Levine, 39.

62   the individual was now central: Alofsin, "Taliesin," 60. At Taliesin, says Alofsin, a "vision of the self replaces the centrality of family in [Wright's] life."

62 "a sacred thing that was happening": Qtd. in "Taliesin, 1911-1925." Online, www.pbs.org/flw/buildings/taliesin/taliesin_interior.html (accessed
June 2002).

63 "it must be untrue": Qtd. in Secrest, 212. The story about Frank and
Mamah at Taliesin, entitled "Architect Wright in New Romance with
'Mrs. Cheney,'" had appeared in the *Chicago Tribune*, 24 December 1911.

63 a robe of bright crimson: Farr, 124.

63 "spiritual hegira": Wright himself seems to have coined the unfortunate
phrase, which was immediately picked up by the 8 November 1909 *Chicago Tribune* and thereafter repeated endlessly; see Twombly, *FLLW: His
Life*, 169, n.1, and Alofsin, "Taliesin," 45.

Chapter 3. "A Peculiar Establishment"

71 "Law for Ordinary Man": *Chicago Tribune*, 26 December 1911; the main
headline is "Spend Christmas Making 'Defense' of 'Spirit Hegira.'" All
quotes and paraphrases from Wright's "Christmas message," as it came
to be called, are from this edition. Subsequent treatments of the interview (and its successors) include Secrest, 212; Alofsin, *FLLW: Lost Years*,
95-97; Gill, 221-23; Twombly, *FLLW: Interpretive*, 91; Twombly, *FLLW
in Spring Green*, 6-8; N. Smith, 101; Alofsin, "Taliesin," 44-55; and Jacobs, 73, who too credulously parrots Wright's own apologia: "It was the
familiar story of the too-young marriage and the later disillusionment, as
each partner developed into a somewhat different person." Also see the
Chicago Tribune of 26, 27, 29, 30, and 31 December 1911, and of 1 January
1912; *Spring Green Weekly Home News*, 28 December 1911; the *Wisconsin
State Journal*, 30 December 1911; and the *Chicago Record-Herald*, 29, 31
December 1911, and 26 January 1912.

About five eventful years later, Anna Lloyd Wright, in a letter to her
son, echoes almost exactly the sentiments of his Nietzschean remark: "I
feel when certain ones reach as high a moral state as yourself," she wrote
on 4 February 1917, "they will not then feel their humiliation because of
their touch with you"; see the Anna Lloyd Wright correspondence,
Frank Lloyd Wright Foundation Archives, Taliesin West, Scottsdale,
Arizona.

71 he gets beyond my depth: *Chicago Tribune*, 27 December 1911.

72 "I don't know what is going on there": *Chicago Tribune*, 29 December
1911. Other quotations in the passage are from this edition of the *Tribune*
and from the one of 27 December 1911.

73 the ongoing adultery at Taliesin: *Weekly Home News*, 28 December 1911.
For other treatments of Purdy's heated text, see Alofsin, *FLLW: Lost
Years*, 96; Twombly, *FLLW in Spring Green*, 8; and Twombly, *FLLW:
Interpretive*, 110.

73 the "uttermost depths of his soul": *Wisconsin State Journal,* 30 December 1911. The statement also appears in the *Chicago Tribune,* 31 December 1911; oddly, however, the two accounts, while essentially similar in tone and content, often differ in wording and occasionally in fact. The *State Journal* version, for example, quotes Wright to the effect that Edwin Cheney had divorced Mamah while she was in Europe, so that she was homeless and destitute upon her return to America, and "Because she was the woman of his passion," Wright gave her shelter at Taliesin. In the *Tribune* account, conversely, Wright stipulates that Mamah initiated the divorce proceedings after she confronted Edwin in Canada well after her return from Berlin. Future quotations here rely on the *Tribune's* presentation. For more on this second statement, see Alofsin, *FLLW: Lost Years,* 96–97; Twombly, *FLLW: Interpretive,* 91; and Jacobs, 73.

73 "a universal legend": Secrest, 212.

75 the willing signatures of Edwin and Catherine: *Chicago Tribune,* 29 December 1911 and 1 January 1912.

75 "set [his] life in conventional order": *Weekly Home News,* 4 January 1912.

75 Calm had descended over Taliesin: F. L. Wright, "Taliesin, the Chronicle of a House with a Heart," *Liberty* 6 (23 March 1929), 26; qtd. in Alofsin, "Taliesin," 60.

75 Wright's abrupt introduction of his mistress: Secrest, 213.

75 conventional modes of behavior: Twombly, *FLLW in Spring Green,* 8. "If in Oak Park [Wright] had donned the trappings of the upper middle class," says Twombly, 10, "he now coveted membership in the life of a farming community."

76 "the social sanction he so desperately seemed to need": Alofsin, "Taliesin," 44.

76 "Wright had jeopardized his acceptability": N. K. Smith, 101.

76 Frank and Mamah's day-to-day life: K. Smith, *FLLW's Taliesin,* 49; also see Twombly, *FLLW: His Life,* 166. Echoing Smith, Anthony Alofsin, "Taliesin," 60, remarks, "The details of [Wright's] life with Mamah Borthwick remain unknown."

76 press coverage . . . ceased: Still, local papers kept an eye cocked toward Taliesin. On 18 January 1912, for example, the vigilant editor of the *Baraboo Daily News* makes a suggestive note of Wright's recent "several mysterious trips" from Spring Green to Madison.

76 a scant three by 1912: Secrest, 213–14; also see Twombly, *FLLW in Spring Green,* 10, who calculates that, overall, Wright's total commissions plummeted from "an average of seventeen a year (1905–1909) to ten (1910–1914)."

76 "a ritual demonstration": Twombly, *FLLW: Interpretive,* 111.

77 "not the kind that would bring clients to his door": Jacobs, 75.

77 less than half his output: Twombly, *FLLW: His Life,* 157.

77   offered him the lucrative job: Wright, *Autobiography*, 193.

77   upper echelons of the imperial Japanese government: Secrest, 214.

77   "The glory of Wright's whoppers": Gill, 225.

78   "they left the deserted wife of the architect": *Sauk County Democrat*, 16 January 1913. On the Tokyo trip, also see the *Baraboo Daily News*, 19 June 1913, and the *Weekly Home News*, 8 May 1913.

78   the agreement would not be finalized: Secrest, 214. Secrest cites the fee mentioned by Wright in a 10 January 1913 letter to Darwin Martin; Gill, 236, suggests that the fee "was to be between three and four hundred thousand dollars"—in those days, a truly staggering sum.

78   nothing even remotely like the place: Wright entertainingly tells "The Tale of the Midway Gardens" in his *Autobiography*, 175–84. The standard (and quite wonderful) study of the building is Paul Samuel Kruty's *Frank Lloyd Wright and Midway Gardens;* also see Blake, 64–66; Tafel, *Apprentice*, 81; Gill, 225–28, 235–36; and Twombly, *FLLW: His Life*, 152–54.

79   "had simply shaken itself out of my sleeve": Wright, *Autobiography*, 176–77.

79   "like the battlements of some castle in Graustark": Gill, 226; also see Blake, 64, and Gill, 228.

79   "sculptural art into the twentieth century": Twombly, *FLLW: His Life*, 153–54; also see Gill, 228; Tafel, 81. Wright's son John ended up falling in love with and marrying one of the models for Ianelli's sculpted "sprites."

80   "I [was] up and doing": Qtd. in Secrest, 214.

80   back in debt and perfectly content: The anecdote is told in Willard, 67–68.

81   a purely "economic basis": Alofsin, *FLLW: Lost Years*, 95–96; Alofsin quotes from the *Chicago Tribune*, 29 and 30 December 1914.

81   this clumsy forgery: Secrest, 214.

81   on the grounds of desertion: Qtd. in Secrest, 215. For a contemporary news account of Wright's quest for a quiet divorce, see "'Family Caucus'; Plan of Wright," *Chicago Tribune*, 30 December 1911.

81   he would eventually come back to her: Secrest, 215.

81   "that one cannot forgive in a weaker": Ashbee, 16–19.

82   "[their] errant member": Secrest, 213, paraphrasing the *Chicago Record-Herald*, 28 December 1911.

82   its "deadliest blow": Frank Lloyd Wright archives, State Historical Society, Madison.

82   "and an entertainment center": Lind, *FLLW's Life and Homes*, 36.

83   "a step ahead in the matter of sex": Qtd. in Alofsin, "Taliesin," 51.

83   and *The Woman Movement:* A fifth translation by Borthwick, that of Key's "Romain Rolland," appeared posthumously in the October 1915 number of the *Little Review*. For a complete bibliography of Borthwick's translations of Key, see Sweeney, 18, 21, 25; for a biography of Key, see

Louise Nystrom Hamilton, *Ellen Key, Her Life and Work,* trans. A. E. B. Fries (New York: Putnam's, 1913).

83 "no function whatever in any true Democracy": Wright, *Autobiography,* 163; qtd. (except for the last clause) in Alofsin, *FLLW: Lost Years,* 93, and in Gill, 206. A sympathetic analysis of Key's influence on Wright is provided in Alofsin's "Taliesin," 50–54; for a hostilely competing view, see Gill, 206–8.

83 "lack of intellectual rigor": Gill, 207.

83 "anybody's sake but his own": Qtd. in Alofsin, "Taliesin," 51.

83 Mamah as the local newspaper editor: Secrest, 215.

Chapter 4. "A Summer Day That Changed the World"

86 sometimes even "I guess": Prior to this study, the fullest account of the murders has been McCrea's seminal online article, "Murders at Taliesin," originally published in the *Madison Capital Times* on 15 August 1998. Other recent treatments—all of which have been consulted in compiling my own retelling (and some of which are infinitely more reliable than others)—include Secrest, 216–22; Gill, 229–34; Farr, 134–40; Twombly, *FLLW: His Life,* 167–69; Twombly, *FLLW in Spring Green,* 6–11; Barney, 145–47; J. L. Wright, 80–86; and, of course, Wright, *Autobiography,* 184–89. Because so many initial journalistic accounts necessarily overlap on many points of pertinent detail—to the extent that such matters wander into the realm of common knowledge—mostly contributions of latter-day investigators will be cited in the text.

86 finishing touches on Midway Gardens: *Chicago Tribune,* 16 August 1914.

87 had worked adjoining farm fields: Meudt, 5.

87 "Are not the children innocent?": Qtd. in Secrest, 216; Meudt, 174.

87 occasional foreman for Wright: Two of Brunker's children were still minors. Almost everyone gets Brunker's age wrong. He was born in Ridgeway in 1848; see the *Dodgeville Chronicle,* 21 August 1914. His wife had died four years before.

87 rode their bicycles four miles: Marcus Weston, "Marcus Weston," in Tafel, *About Wright,* 182.

87 "Billy was one of them": Wright, *Autobiography,* 172; Secrest, 216. Actually, when he was first hired at Taliesin by chief carpenter Johnnie Vaughn, Billy had a broken arm: "I couldn't do anything—they just wanted my tools," he told his son Marcus; qtd. in Tafel, *About Wright,* 182.

88 sad but mitigating cachet: About seventy thousand blacks lived in Chicago at the time. The Barbados Department of Archives, which runs a tight ship, can find no record of a Julian Carlton having been born there during the requisite time frame. Carlton's Wisconsin death certificate,

under the rubric "Birthplace," lists "Alabama," followed by a question mark. Wright at one point refers to him as "a Cuban negro"; see, e.g., the *Chicago Tribune*, 16 August 1914. Storrer, 173, suggests that Carlton's father, not Carlton himself, "may have [once] been a slave, from Cuba or Barbados." Burns, 316, says only that Carlton was "West Indian." One area newspaper—the *Baraboo Daily News* for 18 August 1914—calls Carlton a "mullatto." The speculation here that Carlton was African American as opposed to a West Indian of any sort is my own.

88 He did not know much more about them: Although it seems unlikely, it may just be that Carlton had initiated the contact with Wright, having somehow learned of the vacancy at Taliesin. Following the murders, Vogelsang told reporters that "After [Carlton] sought work with Mr. Wright, he asked for a recommendation, which we gladly gave him" (*Dodgeville Chronicle*, 21 August 1914). More plausibly, Vogelsang was simply trying to distance himself a bit from a recommendation that had ended in such disaster for his friend Wright, who, in his *Autobiography*, 185, implicitly faults Vogelsang for referring Carlton to him.

89 a Pullman porter, headquartered in Chicago: See Gertrude's statement in the *Chicago Tribune*, 17 August 1914.

89 an assistant janitor at the Frances Willard School: *Chicago Tribune*, 17 August 1914. The school was named after the most famous woman in America in the last quarter of the nineteenth century. Almost forgotten now, Willard was a celebrated educator, Prohibition activist, and feminist. Except in matters of religious faith—Willard was a devout Methodist—Mamah would have admired her. By coincidence, the first Frances Willard School was co-designed by an architect named Cheney.

89 his desire to ingratiate himself: Alofsin, *FLLW: Lost Years*, 97.

89 the same time that the children arrived: For the children's departure date, see Farr, 136. Carlton seems to have confirmed to Iowa County sheriff Williams that he had, in fact, gone to Chicago a week or two before the murders, but he would not tell Williams the reason for the trip: see the *Chicago Tribune*, 17 August 1914.

90 "All Europe Aflame": *Baraboo Daily News*, 5 August 1914.

90 "a black son of a bitch": Secrest, 217.

90 intended as a sitting room for Anna: This whole matter of the precise location of the workmen's dining area is decidedly a mare's nest. Whatever room it was would seem to have to meet the various criteria suggested immediately after the fire by Herb Fritz's statement, by reports in the *Chicago Tribune*, and by various other contemporary testimonies. Taken together, these sources indicate the following: the room was small, perhaps twelve by twelve feet; it was located toward the western corner of Taliesin; the room featured only two doors—one leading to a "kitchen" and the other to what Fritz referred to as the "court"; the room had at

least one window (probably more) overlooking a steep decline that led down to a "creek"; there were rocks directly beneath the room's windows, which were positioned about a storey-and-a-half above ground; and, finally, the room had originally been intended as part of Anna Lloyd Wright's living quarters.

With reference to the handful of surviving floor plans of Taliesin I, no one room perfectly meets all these particulars. But the one that seems to come closest is the so-called sitting room, located in the working wing to the west (roughly) of the main house. This room, situated between the drafting room to the east and the carriage barn to the west, apparently shares one wall, cut on a bias, with an adjacent kitchen, features two windows overlooking the hill, and has only one door, which opens on the driveway "court." For these reasons, this "sitting room" long seemed to this author to provide the most likely site for the dining area of the workmen, apprentices, and draftsmen. But a conversation in November 2002 with Craig Jacobsen, public access manager for Taliesin Preservation, Inc., dissuades me. Jacobsen notes—as Wright himself had—that while the residential area of Taliesin was gutted by the fire, the working wing—along with its "sitting room"—was largely spared, as a photograph taken on August 16 clearly shows. Further, I have subsequently come across a floor plan of Taliesin drawn by Wright immediately after the disaster; this plan labels (for the first time) a room at the far southeast end of the residential wing as housing the "Men's Dining Room." Accordingly, I now join such previous researchers as McCrea, 3; Twombly, *FLLW: His Life,* 172, n.29; and Secrest, 218, in locating the impromptu dining room at the far end of the residence itself.

Alas, this room presents significant difficulties of its own in terms of the logistics of the murders: it is remote from the main kitchen, for example, and it provides easy access to an adjoining bathroom and one of two connecting bedrooms, supplying thereby other potential sources of escape for the embattled workmen and further clouding the whole issue. A mare's nest, indeed—and another Wrightian conundrum.

Yet another nettlesome issue is the matter of Taliesin's precise directional orientation. In her review of a draft of this study, Keiran Murphy, a historic researcher for Taliesin Preservation, Inc., helpfully points out that "a completely accurate drawing of the entire Taliesin I complex was never executed"; further, because Wright fiddled with the "directional designations of the building at some point during the Taliesin II era," no existing floor plan of Taliesin reliably indicates cardinal direction points with respect to the complex, which sat about "forty-five degrees east of true north."

For clarity's sake, and leaning heavily on Murphy's expertise and remarks, I have revised my narrative here in an effort to refer to true cardinal direction points—as closely as I can get to them—throughout. If I occasionally fail in this respect, the fault and confusion are mine, not Murphy's.

91 by some eighty feet: I believe that this matter of the physical distance between the family and the workmen has been a source of much confusion, both in the initial accounts and, therefore, in later ones. See my discussion in the text, below.

93 bringing him, dying, to his knees: Secrest, 219. Secrest (ibid.) suggests that Carlton also attacked Billy Weston as he came through the window and that the murderer had already assaulted David Lindblom. Actually, a good case can be made that Weston did escape through the window; The *Spring Green Weekly Home News* for 20 August 1914 twice makes that assertion, on one occasion indirectly quoting Weston himself to that effect. But the *Home News* reporter then records that Weston, following the attack upon him, "got up and ran across the *court* [my emphasis] to the studio," a comment that decidedly muddles the issue. Further, in his own statement, Herbert Fritz implies that only he and Brodelle used the window to exit the room. The *Wisconsin State Journal* of 16 August 1914 quotes Weston as declaring that he "stumbled *going through the door directly behind Brunkert* [*sic*] and for that reason Carlton's blow missed [Weston]" (my emphasis). Finally, if Weston did use the window, we must then imagine that he consciously abandoned his young son Ernest in the burning room. In sum, the door is a more likely venue here.

94 "The Lord is with *me*": Meudt, 174-76.

94 under her right eye: Secrest, 218.

95 presumably dead at last: *Weekly Home News*, 20 August 1914. Ferris's odd account—nowhere corroborated in print by the three men who arrived with him—further complicates an already confused situation. For Ferris also told the *Home News* reporter that he saw young Ernest Weston, "covered with blood," still "running down the court" when he arrived; Ferris claimed that he carried the fainting boy to the shade of a tree and laid him down there. And all this was after Carlton had already gone to ground: Ferris said "he saw nothing of the negro." (Ferris's testimony regarding Martha Cheney is discussed in the text, below. In most sources, his name is spelled *Farries*, but the spelling offered here is that found in the Iowa County jail and court records.)

96 Brodelle's savage murder: In its essential outlines, this is the chronological and logistical account of the murders offered by, e.g., Farr, 137-38; McCrea, 3-4 (although McCrea correctly has Brunker attacked in the courtyard, not, as in Farr, at the windows); Secrest, 218-19 (again, Secrest, in keeping with the *Weekly Home News* report of 20 August 1914, adds Billy Weston to those seeking escape through the window); and Willard, 69: namely, all these sources agree that Carlton first set the fire

in the men's dining room, *then* assaulted the family group, and then finally returned to the dining room to attack the workers. (To her credit, Secrest adopts the sensibly agnostic position, 218, that "the exact sequence [of the murders] is unclear.") Indeed.

97 "the negro had gone": It is quite possible to credit the earlier part of Fritz's statement while entertaining some doubts as to its closing comments, in which he claims to have climbed the hill in time to witness the last of the assaults. Indeed, some early accounts suggest that Fritz — understandably — hid out on the hill until a rumor reached him that Carlton was gone, having escaped in a canoe on the river; see, e.g., the town of Lancaster's *Grant County Herald*, 19 August 1914, and Mineral Point's *Iowa County Democrat*, 20 August 1914. (How he could have possibly received such a report, however, remains unstated.) But whether or not he hobbled back into the courtyard during the carnage, there is no reason to question his testimony regarding the start of the fire in the dining room. In a few instances, I have regularized spelling and punctuation in Fritz's narrative and added italics for emphasis.

In her review of my typescript, Keiran Murphy also questions — largely on logistical grounds — Fritz's claims about witnessing the subsequent murders. She is even dubious about Fritz's account of his fall from the window, arguing that had Fritz "gone out that window, he would have fallen into the walled-in garden, which was probably [only] a foot below the floor level of the men's dining room." Nonetheless, she concedes that "it's possible that he either ran into another room and out through [a] window (on the southeast façade?) or first crashed out of the window of the men's dining room, then jumped over the parapet wall of the walled-in garden." Of these two options, the former strikes me as distinctly more likely.

98 misleading *Tribune* article: That article was probably written by the *Tribune*'s fabled Walter Noble Burns, the paper's star reporter, "whose last name Charles MacArthur and Ben Hecht bestowed upon the irascible city-desk editor in their play *The Front Page*": Gill, 231.

99 "Taliesin I," as it came to be called: Taliesin burned in 1914 and was reconstructed as Taliesin II, which burned in turn, due to faulty electrical wiring (perhaps in a telephone), in 1925, giving way to the Taliesin III that visitors are shepherded through today. After both fires, Wright built the succeeding residences generally along the lines of the unconsumed masonry work, so that the current Taliesin, while in some ways distinctly different from the one in which Wright and Mamah Borthwick lived, is in other fundamental ways quite similar to it, at least in its general outlines; see McCarter, 120. (Since 1938, with the construction of Taliesin West in Scottsdale, Arizona, the Wisconsin Taliesin is most often referred to in the literature as "Taliesin East.")

99 Wright's original floor plan: Storrer, *FLLW Companion*, 173. Secrest, xiv, calls Storrer's *Companion* "the definitive catalogue of Wright's works," and the book has been lauded by the *New York Times*'s Paul Goldberger for "a level of accuracy that goes beyond even what is in the Wright archives." (Still, Keiran Murphy points out that Storrer, apparently following an earlier rendering supplied by Henry-Russell Hitchcock, neglects to include the "walled-in garden" just outside the workmen's dining area.) A version of Storrer's compendium is also available in multimedia format on a compact disc put out by Prairie Multimedia, Inc. McCarter, 119, provides a floor plan that helpfully includes some of the surrounding landscape, including an indication of the "wooded hillside" down which Herb Fritz seems to have taken his fiery tumble. An aerial view of Taliesin I and its grounds can be found in "Taliesin, the Home of Frank Lloyd Wright and a Study of the Owner," 17, the article largely written by the British Arts and Crafts advocate C. R. Ashbee.

100 "practically burned off her body": *Weekly Home News*, 20 August 1914.

101 both . . . named Carlton as the killer: By one journalistic account, however, Brunker, his leg "burned to a crisp" below the knee, never regained a sufficient level of consciousness to give a statement; see the *Chicago Tribune*, 19 August 1914, p. 12.

101 "Frank Lloyd Wrong": Burns, 316, captures this much-voiced epithet in print.

101 "one of the most despised men": Qtd. in Dennis Boyer, "Taliesin's Ghost Moves to the East," *Madison Capital Times*, 30 October 1997, p. 13A. His reputation in neighboring Sauk County is often no better; typical is a comment by a Spring Green resident whose chief "recollection upon hearing the mention of Wright's name recently was that he never paid his grocery bills"; see the *Chicago Sun-Times*, 25 September 1994, "Travel" sec., 8.

102 "as 'their son, their neighbor'": Pfeiffer, *FLLW: Monograph*, viii.

102 "As a witness only against her husband": *Dodgeville Chronicle*, 4 September 1914; cf. McCrea, 4.

103 struck him as deeply suspicious: This according to a personal communication to the author from Ron McCrea, August 2000.

103 taken over by the workmen: See, e.g., Gill, 234; and Twombly, *FLLW: His Life*, 172 (n. 29), 183. That said, it is conceded that Anna was often at Taliesin and seems to have overseen operations there when Wright was away; see Secrest, 225.

103 "is trying to find an answer": *Dodgeville Chronicle*, 21 August 1914.

103 "growing as they traveled": *Weekly Home News*, 20 August 1914.

104 seems to have remained unconscious: A nettlesome point, this: the August 16 *Chicago Tribune* reports that Fritz joined David Lindblom in dragging the dead and dying from the cinders; but if Fritz was able-bodied

enough to exert himself in this way, why did not he—rather than the much more severely injured Lindblom—join Weston in the run for help? Implicit here is further evidence for the idea that Fritz may have been still hiding out on the hillside by the time Weston awoke; cf. note to "the negro had gone," above.

104 Rieder, they knew, had a telephone: Wright, *Autobiography*, 185. Although an early newspaper account (*Iowa County Democrat*, 20 August 1914) has one of the workmen, Fritz, phoning for help from Taliesin, it is clear from Weston's actions that the telephone there had been rendered useless. Further, shortly after the fire, Wright tried calling the house from Chicago and could not get through; see the *Chicago Tribune* 16 August 1914; and cf. Secrest, 219. Rieder's name is on the deed as the person who sold Anna the land on which Taliesin would be built.

104 "Will Weston saved that": Wright, *Autobiography*, 185. Wright makes similar comments in a 1929 *Liberty* magazine article; see Lind, *Lost Wright*, 21.

105 the aforementioned Jake Ferris: Secrest, 219.

105 Attendants came swiftly: Secrest, 219.

105 injuring his hands and arms: *Dodgeville Chronicle*, 21 August 1914.

105 her hair burned away: Secrest, 220.

106 "like unbaked ladyfingers": Meudt, 176. Little Edna Kritz grew up to be Edna Meudt, a prominent Wisconsin poet. The quotes here and above are from her poem, as reprinted in her autobiography *The Rose Jar*, 174-78. Reluctantly, for purposes of fluidity, I have not demarcated the lineation of Meudt's poem in my own prosaic text.

106 to Tan-y-Deri, the Porter's place across the Valley: This direct removal of the wounded to Tan-y-Deri is widely asserted in the literature. Other versions have the victims transported first to a different neighboring cottage (e.g., Secrest, 220; J. L. Wright, 83) or, alternately and less likely, to the Hillside Home School (e.g., the *Chicago Tribune*, 16 August 1914). Almost certainly, the victims were taken directly to Tan-y-Deri; we know for a fact that the majority of them, at least, were there by Saturday night; see, e.g., the *Chicago Tribune*, 17 August 1914. For the bodies in the courtyard, see Pfeiffer, *FLLW: Collected Writings*, 17.

106 The call was from Frank Roth: Willard, 69; Farr, 138. Curiously, Wright himself, in his *Autobiography*, 184, records that the fateful call originated directly from Spring Green. More likely, the news from the murder site was first conveyed to Roth in Madison, who in turn called Wright. A perennial, dramatically satisfying, but totally apocryphal story is that Wright first learned of the Taliesin fire when he called Catherine in Oak Park to renew his pleas for a divorce; see, e.g., *Milwaukee Journal*, 9 April 1959, 1.6.

106 at work on a polychromatic mural: J. L. Wright, 80-81. John had served as part-time superintendent of the Gardens project, often to the

exasperation of chief contractor Paul Mueller; see Wright, *Autobiogra-phy*, 182.

106   whip the Gardens into its final shape: Wright, *Autobiography*, 184.

107   John summoned a taxi: J. L. Wright, 81. Of course, Frank's reported statement, "Why did I leave them today?" makes no literal sense—he had departed from Mamah and Taliesin four days previously. Also, the content of Roth's message varies from source to source. The *Tribune* of 16 August expansively suggests, "This is Frank Roth at Madison. Be pre-pared for a shock. Your wife—that is, Mrs. Cheney—the two children, and one of your draftsmen have been killed by Carleton [*sic*]. Carleton set fire to the bungalow and got away. He must have gone crazy. A posse is chasing him. You'd better get to Spring Green right away." Wright himself (*Autobiography*, 184–85) records the more economical "Taliesin destroyed by fire." Whatever Roth said to Wright, it is likely that the lat-ter did not comprehend the full extent of the tragedy until he was well underway to Spring Green; see Wright, *Autobiography*, 185, and J. L. Wright, 82.

107   "grief-stricken, mute understanding": J. L. Wright, 81.

107   Edwin had nothing to say to Frank: J. L. Wright, 81–82; Gill, 230.

107   the train chugged away: See Indira Berndtson's "Telephone Interview with John S. Christensen . . . ," 9 August 1995, Frank Lloyd Wright Archives, Taliesin West. All further references to Frances Inglis in this chapter are from this source; Christensen is Frances Inglis Thayer's grandson.

108   had arrived early at the scene of the fire: Bossard is a fascinating charac-ter. He was a doctor of the old school, tending patients more often in their homes than in his office, and he served the Spring Green area for an indefatigable sixty years—from 1887 to 1947. He charged a total of twenty-five dollars for his work that day with the wounded. Over the next three days, he continued to treat Brunker and Brodelle, and he was still dressing Billy Weston's burns as late as August 20. His papers (jour-nals and daybooks) are housed at the State Historical Society, Madison. According to a personal communication from Ron McCrea to the au-thor, Bossard wrote a memoir that oddly omits any reference to the crime. Until recent years, Spring Green's town library was named after Bossard.

108   too injured to attend his son's funeral: For the condition of the injured as of August 15, see the *Chicago Tribune*, 17 August 1914.

108   to escape the scene once night had fallen: *Chicago Tribune*, 16 August 1914; *Dodgeville Chronicle*, 21 August 1914. Ron McCrea (as well as some contemporary accounts) suggests that a more precise description of Carlton's hiding place might be the "boiler" or "fire pot" of the furnace; cf. Willard, 69. Spring Green's *Weekly Home News* (20 August 1914) asserts

that Carlton took the acid "when the heat [in the boiler] became unbearable and he thought he would roast to death."

108 "Acid," Carlton murmured: Sources vary regarding Carlton's exact words (if any) as he was hoisted from the furnace, but "Acid" is credibly economical and most common in the literature. Farr, 139, suggests, "Acid, from the household stores," which strikes the ear as overly particular. Madison's *Wisconsin State Journal* (16 August 1914) records "Muriatic acid," which seems too pharmacological. Bracingly direct and therefore wholly believable is the *Iowa County Democrat*'s "Help! Give me a drink!"; but that account (20 August 1914) is nowhere else repeated in print.

108 "both in number and in feeling": *Iowa County Democrat*, 20 August 1914.

109 "if they expect to find out something": *Dodgeville Chronicle*, 21 August 1914. Richland Center's *Richland Rustic* for 21 August 1914 chauvinistically defends the demeanor of the crowd, "which [while] it held itself in readiness to do great violence to [Carlton] all the afternoon, acted very sensible and conducted itself in a manner creditable to American manhood." The *Weekly Home News* (20 August 1914) makes it clear, however, that Carlton "feared mob violence," and the *Chicago Tribune* (16 August 1914) confirms that the crowd of farmers was "ready in a moment . . . to 'string [Carlton] up.'"

109 before finally giving up the chase: See, e.g., the *Wisconsin State Journal*, 16 August 1914, and the *Chicago Tribune* of that same date.

109 in the nearby fields and woods: Farr, 140; Twombly, *FLLW: His Life*, 167.

110 such "a mild-mannered man": *Wisconsin State Journal*, 16 August 1914; cf. McCrea, 3. The *State Journal* reports that both Nell and Jane Lloyd Jones were in Madison with Porter; the *Chicago Tribune* of the same date has it that Porter was telephoned in Madison by one of the Aunts from Spring Green and told to return with "nurses and medical supplies." The on-site *State Journal* account is more reliable on this point; further, both Aunts seem to have greeted Wright at the Madison train station that evening: see Secrest, 221.

110 wide-eyed, all night: Secrest, 221.

110 "Don't worry. Herbert": *Chicago Tribune*, 16 August 1914.

110 "at the hands of one Julian Carlton": *Chicago Tribune*, 16 August 1914; *Dodgeville Chronicle*, 21 August 1914. O'Neill's first name is given as Thomas in some sources.

110 "seems infinitely sad": Qtd. in Secrest, 221–22.

111 "*Taliesin Burning to the Ground*": J. L. Wright, 82. Frank could hardly have heard it exactly that way: no more than five of the eventual seven victims were dead by that time; as we shall see, John — like his father — plays fast and loose with facts on occasion. Still, the journey must have been as impossibly morose as he suggests.

111 "buoys my hopes": *Chicago Tribune,* 16 August 1914.

112 vary significantly from source to source: For example, a shorter version of Wright's alleged remarks is carried in the *Dodgeville Chronicle* of August 21, making no reference to Wright's plan to pay off Carlton or to the troublesome "telegram."

112 "someone signed her name to the wire": *Wisconsin State Journal,* 18 August 1914. Secrest, 217, echoes Wright's alleged speculation: "Perhaps Mamah Borthwick sensed that something was going very wrong, that August Saturday morning."

113 and, finally, "sadists": J. L. Wright, 82. John's odd book first appeared in 1946, before which time it was forecasted on some sides that Frank would be infuriated by his son's candid, critical, "warts and all" approach. To the contrary, the book proves to be routinely defensive of Frank, fawning and obsequious. The book was reissued as *My Father, Frank Lloyd Wright* by Dover in 1992 and then reprinted under its original title by Southern Illinois University Press two years later.

113 had never been to Taliesin in his life: J. L. Wright, 80.

114 "happy about the whole thing": J. L. Wright, 87.

114 "only yearn and refrain": J. L. Wright, 83.

114 "get hold of yourself": J. L. Wright, 83; Secrest, 221. Secrest apparently errs in placing this encounter at the train station in Madison, not Spring Green.

114 a "scene of devastating horror": Wright, *Autobiography,* 187.

114 "upon which Taliesin once stood": J. L. Wright, 83.

115 "themselves tragic": Wright, *Autobiography,* 185. In her description of the ruin, Wright's sister Maginel also emphasizes the monolithic remains of the masonry work: "[O]nly the great stone chimneys with their yawning fireplaces stood undamaged" (Barney, 146). Of course, Wright's comment about "thirty-six hours" cannot be true; he had been away from Taliesin since the previous Tuesday.

115 strewn about under sheets: J. L. Wright, 83.

115 over Mamah Borthwick's corpse: *Chicago Tribune,* 17 August 1914.

115 shredded much of the area's corn crop: *Baraboo Daily News,* 17 August 1914; *Richland Center Observer,* 20 August 1914; Secrest, 222.

115 the celebrated Walter Noble Burns: Gill, 231.

116 "and strode away": *Chicago Tribune,* 17 August 1914.

116 the sexton at Hillside Chapel: *Chicago Tribune,* 17 August 1914.

117 "who was once his wife lay dead": *Chicago Tribune,* 17 August 1914. John Lloyd Wright's account of the departure, 82, mirrors the *Tribune*'s report, to the point of borrowing some of the reporter's diction.

118 Enos had said it would be all right: Wright, *Autobiography,* 185.

118 "It helped a little": Wright, *Autobiography,* 186. Other accounts of Mamah's burial can be found in J. L. Wright, 83–85; Secrest, 222; Gill,

231–32; Burns, 318; Farr, 139; McCrea, 5; and the *Chicago Tribune*, 17 August 1914.

118 "he made no sound": J. L. Wright, 84.

118 "It was friendly": Wright, *Autobiography*, 186.

119 "was of noble character": J. L. Wright, 86.

119 "to make his home elsewhere": J. L. Wright, 87.

119 As for Frank, he was devastated: Wright, *Autobiography*, 188; cf. Secrest, 222, and Alofsin, *FLLW: Lost Years*, 97, 100.

119 into the ruined Valley below: Barney, 146–47.

120 "release from anguish of mind": Wright, *Autobiography*, 187–89. Cf. Burns, 318, and K. Smith, 49.

120 "as he stood in the night": *Chicago Tribune*, 17 August 1914.

120 "bow its head in silence": *Oak Park Leaves*, 22 August 1914.

120 "and the state free of disgrace": *Mineral Point Tribune*, 20 August 1914. The same newspaper calls Carlton a "devilish nigger."

120 "receiving punishment for his life and life style": Pfeiffer, *FLW: Monograph*, viii.

121 "the spirit that would not be quelled": Wright, *Autobiography*, 188–89.

121 "Why Taliesin?": Wright, *Autobiography*, 189. Later, in a magazine article, Wright meditated along similar lines: "And I? Unconventional believer in the Good, the True, and Beautiful, thus struck at, if not struck down, in the midst of all three?"; see Alofsin, "Taliesin," 55. Gill, 233, sides with Frank and John Lloyd Wright in his assessment of Spring Green's judgmental attitude, as fueled by the local press and clergy: "the newspapers did what they could to stir up excitement by stirring up the moral indignation of an assortment of Mrs. Grundys, male and female. . . . [D]eath [they thought] had been too good for Wright; what he needed was to be tortured forever by a sense of his infinite sinfulness."

121 "pull something down that would destroy me": Barney, 146–47. In her memoir, Maginel, 146, cannot bring herself to record Mamah's name; she refers to her only as "the woman Frank loved."

122 "refuge upon the Jeffersonian farm": Scully, 22. Scully argues, "Taliesin, in its own way, was the successor of Monticello."

122 "the wrathful God of . . . Isaiah": Secrest, 222.

122 preparing a press release: Gill, 233.

122 "He still, it seemed, wanted to live": Secrest, 222.

122 Brodelle was being buried: Brodelle's Milwaukee address is commonly given as 3519 (or 3510) Clark Street—see, e.g., the *Dodgeville Chronicle*, 19 August 1914, and the *Reedsburg Free Press*, 20 August 1914—but this was actually the address of Clarence Boettcher, his fiancée's brother, to whose home Brodelle's body was transported by Boettcher on Sunday, 16 August.

123 "inchoate friendliness": Twombly, *FLLW in Spring Green*, 11; Twombly asserts that "Wright's principal consolation was Spring Green's

sympathy"—a dubious claim, I think. See Twombly's similarly happy assessment of the *Home News* statement in his *FLLW: His Life*, 167–69.

123 an outright "war cry thinly disguised": Gill, 233.

125 "The pain was too great": Wright, *Autobiography*, 188.

125 dedicated to Mamah Borthwick: Wright, *Autobiography*, 188.

Chapter 5. "I Guess You Solved the Question"

132 "[and] he died there": Wright, *Autobiography*, 185. Yet another oddity in an already odd autobiography is Wright's remarkable lack of interest in the fate of a man who had killed Wright's lover, her children, and so many of his friends.

132 "left no explanation of his crimes": Gill, 230.

132 not so very hard a question to answer after all: This confident assertion runs counter to conventional assumptions: echoing a host of scholars and biographers, Alofsin, "Taliesin," 55, for example, assumes that Carlton's motives "will never be known."

132 "and that is 'insanity'": *Dodgeville Chronicle*, 21 August 1914.

133 for the long legal haul: See, e.g., the *Wisconsin State Journal*, 18 August 1914. Even in jail, Carlton's safety was less than certain: the 17 August 1914 issue of the *Baraboo Daily News* reports, "It is feared that [an] attempt may be made to take the slayer from the county jail at Dodgeville and lynch him."

133 "influenced by an outside source": *Wisconsin State Journal*, 18 August 1914. The *State Journal* may have taken the idea from the *Chicago Tribune*, which alleged on 16 August that Julian had been fired. Thereafter, the theory appears everywhere: see, e.g., the 20 August 1914 editions of, respectively, the *Richland Observer* ("The negro . . . is believed to have become enraged at some rebuke from Mrs. Borthwick"); the *Reedsburg Free Press* ("The [fact that] the negro had been discharged from the employ of the family is the only cause besides insanity offered for the crime"); the *Mineral Point Tribune* ("The Negro [was] maddened it [is] thought because of the discharge of himself and [his] wife."); and the *Iowa County Democrat*.

133 "their time would be up": *Chicago Tribune*, 16 August 1914.

134 "they would have to leave": Burns, 316.

134 "something was going very wrong": Secrest, 217.

134 "too good to be true": *Chicago Tribune*, 16 August 1914.

134 had been urged to stay beyond August 15: Unattributed newspaper clipping in the "Taliesin: Tragedy of 1914" file (4103.299), Frank Lloyd Wright Archives, Taliesin West.

134 "because I was lonesome": *Chicago Tribune*, 17 August 1914.

134 and homesick for Chicago: The 20 August 1914 *Spring Green Weekly Home News* is among the contemporary sources that gets this salient fact

wrong, stating that Gertrude (only) was homesick for Chicago. But the same edition is accurate about the basic situation—namely, that the Carltons had planned after only a couple of weeks at Taliesin to leave Wright's employ. While Secrest, 217, finds the *Chicago Tribune/Dodge-ville Chronicle* scenario of a sudden flare-up between Mamah and Julian more plausible than the *Weekly Home News* assertion of an early planned departure, the latter paper is almost certainly right on this point. Also see Willard, 69: "Julian Carlton hated the isolation at Taliesin and had often demanded that they leave"; see also Farr, 136.

134   "Increase if satisfactory": Qtd. in McCrea, 3.

135   "have quit our employ today": *Chicago Tribune,* 16 August 1914; *Dodge-ville Chronicle,* 21 August 1914.

135   "there was no sudden firing": McCrea, 3.

135   "a servant of the Lord": Barney, 145–46.

135   "do something about the unconventional household": Jacobs, 85.

135   "driven mad by the unconventional lovers": Hurder, 3.

135   "why he acted in the architect's absence": Twombly, *FLLW: His Life,* 167.

135   the sleeping arrangements of his employers: McCrea, 3.

136   a common-law arrangement: *Dodgeville Chronicle,* 9 October 1914.

136   "was the tool of enemies": Unattributed news clipping (4103.288) among the William C. Marlin papers, Frank Lloyd Wright Archives, Taliesin West.

136   and he hung up: Personal communication from Joe Warnkerl of Plain, Wisconsin, 24 January 2002. Gill, 218–19, suggests that Wright was himself essentially broke during the Taliesin I years.

137   failed to pay even his own son: Farr, 131.

137   "Wright's callousness concerning pay": Brooks, *FLLW and the Prairie School,* 15.

137   claims that money was an issue: Hurder, 3.

137   "no evidence . . . has ever come to light": McCrea, 3.

137   "the idea that he was . . . mad seemed unbelievable": McCrea, 3.

137   "seemed rational at all times": *Dodgeville Chronicle,* 21 August 1914.

138   an absurd mistake: *Wisconsin State Journal,* 16 August 1914.

138   education and self-evident intelligence: Farr, 135.

138   "talked intelligently to them": *Iowa County Democrat,* 20 August 1914.

138   "I do not believe the negro is insane": *Chicago Tribune,* 16 August 1914.

138   "evidence of his fiendish propensities": See, e.g., the 20 August 1914 editions of the *Iowa County Democrat* and the *Weekly Home News.*

138   "[and] he had been pleasant": *Wisconsin State Journal,* 16 August 1914.

139   "she feared for her life": The statements from Carlton's Chicago neighbors are easily found in the *Chicago Tribune,* 17 August 1914; oddly, however, these highly pertinent testimonies seem to have been overlooked (or ignored) by most previous researchers.

139 "he'll fly off the handle": *Dodgeville Chronicle*, 21 August 1914, where the
tavern owner's name is misspelled "Rouchlin" and where Billy Weston is
presented as the speaker. But according to the *Weekly Home News* coverage of 20 August, Reuschlein actually attributed the warning to Lindblom, not Weston. And given Lindblom's reported problems with Carlton (and Weston's later statement that Carlton was "pleasant"), the *Home
News* account seems more trustworthy.

139 "would send him to hell in a minute": *Weekly Home News*, 20 August
1914.

139 "and then Carlton left": For Grauvogl's statements, see the *Weekly Home
News*, 20 August 1914.

139 ended with Brodelle's striking Carlton: *Weekly Home News*, 20 August
1914. Decades later, Herb Fritz repeated the same "black son of a bitch"
story to Meryle Secrest; see Secrest, 217.

139 had been "disliked and mistrusted": *Iowa County Democrat*, 20 August
1914; cf. Secrest, 217.

140 "until I was arrested on the road to town": *Chicago Tribune*, 17 August
1914.

140 "frequent threats of violence": *Chicago Tribune*, 17 August 1914.

140 "had been entertaining queer notions": *Richland Rustic*, 21 August 1914.

140 "into the darkness with wakeful eyes": Farr, 136.

140 "talkin' 'bout killin' folks": *Dodgeville Chronicle*, 21 August 1914; qtd. in
part in Secrest, 217–18.

140 It took two deputies: *Grant County Herald*, 2 September 1914.

140 obviously unbalanced: For a very long time, the official jail and court
records pertaining to Carlton's arrest, imprisonment, and hearings appeared to have been lost, compelling researchers to reconstruct the various charges and proceedings largely from reports in the local press. Some
years ago, it seems that Iowa County divested itself of its older archives,
distributing them between the State Historical Society in Madison
and the Karrmann Library at the University of Wisconsin-Platteville.
Searches in both these repositories, however, could not turn up the court
records pertaining to Carlton's case, despite the able assistance of librar-
ians and archivists at both institutions and the remarkable cooperation of
Dodgeville resident and Wright scholar Carla Lind, the Iowa County
Circuit Court, the Iowa County Sheriff's Office, the Iowa County Historical Society, and Dodgeville's Therese Evans, who has compiled and
shared a useful typescript reflecting the complete contemporary coverage
of the various hearings by the *Dodgeville Chronicle*. Finally, acting upon a
tantalizing footnote in Alofsin's *FLLW: Lost Years*, the present author
was able, through the help of archivists Indira Berndtson and Margo
Stipe, to locate photocopies of all the relevant court documents among
the William C. Marlin papers (4103.298) at Taliesin West in Scottsdale,

Arizona. All subsequent references in the text to the various orders, sub-poenas, warrants, complaints, and affidavits emanating from Sheriff Williams, Justice of the Peace Arthur, District Attorney O'Neill, and Circuit Court judge Clementson derive from this invaluable source.

140   ill in his jail cell: *Baraboo Daily News,* 18 August 1914; *Dodgeville Chronicle,* 21 August 1914.

141   would die from the acid: Later, Dr. Lincoln seems to have wavered in his prognosis; the *Dodgeville Chronicle* of 21 August 1914 has the same physician predicting Carlton's eventual recovery.

141   "drank the acid and gave himself up": Unattributed news clipping (*Chicago Tribune?*), dated 17 August 1914 and contained in the "Taliesin: Tragedy of 1914" file (4103.299), p. 1, Frank Lloyd Wright Archives, Taliesin West. The subhead is "Murderer May Die."

141   "outside the grated door": *Dodgeville Chronicle,* 21 August 1914.

141   no attorney was appointed: For press coverage of this first hearing, see the *Dodgeville Chronicle,* 21 August 1914; the *Iowa County Democrat,* 20 August 1914; the *Baraboo Daily News,* 18 August 1914; and the *Dodgeville Sun-Republic,* 21 August 1914.

142   "against whom he admits he was enraged": *Baraboo Daily News,* 18 August 1914.

142   "Borthwick and the other victims": *Mineral Point Tribune,* 3 September 1914.

142   "for the murder of Emil Bourdelle": *Grant County Herald* 2 September 1914.

143   "he would "get" [Brodelle]": *Dodgeville Sun-Republic,* 28 August 1914.

143   and then burning down the house: *Grant County Herald,* 2 September 1914.

143   "and I waited for my chances": *Baraboo Daily News,* 17 August 1914.

143   "decided to end the lives of the party": *Baraboo Daily News,* 17 August 1914. Cf., e.g., the *Sauk County News,* 20 August 1914. Also see the *Baraboo Daily News,* 18 August 1914; Twombly, *FLLW: His Life,* 167; and Twombly, *FLLW in Spring Green,* 11.

143   signed a statement to that effect: *Dodgeville Chronicle,* 21 August 1914.

143   "I guess you solved the question": *Dodgeville Chronicle,* 9 October 1914.

143   "They all imposed upon me": *Richland Rustic,* 21 August 1914.

144   "tried to burn myself up": *Wisconsin State Journal,* 18 August 1914. The *State Journal* reporter quotes Carlton to the effect that the workmen and apprentices were allegedly telling lies about him to Wright. Cf. Farr, 136.

144   "The fire . . . was an accident": *Weekly Home News,* 20 August 1914.

144   banned access to the jail: *Dodgeville Chronicle,* 21 August 1914. The jail was not in good shape. On 7 December 1914, John P. Lewis filed a report on the condition of the facility with the State Board of Control, noting that the building was old and lacked "a heating plant and also bath tub

and lavatory." Further, female prisoners—including Gertrude Carlton, presumably—were "kept in the residence part of the jail," in violation of state requirements. Lewis concludes by urging Iowa County to finance "a new, up-to-date jail"; but citing what he calls "the general spirit of the times in Wisconsin"—no doubt referring to an economic downturn—he is willing to leave the matter to the county. The report can be found among the Iowa County documents archived at the University of Wisconsin-Platteville's Karrmann Library.

144   "largest crowd": *Grant County Herald,* 2 September 1914.

144   the "colored slayer": *Dodgeville Sun-Republic,* 28 August 1914.

145   "he had not understood the charges": *Weekly Home News,* 27 August 1914; *Grant County Herald,* 2 September 1914.

145   setting bail at $5,000: *Weekly Home News,* 27 August 1914.

145   "no special attention": *Grant County Herald,* 2 September 1914.

145   revenge-minded coterie: *Weekly Home News,* 27 August 1914.

145   "A personified enigma": *Dodgeville Chronicle,* 21 August 1914.

145   caused by his ingestion of the acid: *Baraboo Daily News,* 17 and 20 August 1914; also see the *Sauk County Democrat,* 20 August 1914.

146   taking little nourishment: *Baraboo Daily News,* 18 August 1914; *Dodgeville Chronicle,* 21 August 1914.

146   the inevitability of the servant's death: *Dodgeville Chronicle,* 21 and 17 August 1914.

146   as "eating better . . . and . . . gaining strength": *Dodgeville Chronicle,* 25 September 1914.

146   "he could endure that": *Dodgeville Chronicle,* 2 October 1914. All future references to the remarks made at Carlton's 1 October hearing are from this source.

147   they laid him on a makeshift cot: *Dodgeville Chronicle,* 2 October 1914.

148   no doubt to life imprisonment: See, e.g., the *Dodgeville Chronicle,* 25 September 1914. Then, as now, Wisconsin had no death penalty. In fact, Wisconsin enjoys the nation's longest uninterrupted history of an outright ban on capital punishment.

149   "The way of the transgressor is hard": *Dodgeville Sun-Republic,* 9 October 1914.

149   "and starved himself to death": *Weekly Home News,* 8 October 1914.

150   Driver and Diederich the "lowers": I am indebted for this information to Kristen Zehner, Jim Petterson, Robert Schlotthauer, Phil Schadler, and Wayne Roohr—all members, active or retired, of the University of Wisconsin-Madison Department of Anatomy.

150   "examined for [any] abnormalities": *Dodgeville Chronicle,* 16 October 1914.

151   "there had been flare-ups": McCrea, 3.

151   and "negro maniac": See, e.g., the *Mineral Point Tribune,* 20 August 1914;

the *Weekly Home News,* 20 August 1914; the *Reedsburg Free Press,* 20 August 1914; the *Reedsburg Times,* 21 August 1914; the *Sauk County News,* 20 August 1914; and the *Wisconsin State Journal,* 15 August 1914. This was more than a regional tendency, however: even the *New York Times* coverage of the murders, 16 August 1914, was headlined "Wild Negro Chef Kills 6, Wounds 4."

151 On the death certificates of: Dr. Frank Nee submitted and signed the death certificates for Mamah Borthwick, Emil Brodelle (misspelled "Burdell" on the form), Martha Cheney, and Tom Brunker; Dr. Marcus Bossard wrote the ones for Ernest Weston and David Lindblom (misspelled "Lindblum"); again, no death certificate was ever issued for young John Cheney.

151 Thomas Wolfe's short story: In 1939, Wolfe expanded the story into the eighth chapter of his novel *The Web and the Rock.*

152 "like an infuriated tiger": *Iowa County Democrat,* 20 August 1914.

152 "one of the most . . . enjoyable meetings": *Weekly Home News,* 10 September 1914.

153 Carlton's ashes were then disposed of: I am grateful to Wayne Roohr, late of the University of Wisconsin–Madison's Department of Anatomy, for this information.

Epilogue: The Legacy of Fire

154 the ironically benign prelude: Fussell, 18–29.

154 "Never before or since": Qtd. in Fussell, 19.

155 the imperatives of the individual: See, e.g., N. K. Smith, 61.

155 "an unrelievedly morose diatribe": N. K. Smith, 102.

155 "few recognized Wright as the driver": Twombly, *FLLW: His Life,* 163.

155 "treachery and evil intent": Twombly, *FLLW: His Life,* 163, 165.

156 "the absolute individualist": Wright, "In the Cause of Architecture," *Architectural Record* 35:5 (May 1914), 412. For Wright's and Whitman's views on democracy as an unfulfilled American dream, see Menocal, 150–51.

156 the great Wasmuth monograph: Wright, *Autobiography,* 192; also see Sweeney, 16. But Alofsin, in a chronological appendix to his *FLLW: Lost Years,* suggests that some of the editions may already have been in circulation in America.

156 "where desolation ended and began": Wright, *Autobiography,* 186. Years later, Wright had a small, simple marker placed at Mamah's gravesite, at the foot of a pine; see Gill, 232.

156 Wright knew no German: Gill, 209; Alofsin, *FLLW: Lost Years,* 348. Goethe was important in Wright's life. He had been reading the great Romantic's novels in translation since his boyhood days in Madison and,

around 1925, was first bewitched by Olgivanna Hinzenberg, his third wife, when she danced sinuously before the fireplace at Taliesin to the strains of "The Elf King," Schubert's musical setting of Goethe's poem; see Secrest, 73, 302. Actually, there seems to be some debate over the authorship of the "Hymn," some authorities attributing it to Goethe's friend Tobler.

156 the poem's Whitmanesque tone: Gill, 233.

157 "The Present is her Eternity": see Twombly, *FLLW: His Life,* 169.

157 "with the death of Mamah Borthwick": Twombly, *FLLW in Spring Green,* 14.

158 shooting out over the ravines: Hitchcock, 66–67; also see Gill, 223–24.

158 of the land on which it sat: Twombly, *FLLW in Spring Green,* 14.

158 "Wright's newest efforts": Twombly, *FLLW in Spring Green,* 15.

159 "discourage penetration": Twombly, *FLLW in Spring Green,* 15.

159 "lacking [in] joy": For the Storer House, see Gill, 272–74, 277.

159 "made necessary by Mamah Borthwick's death": Twombly, *FLLW in Spring Green,* 17.

159 "far within his own thoughts": Tafel, *Apprentice to Genius,* 81.

160 "he went on living": Blake, 67.

160 "toward the Lloyd Jones family Chapel": Wright, *Autobiography,* 189.

160 "God was testing his character": *Dubuque (Iowa) Telegraph Herald,* 26 August 1990: 1C.

160 standing "tall against the storms": Heinz, *Vision,* 281.

160 and all their works have vanished: Heinz, *Vision,* 283; Jacobs, 64–65. Wright entertainingly tells the "Romeo and Juliet" story in his *Autobiography,* 132–38. The windmill was dismantled in 1990 and reconstructed the following year.

161 "I've never seen anyone like you": Wright, *Autobiography,* 201–2.

161 "refused to be happy": Secrest, 283–84.

161 spanning the Wisconsin River: Secrest, 279.

161 readers of the *Weekly Home News:* Twombly, *FLLW in Spring Green,* 12.

162 to reopen an investigation: Twombly, *FLLW in Spring Green,* 13.

162 had him arrested: Twombly, *FLLW in Spring Green,* 14.

162 "she had defeated Anna": Secrest, 280.

162 "to come to Taliesin never again": See "Letters of Anna Lloyd Wright to Frank Lloyd Wright 1887–1922," pp. 15–17, Frank Lloyd Wright Archives, Taliesin West.

162 taken off for Los Angeles: Secrest, 277–78.

163 actor, restaurateur, and property manager: See Indira Berndtson's "Telephone Interview with John C. Christensen . . . ," 9 August 1995, Frank Lloyd Wright Archives, Taliesin West. Early in 2007 (too late, alas, for inclusion in this account), the Iowa County Historical Society came in

possession of the unpublished memoir of Grace Mann Larson Lewis, a young woman who, like Frances Inglis, wandered into Taliesin on the day of the murders; Grace Lewis helped tend to the victims, and her account apparently provides additional details regarding the tragedy. Her manuscript, formerly distributed only among family members, is now available for inspection at the Society's office in Dodgeville. I am indebted to archivist Boyd W. Geer for this information.

163 a disciple of Wright's "organic" style: Tafel, *About Wright,* 182.

163 "he never missed a college reunion": Gill, 219.

163 this show of magnanimity: Twombly, *FLLW in Spring Green,* 18; and see the *Weekly Home News,* 15 December 1927.

163 investigated by his own government: For a full treatment of the Ford Expedition, see Barbara S. Kraft, *The Peace Ship: Henry Ford's Pacifist Adventure in the First World War* (New York: Macmillan, 1978).

164 "the voice of 'the Lord'": Qtd. in Secrest, 264.

164 "a bald-headed Soviet mystic": Qtd. in an unattributed news clipping, 1990, Frank Lloyd Wright file, Karrmann Library, University of Wisconsin-Platteville; on Olgivanna's and Wright's association with Gurdjieff, see Secrest, 307-12, 430-31, and Gill, 326-27. No "Soviet," Gurdjieff was actually of Greek-Armenian heritage; he had left Russia during the Bolshevik Revolution.

164 "remembered the promise only later": Tafel, *Apprentice to Genius,* 136.

164 then promptly mortgaged the place: Alofsin, *FLLW: Lost Years,* 350.

165 "its immensity, beauty, and grandeur": Twombly, *FLLW: His Life,* 153.

165 what Wright called an "auto-laundry": Qtd. in Blake, 66.

165 "rising grotesquely out of the waters": Gill, 228.

165 a one-ton carved stone urn: Gill, 387-88.

165 "a full carload": Tafel, *Apprentice to Genius,* n.p.

165 "a quick, fierce reaction": N. K. Smith, 108.

166 "house commissions fell off sharply": Brooks, *FLLW and the Prairie School,* 26.

166 seized for a time by creditors: Brooks, *FLLW and the Prairie School,* 27; also see Scully, 24.

166 quaint, outmoded, irrelevant, and passé: N. Smith, 109.

166 "almost a leitmotif of his life": Secrest, 149.

166 "the expression on Dad's face": Qtd. in Secrest, 150.

166 "thunder rolling as the lightning flashed": Qtd. in Secrest, 149.

167 never to design such a wall again: Tafel, *About Wright,* 312.

167 "Something always happens in the country": Qtd. in Tafel, *About Wright,* 312-13.

167 too near the chimney flue: Tafel, *About Wright,* 314.

167 to a waiting chauffeur below: Secrest, 259-60.

167   "'All my life I have been plagued by fire'": Tafel, *About Wright,* 315-16.

168   "Why should I have bothered?": Qtd. in Gill, 498-99. For a slightly differing account, see Secrest, 563.

168   "and handed over to a representative from Taliesin West": Much misinformation regarding Wright's disinterment abounds in the literature—errors that regrettably recurred in the hardcover edition of this present text. I am obliged to Spring Green's Mrs. Viola Richardson for the corrective details. Also see the relevant article in the *Home News,* 27 March 1985.

168   "near his mother, in those green Wisconsin hills": Tafel, *About Wright,* 316.

168   next to Olgivanna's dust: *Milwaukee Journal,* 8 November 1985, "Home" sec.: 1.

168   "he was plagued by fire": Tafel, *About Wright,* 316.

Selected Bibliography

Aguar, Charles E., and Berdeana Aguar. *Wrightscapes: Frank Lloyd Wright's Landscape Designs.* New York: McGraw-Hill, 2002.

Alofsin, Anthony. *Frank Lloyd Wright: An Index to the Taliesin Correspondence.* 4 vols. New York: Garland, 1988.

———. *Frank Lloyd Wright: The Lost Years, 1910–1922.* Chicago: University of Chicago Press, 1993.

———. "To Fashion Worlds in Little." In *Wright Studies* 1, ed. Narciso G. Menocal, 44–65. Carbondale and Edwardsville: Southern Illinois University Press, 1992.

———. "Taliesin I: A Catalogue of Drawings and Photographs." In *Wright Studies* 1, ed. Narciso G. Menocal, 98–141. Carbondale and Edwardsville: Southern Illinois University Press, 1992.

Anderson, Quentin. *The Imperial Self: An Essay in American Literary and Cultural History.* New York: Vintage Books, 1971.

Ashbee, C. R. "Taliesin, the Home of Frank Lloyd Wright and a Study of the Owner." *Western Architect* (February 1913): 16–19.

Barney, Maginel Wright. *The Valley of the God-Almighty Joneses.* New York: Appleton-Century, 1965.

Blake, Peter. *Frank Lloyd Wright: Architecture and Space.* 1960. Baltimore: Penguin Books, 1964.

Brooks, H. Allen. *Frank Lloyd Wright and the Prairie School.* New York: George Braziller, 1984.

———. *Prairie School Architecture: Studies from the* Western Architect. Toronto: University of Toronto Press, 1975.

Burns, Ken. "The Master Builder." *Vanity Fair* (November 1998): 303–18.

Connors, Joseph. "Wright on Nature and the Machine." In *The Nature of Frank Lloyd Wright,* ed. Carol R. Bolon, Robert S. Nelson, and Linda Seidel, 1–19. Chicago: University of Chicago Press, 1988.

Copplestone, Trewin. *Frank Lloyd Wright.* New York: Gramercy Books, 1999.

Cronon, William. "Inconstant Unity: The Passion of Frank Lloyd Wright." In *Frank Lloyd Wright: Architect,* ed. Terence Riley with Peter Reed, 8–31. New York: Museum of Modern Art, 1994.

Farr, Finis. *Frank Lloyd Wright.* New York: Scribner's, 1961.

Fussell, Paul. *The Great War and Modern Memory.* London: Oxford University Press, 1975.

Gill, Brendan. *Many Masks: A Life of Frank Lloyd Wright.* 1988. New York: Da Capo Press, 1998.

Heinz, Thomas A. *Frank Lloyd Wright.* New York: St. Martin's Press, 1982.

———. *The Vision of Frank Lloyd Wright.* Edison, NJ: Chartwell Books, 2000.

Hitchcock, Henry-Russell. *In the Nature of Materials: The Buildings of Frank Lloyd Wright, 1887–1941.* 1942. New York: Da Capo Press, 1973.

Hoffman, Donald. *Understanding Frank Lloyd Wright's Architecture.* New York: Dover, 1995.

Hurder, Steven. "Brief Biography of Frank Lloyd Wright." 1996–2001. www.oprf.com/flw/bio. Accessed 24 January 2001.

Jacobs, Herbert. *Frank Lloyd Wright: America's Greatest Architect.* New York: Harcourt, Brace and World, 1965.

Kruty, Paul Samuel. *Frank Lloyd Wright and Midway Gardens.* Urbana: University of Illinois Press, 1998.

Larson, Erik. *The Devil in the White City: Murder, Magic, and Madness at the Fair That Changed America.* New York: Vintage, 2004.

Levine, Neil. "Frank Lloyd Wright's Own Houses and His Changing Concept of Representation." In *The Nature of Frank Lloyd Wright,* ed. Carol R. Bolon, Robert S. Nelson, and Linda Seidel, 20–69. Chicago: University of Chicago Press, 1988.

Lind, Carla. *Frank Lloyd Wright's Life and Homes.* San Francisco: Pomegranate Artbooks, 1994.

———. *Lost Wright: Frank Lloyd Wright's Vanished Masterpieces.* New York: Simon and Schuster, 1996.

A Lloyd Jones Retrospective. Spring Green, WI: Unity Chapel, 1986.

Manson, Grant Carpenter. *Frank Lloyd Wright to 1910: The First Golden Age.* New York: Reinhold, 1958.

McCarter, Robert. *Frank Lloyd Wright.* London: Phaidon Press Ltd., 1997.

McCrea, Ron. "Murders at Taliesin." *Madison Capital Times.* 15 August 1998.

Meehan, Patrick J. *Frank Lloyd Wright: A Research Guide to Archival Sources.* New York: Garland, 1983.

Menocal, Narciso G. "Frank Lloyd Wright's Concept of Democracy: An American Architectural Jeremiad." In *Frank Lloyd Wright: In the Realm of Ideas,* ed. Bruce Brooks Pfeiffer and Gerald Norland, 149–64. Carbondale and Edwardsville: Southern Illinois University Press, 1988.

———, ed. *Taliesin, 1911–1914. Wright Studies* 1. Carbondale and Edwardsville: Southern Illinois University Press, 1992.

Meudt, Edna. *The Rose Jar: The Autobiography of Edna Meudt.* Madison, WI: North Country Press, 1990.

Morgan, Keith. "The Charnley-Persky House: Architectural History and the Society." *Journal of the Society of Architectural Historians* 54 (September 1995).

Pfeiffer, Bruce Brooks. *Frank Lloyd Wright: Monograph, 1914–1923.* Frank Lloyd Wright Series, vol. 4. Tokyo: A. D. A. Edita, 1985.

———. "The Second Career: 1924–1959." In *Frank Lloyd Wright: In the Realm of*

Ideas, ed. Bruce Brooks Pfeiffer and Gerald Norland, 165–75. Carbondale and Edwardsville: Southern Illinois University Press, 1988.

Scully, Vincent, Jr. *Frank Lloyd Wright.* New York: George Braziller, 1960.

Secrest, Meryle. *Frank Lloyd Wright: A Biography.* New York: Knopf, 1992.

Smith, Kathryn. *Frank Lloyd Wright's Taliesin and Taliesin West.* Photo. Judith Bromley. New York: Harry N. Abrams, 1997.

——. *Frank Lloyd Wright: Hollyhock House and Olive Hill.* New York: Rizzoli, 1992.

Smith, Norris Kelly. *Frank Lloyd Wright: A Study in Architectural Content.* Englewood Cliffs, NJ: Prentice-Hall, 1966.

Steiner, Frances. *Frank Lloyd Wright in Oak Park and River Forest.* Chicago: Sigma Press, 1983.

Storrer, William Allin. *The Architecture of Frank Lloyd Wright: A Complete Catalog.* 2nd ed. Cambridge, MA: MIT Press, 1978.

——. *The Frank Lloyd Wright Companion.* Chicago: University of Chicago Press, 1993.

Sweeney, Robert L. *Frank Lloyd Wright: An Annotated Bibliography.* Los Angeles: Hennessey and Ingalls, 1978.

Tafel, Edgar. *About Wright.* New York: John Wiley and Sons, 1993.

——. *Apprentice to Genius: Years with Frank Lloyd Wright.* New York: McGraw-Hill, 1979.

Twombly, Robert C. *Frank Lloyd Wright: An Interpretive Biography.* New York: Harper and Row, 1973.

——. *Frank Lloyd Wright: His Life and His Architecture.* New York: John Wiley and Sons, 1979.

——. *Frank Lloyd Wright in Spring Green, 1911–1932.* 1968. Wisconsin Stories Series. Madison: State Historical Society of Wisconsin, 1980. Rpt. from *Wisconsin Magazine of History* 51 (Spring 1968): 200–217.

Wickes, Molly, and Kate Irvin, eds. *Guide to Oak Park's Frank Lloyd Wright and Prairie School Historic District.* Oak Park, IL: Oak Park Historic Preservation Commission, n.d.

Willard, Charlotte. *Frank Lloyd Wright.* New York: Macmillan, 1972.

Wright, Frank Lloyd. *An Autobiography.* New York: Duell, Sloan and Pearce, 1943.

——. *Frank Lloyd Wright: Collected Writings.* Ed. Bruce Brooks Pfeiffer. Vol. I. New York: Rizzoli, 1992.

——. *A Testament.* New York: Horizon Press, 1957.

Wright, Gwendolyn. "Frank Lloyd Wright and the Domestic Landscape." In *Frank Lloyd Wright: Architect,* ed. Terence Riley with Peter Reed, 80–95. New York: Museum of Modern Art, 1994.

Wright, John Lloyd. *My Father Who Is on Earth.* New York: Putnam's, 1946.

Wright, Olgivanna Lloyd. *Frank Lloyd Wright: His Life, His Works, His Words.* New York: Horizon Press, 1966.

——. *The Shining Brow: Frank Lloyd Wright.* New York: Horizon Press, 1960.

Index